A Hand Book of Education

A Hand Book of Education

Edited by

Romila Chawla

Raj Publications

New Delhi - 110002 (India)

A Hand Book of Education

First Published in 2006

ISBN 81-86208-40-2

Published By : **Poonam Goel**
Raj Publications
4855/24, Ansari Road,
Daryaganj, New Delhi - 110002
Tel : 011 - 30120939

Price : 225/-

Laser Typesetting : **Classic Computers**
D-120/C, South Ganesh Nagar
Delhi - 110092
Tel. 9891458179

Printed at : **Balaji Offset,** Naveen Shahdara, Delhi.

Printed in India

Contents

Preface

Education every where has undergone profound changes. Technological revolution and advance in information technological have necessitated radical changes in education.

Aim of this book is to present some important and innovative aspects of education. In selecting these essays special care has been taken to ensure its usefulness to students and teachers.

How children education have been revolutionised in the East and the West has been examined. Importance of planning in education, education of teacher, national and international dimensions have been studied. Perspective of primary education secondary education, cultural education and the administration of education have been highlighted.The development of comparative education and some of the Western education systems have been included.

In preparing this book we have increased indebtedness of the authorities on the topics covered in this worked. We record our grateful acknowledgments.

Librarians and their staffmembers have rendered all possible help and assistance. We are thankful to them.

My publisher Poonam Goel and his staff members have worked hard. We shall all feel fully rewarded if the book proves useful to our readers.

— Romila Chawla

1

Ancient Thinking

Western European and American education shows traceable continuity from the period of the Greek philosopher Socrates, 469-399 B.C., and his later contemporaries, Plato and Aristotle, to the present time. It is rather puzzling that we can no longer trace the impact of the Chinese, Egyptian, Indian, and Iranian systems of education, some of which antidated Socrates and the Athenian system by atleast 1500 years.

The fact is that the thinking of these older peoples had only an indirect influence on Western Europe, and the body of Oriental thought became so absorbed in the stream of Western ideas that it is now impossible to identify it as Oriental.

The "Western" mind seems either to reject or to digest and make its own every set of ideas it encounters: it never adopts them as is.

Even Hebrew conceptions of reality as represented by early Hebrew Christians had to be fitted into the Greek mold in order to have appeal to the great educators of the western world.

Hence little is to be gained by reviewing systems

antidating the educational structure in the Athens of the fifth and fourth centuries B.C.

The city of Athens was a tiny democracy of well-to-do citizens, proud of its independence, its system of jurisprudence, its art, music, recreations, especially of its knowledge of the visible world and its conception of the world to come.

Justice and virtue were held in the highest esteem.

It was quite unlike the educational system of the republic of Sparta, which emphasized strength, ruggedness, militancy, and the harsh legal code of Lycurgus.

The Athenians were aesthetic, contemplative, hospitable to new ideas, stressed poise and balance in all things, and were highly appreciative of the graces of life.

From them came the ingredients of what we now call the liberal arts approach to education.

Teachers of high reputation gathered about them well-born, promising youths mainly to prepare them for public usefulness.

Schools were entirely private; classes were held in the home of the instructor, or as they went about the city observing state, religious, and recreational activities.

The daily session lasted from early morning until late afternoon.

Students visited the assembly to hear, and in some cases to participate in, the debates, the juries, where cases of law were adjudicated; the theatres, where the greatest dramas of that day were enacted; the Olympic, Ishmean, and Nemean games, where contests in the various sports of the day were held, or where in the intervals orations, legends, and drama could be heard.

In the field of primary education the student was usually accompanied by his pedagogus, a kind of slave, tutor, and mentor, who was responsible for the conduct of his charge at all times.

The student also was required to attend the Palestra, a gymnasium for physical training.

The latter included more than the development of the body in the sports of running, jumping, throwing the discus, and wrestling.

Such exercises were considered incidental to the perfecting of muscular correlation, the development of grace and symmetry of movement, the carriage, and poise of the body.

They were thought to improve the student's mental ability, his perception, and judgment, and above all, to establish the harmony and balance which to the Greek was the key to human virtue.

The boy had access also to the music school, i.e., the school over which the muses presided.

Here he learned to read Homer, to write, to appreciate music, and to compute by the dexterous use of his fingers.

Schools for secondary education developed about the middle of the fourth century B.C.

These schools were mainly for the children of the well-to-do.

Boys whose parents were not well off were usually apprenticed to artisans who assumed responsibility for their education.

The "rich" continued in the academy and the Lyceum with studies in literature, drawing, geometry, geography, and grammar; and with advanced training in gymnastics.

In the higher schools the final objective of instruction seems to have been preparation for citizenship and statecraft.

These schools were administrated by state officials, who participated in the instruction.

Students were a part of the garrison and the police force.

They were under rigid military discipline.

Not unfrequently they participated in the assembly and through systematic instruction became familiar with the Gods and Muses. Thus education in Athens was a process of learning by doing.

At the close of the Periclean period, about 500 B.C., there arose what are now called the schools of the philosophers.

They came into being after the Persian wars, when Athens was enjoying an era of peace, of phenomenal trade with its accompanying prosperity.

In 507, the city became a democracy, with citizenship rights available to all free men.

There was a growth of cosmopolitanism due to the influence of strangers from other countries touching the Mediterranean.

The city was the center in which foregathered the wealthy, wise, adventurous, and cultured of the ancient world.

Strangely enough, the Greeks welcomed aliens.

Especially they made a place for the learned, the scholars, or sophists, as they were called, who presumably could enrich Greek education and contribute to the sum of Greek knowledge.

Unlike the state officials in the higher schools, these foreign scholars built up a following and collected a fee for their teaching.

They also introduced a new concept of the purpose of education.

To them, the principal objective of education was to prepare the student to anticipate and capitalize on the changing conditions of his time, thus contributing to his personal advancement.

Opportunities for personal advancement were multiplied by Greek leadership in the Delian League, including all Ionian states and all islands in the Aegean sea.

The purpose of the higher education thus became frankly individual aggrandisement, not, as formerly, state service.

To this end, emphasis for the first time was placed on the art of speech, the ability to sway people's thinking-declamation, oratory, rhetoric, and debate, as a means to civic and political preferment.

PROTAGORUS AND PYTHAGORAS

One of the most outstanding foreign sophist teachers was Protagorus, widely travelled, familiar with the scientific and political thinking of his time, a grammarian, mathematician, and philosopher.

Protagorus should not be confused with the earlier, highly esteemed philosopher, Pythagoras (600 B.C.) who had emphasized the value of applying measurement to all things, in order to demonstrate the oneness of nature in its obedience to the eternal truths and thus to bring man's behavior into harmony with the ways of the gods and the ways of Nature.

Some indication of Pythagoras' balanced philosophy may be seen in his instruction to his students, referred to by them as:

The Golden Words*

The Gods immortal, as by law disposed,
First venerate, and reverence the oath:
Then to the noble heroes, and the powers
Beneath the earth, do homage with just rites.

Thy parents honor and thy nearest kin,
And from the rest choose friends on virtue's scale.
To gentle words and kindly deeds give way,
Nor hate thy friend for any slight offence.
Bear all thou canst; for Can dwells nigh to Must.
These things thus know.

---

* The Golden Words (ascribed to Pythagoras, 6th century B.C)
Thomas Davison, "Aristotle," Scribners, New York, 1905, p. 57.

What follow learn to rule:
Thy belly first, then sleep and lust and wrath.
Do nothing base with others or alone:
But most of all thyself in reverence hold.
Then practice justice both in deed and word,
Nor let thyself wax thoughtless about aught:
But know that death's the common lot of all.

Be not untimely wasteful of thy wealth,
Like vulgar men, nor yet illiberal.
In all things moderation answers best.
Do things that profit thee: think ere thou act.

Let never sleep thy drowsy eyelids greet,
Till thou hast pondered each act of the day:
"Wherein have I transgressed? What have I done?
What duty shunned?" - beginning from the first,
Unto the last. Then grieve and fear for what
Was basely done; but in the good rejoice.
These things perform; these meditate; these love.
These in the path of godlike excellence
Will place thee, yea by Him who gave our souls
The number Four, perennial nature's spring!
But, ere thou act, crave from the gods success.

These precepts having mastered, thou shalt know
The system of the never-dying gods
and dying men, and how from all the rest
Each thing is sunder'd, and how held in one:
And thou shalt know, as it is right thou shouldst,
That nature everywhere is uniform,
And so shalt neither hope for things that lie
Beyond all hope, nor fail of any truth.
But from such food abstain as we have named,
And, while thou seek'st to purge and free thy soul,

Use judgment, and reflect on everything,
Setting o'er all best Thought as charioteer.
Be glad to gather goods, nor less to lose.

Of human ills that spring from spirit-powers
Endure thy part, nor peevishly complain.
Cure what thou canst: "til well, and then reflect:
"Fate never lays too much upon the good.

Words many, brave and base, assail men's ears.
Let these not disconcert nor trammel thee;
But when untruth is spoken, meekly yield.

What next I say in every act observe:
Let none by word or deed prevail on thee
To do or say what were not best for thee.
Think ere thou act, lest foolish things be done;-
For thoughtless deeds and words the caitiff mark;-
But strongly do what will not bring regret.
Do naught thou dost not know; but duly learn.
So shall thy life with happiness o'erflow.

Be not neglectful of thy body's health;
But measure use in drink, food, exercise-
I mean by "measure" what brings no distress.

Follow a cleanly, simple mode of life,
And guard against such acts as envy breed.

Then, if, when thou the body leav'st, thou mount
To the free ether, deathless shalt thou be,
A god immortal, - mortal never more.

To Pythagoras' doctrine of eternal truths, Protagorus set up an opposing thesis that "man (himself) is the measure of all things."

Man's knowledge, (Protagorus maintained), is acquired through the use of his senses.

In as much as the senses in no two people are alike, the natural conclusion is that there can be no timeless principles or universal truths.

Truth, from this strictly sensory approach, is subjective and ultimately a matter of individual opinion.

The high standing of Protagorus among the Sophists permits the conclusion that his thesis was typical of the movement; that individualism was the cornerstone of the ethical and political doctrines of the Sophists.

Sophist students were taught to argue equally well on either side of a question, if need be making the weaker appear the stronger argument.

Even today we apply the term Sophistry to fallacious or specious argument.

Sophistry was an expedient philosophy and, strangely enough, was received in Greece with open arms.

By it each Greek was justified in his own views and actions and not motivated solely by the welfare of the state.

As noted before, Athenian education became an instrument for personal advancement, not for civic duty.

The prevailing ideals in philosophy, ethics, and religion were shattered by this comfortable and tolerant philosophy, as under such a system there could be no rigid religious canons, no stable morality, no universal truth.

This ancient conflict in ideas was peculiarly prophetic of the educational controversy with which we are faced today-ideas unlike old soldiers, never die or pass away.

SOCRATES (468-399 B.C.)

Socrates and his later contemporaries Plato and Aristotle were much concerned about this superficial and dangerous philosophy and sought to reconcile the conflict of individual liberty and social stability by emphasizing knowledge, the elements of which every man possesses.

Socrates was born in Athens, the son of a stonemason.

After an apprenticeship in his father's craft, Socrates' youth was spent as a soldier in the Peloponnesian war.

On his return he became a distinguished educator.

He gathered about him a group of the most promising young men in the city and taught them by the method of questions and answers.

While none of his own writings have survived, many references to the precepts of the Great Master are found in the writings of Xenophon and Plato.

Socrates opposed the Sophists and exhorted his students to seek virtue through knowledge of universal morality and eternal truth. While not rejecting the concept of Protagoras that man himself was the measure of all things, Socrates held that only the good man could be a good measure.

And to be good, man must first understand the measure; hence Socrates insisted,"know thyself"

Knowledge, he urged, is real, a guide to right conduct and virtue.

Its elements are the possession of every man, and thus universal and valid.

Truth and right conduct cannot, therefore, be matters of individual opinion or caprice.

In the judgment of Socrates, knowledge of the right will be followed by the doing of the right.

Everybody has within him the power to arrive at knowledge.

It is the function of education to develop this power of right thinking.

The educator cannot achieve the purpose by lectures, the passing on of predetermined conclusions as the Sophists did, but by raising issues and challenging the validity of opinions concerning them.

Fallacious opinions were reduced to absurdity, imperfect opinions were modified or elaborated into their defensible counterparts. He led his students from unconscious ignorance to conscious ignorance, and then to clear and reasoned truth.

It is little wonder that Socrates referred to himself as an intellectual midwife.

PLATO (427-347 B.C.)

Plato was perhaps the most illustrious of Socrates' disciples. He was aristocratic by birth, rich by good fortune, and authoritarian by nature.

In his "Republic" he elaborated in Socratic dialogue form a picture of his ideal political state–a state to be ruled by an elite of learned men– a state in which he made education not a minor duty of government but its major function, because to Plato the prime purpose of education was preparation for service to the state.

Plato was convinced that the "masses" can only be happy when ruled by their "betters."

He justified this by pointing out that virtue and goodness can come only through knowledge of the supreme good– a knowledge that can be attained only by a select few possessing superior intellectuality.

These select few should rule and should educate the less-gifted many in the ways of good citizenship.

In this way the good society would create good citizens.

There were various safeguards against tyranny and corruption, notably that the ruling scsholars should live as priests without the temptations of wealth or women.

Plato's ideas on politics must have been persuasive because in 384 B.C. the King of Syracuse offered him the chance to put his theories to work.

The experiment met with dismal failure, and thereafter Plato's political writings became much more conservative.

However, the early works are the ones that continue to be influential.

Plato's conception of the learning process (as previously noted) was dominated by his conception of the soul and the mind.

He regarded them as being indivisible, and he believed that after death they were housed in a new-born body.

For this reason, he thought, in the mind of every infant lay the wisdom of the ages, waiting to be "recollected" under the skilled guidance of the teacher.

In the Platonic theory of education, the specific value of knowledge lay in building up inner harmony, completeness, and happiness.

He recognized that every individual naturally is possessed of two fundamental and apparently contradictory characteristics, namely, gentleness and high, unruly spirits.

It is the function of education to harmonize these conflicting tendencies, to nurture the gentle element and to bridle the unruly; to develop both so that they are mutually attuned and obedient to the things accounted good and true and beautiful, and in addition, to develop the student's intellectual discipline so that it controls his whole inner life and enables him to recognize his relationship to the whole universe.

Plato was an idealist, he insisted that reality exists only in ideas.

To repeat the example previously used, an idealist would believe that there could be no God until the mind of man generated the *idea of God*.

As one can readily see, this conception of the mind as the great creator applied to the general learning process places contemplation and thought ahead of observation and reason.

ARISTOTLE (384-322 B.C.)

As the son of a prominent, highly placed physician, Aristotle was raised in a world of science and demonstrable truth, thus laying the base for his devotion to reason as the highest function of man.

Being a student of Plato's, he had the advantage not only of his master's thoughts, but of those of his master's master Socrates.

While Aristotle transmitted many of the teachings of these two great men, he differed from both on the content of education, its method and purpose.

Ideas, he insisted, are not realities but pictures of reality: any knowledge of reality must come through the five senses-through observation and reason.

The highest function of man is reason; so to fulfill this function, to attain virtue or rightness, man must act in accordance with reason.

In his personal conduct and his relations with others he must observe those principles which reason indicates are right.

Whereas Plato taught that the welfare of the citizens depends upon the good state, Aristotle taught that the welfare of the state depends upon the good citizen.

The chief means, therefore, of securing the welfare of the state is to educate its citizens.

Such education should be functional and exactly suited to the needs of different beings.

For this reason the education of adults should differ from that for children, that for males should differ from that for females, as each have differing functions.

It should begin with physical training, pass through the irrational type (literature, music, etc.) and culminate in the moral.

To Aristotle the practice was always to precede theory-doing before reasoning about it.

Only after the *right habits* of feeling and acting have been acquired can the individual be taught the *right basis* for such behavior.

Proper behavior being in harmony with the laws of nature, man should observe nature and society and reflect upon his observations.

Reflection is not an unbridled exercise.

It proceeds according to the universal laws governing proper thinking, i.e., logic.

Aristotle set out the rules for right thinking in great detail.

These rules were the greatest contribution to clear thinking that had ever before been made by any man.

It must be remembered that Aristotle lived in a shaken and tottering world, in which all conventional standards were being called in question.

The appeal of use and wont had little force.

Conventional respectability was impotent to resist the challenge of successful adventurers and gangsters.

The standards of the older generation had lost their moral prestige.

Education was a problem.

Aristotle felt that it was his function to diagnose the social situation of his time, and prescribe a remedy compounded of traditional values and new educational methods.

Sir Walter Moberly has succinctly summarized this educational creed of Aristotle thus: *

*Presidential address delivered to the Classical Association of St. Albans, April, 1944, Oxford Press, 1944.

1. Of all the activities of Natural life, Education is the most important.

2. In education what is most important is not training in particular techniques but general education for life.

3. Yet technical education is a model of method, while what purports to be Education for life is a sham, for it is based on no coherent philosophy of life.

4. The gap must be filled by a true philosophy of life.

5. Responsibility for education belongs inescapably to the community.

6. Education is far wider than schooling as ordinarily understood. To be efficient it must include control of the whole of the people's environment.

7. Intensive education for select few for leadership is the crown of the whole educational process and the only guarantee of its successful working.

It was out of Aristotle's inductive method that the sciences of phsysiology, mechanics, physics, and politics were born.

Why in western Europe he has been so generally given as the authority for the deductive logic of the middle ages is not altogether clear.

The three great Athenian philosophers, Socrates, Plato, and Aristotle, seem to have had a greater influence on the thinking of the educators of the Renaissance and post-Renaissance period in Western Europe than they did on their own immediate society.

Socrates was forced to suicide on the charge of corrupting the youth of Athens.

Plato and Aristotle, who were better understood by their contemporaries, seem to have occasioned little change in the thinking or practice of their time.

Sophist individualism remained, whether in Stoic or Epicurean dress. Schools were established to keep alive the conflict between Greek Sophistry and Classical ideas. The Academy was founded by Plato in 386 B.C., the Lyceum by Aristotle in 335 B.C., the Stoic school by Zeno in 308 B.C., and the School of Epicurus in 308 B.C. These were gradually fused into the University of Athens, which continued to function until the early part of the sixth century A.D. The latter afforded a gathering place and a focus for higher education throughout its long history, and for a part of the period enjoyed a precarious state of subsidy from Athens and, after the conquest, from Rome.

It was one of the five great Greek schools sharing the honors and responsibilities of higher education with Alexandria, Tarsus, Pergamus, and Rhodes.

The University of Alexandria, founded in 280 B.C., had a much larger library (700,000 volumes), was more cosmopolitan in policy and student body, more liberally and consistently supported by the Ptolmies, and before its capture by the Mohammedans in 640 A.D., had produced more illustrious scholars.

Alexandria after the second century B.C. was the Mecca of the knowledge-hungry of the near east and the western world.

Archimedes, the father of physics, and Euclid, of mathematics, Eratosthanes the astronomer, and many of the most outstanding rhetoricians of the period were products of this university.

It was here that the historical books of the Hebrew scriptures were translated into Greek forming the Septuagint.

It embraced also the earliest catechetical schools of Christianity.

Out of none of these schools, however, have come the daring philosophies of the earlier classical writers.

PLATO'S WRITING ON EDUCATION

The Platonic dialogues concern themselves much with education. In the republic, Plato sets forth in detail his views on education in the form in which he held them in his earlier life when his theory of reality carried him away.

For a second time in later life he rewrote his views and plans for education in the *Laws*.

The fact that these two somewhat vague sets of views and plans for education exist makes it difficult to generalize on the educational system he approved of.

Students who are interested in the details must study both the *Republic* and the *Laws*.

It is perhaps sounder, however, to consider not what Plato thought but what he did, and what were the far-reaching results of his work, results which reach down to the very present and mold, in part, the life of every college student through both the form in which the college exists and through the curriculum which it uses.(*An Estimate of Plato's Principles, George Burgess, The Works of Plato, London, 1854, pp. 708-10.*)

This chapter would be incomplete without the inclusion of a typical Socratic dialectic to show the method of teaching in this early period.

As was his custom, Socrates was walking one day in a public place when he met a young man named Euthydemus.

The two entered into a conversation on a typical Socratic subject, that of justice.

"Tell me, Euthydemus, have you really, as I hear, collected many of the writings of the men who are said to have been wise?"

"I have indeed, Socrates, replied he "and I am still collecting, intending to persevere until I get as many as I possibly can."

"By Juno," rejoined Socrates, "I feel admiration for you, because you have not preferred acquiring treasures of silver and gold rather than wisdom; for it is plain that you consider that silver and gold are unable to make men better, but that the thoughts of wise men enrich their possessors with virtue."

Euthydemus was delighted to hear this commendation, believing that he was thought by Socrates to have sought wisdom in the right course.

Socrates, observing that he was gratified with the praise, said," And in what particular art do you wish to become skillful, that you collect these writings?"

As Euthydemus continued silent, considering what reply he should make, Socrates again asked, "Do you wish to become a physician? For there are many writings of physicians."

"Not I, by Jupiter," replied Euthydemus.

"Do you wish to become an architect, then? For a man of knowledge is needed in that art also."

"No, indeed," answered he.

"Do you wish to become a good geometrician, like Theodorus?"

"Nor a geometrician, either," said he .

"Do you wish then to become an astronomer?" said Socrates.

As Euthydemus said "No" to this, "Do you wish, then, "added Socrates,"to become a rhapsodist, for they say you are in possession of all the poems of Homer?"

"No indeed, "said he, "for I know that the rhapsodists, though eminently knowing in all the poems of Homer, are, as men, extremely foolish."

"You are perhaps desirous then," proceeded Socrates, "of attaining that talent by which men become skilled in governing estates, in managing households, able to command, and qualified to benefit other men as well as themselves."

"I indeed greatly desire," said he, "Socrates, to acquire that talent."

"By Jupiter," returned Socrates, "you aspire to a most honorable accomplishment, and a most exalted art, for it is the art of kings, and is called the royal art." "But, "added he,"have you ever considered whether it is possible for a man who is not just to be eminent in that art?"

"I have certainly," replied he, "and it is not possible for a man to be even a good citizen without justice."

"Have you yourself, then, made yourself master of that virtue?"

"I think," said he, "Socrates, that I shall be found not less just than any other man."

"Are there, then, works of just men, as there are works of artisans?"

"There are, doubtless,"said he.

"Then," said Socrates, "as artisans are able to show their works, would not just men be able also to tell their works?"

"And why should not I?" asked Euthydemus, "be able to tell the works of justice; as also, indeed, the works of injustice; for we may see and hear of no small number of them every day."

"Are you willing, then," said Socrates, "that we should make a *delta* on this side, and an *alpha* on that, and then we should put whatever seems to us to be a work of justice under the *delta*, and whatever seems to be a work of injustice under the *alpha*?"

If you think that we need those letters," said Euthydemus, "make them."

Socrates, having made the letters as he proposed, asked" Does falsehood then exist among mankind?

"It does assuredly, "replied he.

"Under what head shall we place it?"

"Under injustice, certainly."

"Does deceit also exist?"

"Unquestionably."

"Under which head shall we place that?"

"Evidently under injustice."

"Does mischievousness exist?"

"Undoubtedly."

"And the enslaving of men?"

"That, too, prevails."

"And shall neither of these things be placed by us under justice, Euthydemus?"

"It would be strange if they should be,"said he.

"But," said Socrates, "If a man being chosen to lead an army, should reduce to slavery an unjust and hostile people, should we say that he committed an injustice?"

"No, certainly," replied he.

"Should we not rather say that he acted justly?"

"Indisputably."

"And if in the course of the war with them he should practice deceit?"

"That also would be just," said he.

"And if he should steal and carry off their property, would he not do what was just?"

"Certainly," said Euthydemus," but I thought at first that you asked these questions only with reference to our friends."

"Then," said Socrates, "all that we have placed under the head of injustice, we must also place under that of justice?"

"It seems so,"replied Euthydemus.

"Do you agree, then," continued Socrates, "that having so placed them, we should make a new distinction, that it is just to do such things without regard to enemies, but unjust to do them with regard to friends, and that towards his friends our general should be as guileless as possible?"

"By all means," replied Euthydemus.

"Well, then" said Socrates, "if a general, seeing his army dispirited, should tell them, inventing a falsehood, that auxiliaries were coming, and should, by that invention, check the despondency of his troops, under which head should we place such an act of deceit?"

"It appears to me," said Euthydemus, "that we must place it under justice."

"And if a father, when his son requires medicine, and refuses to take it, should deceive him, and give him the medicine as ordinary food, and by adopting such deception, should restore him to health, under which head must we place such an act of dec`eit?"

"It appears to me that we must put it under the same head."

"And if a person, when his friend was in despondence, should through fear that he might kill himself, steal or take away his sword, or any other weapon, under which head must we place that act?"

"That, assuredly, we must place under justice."

"You say, then," said Socrates, "that not even toward our friends must we act on all occasions without deceit?"

"We must not, indeed, "said he, "for I retract what I said before, if I may be permitted to do so."

"It is indeed much better that you should be permitted," said Socrates,"than that you should not place actions on the right side. But of those who deceive their friends in order to injure them (that we may not even leave this point unconsidered) which of the two is the more unjust, he who does so intentionally, or he who does so involuntarily?"

"Do you know any person called slave-like?"

"I do."

"Whether for their knowledge or their ignorance?"

"For their ignorance, certainly."

"Is it, then, for their ignorance of working in brass that they receive this appellation?"

"Not at all."

"Is it for their ignorance in the art of building?"

"Nor for that."

"Or for their ignorance of shoemaking?"

"Not on any of these accounts; for the contrary is the case, as most of those who know such trades are servile."

"Is it then an appelation of those who are ignorant of what is honorable and good and just?"

"It appears so to me."

"It therefore becomes us to exert ourselves in every way to avoid being like slaves."

"But, by the gods, Socrates," rejoined Euthydemus," I firmly believed that I was pursuing that course of study by which I should, as I expected, be made fully acquainted with all that was proper to be known by a man striving after honor and virtue; but now, how dispirited must I feel, when I see that, with all my previous labor, I am not even able to answer about what I ought most of all to know, and am acquainted with no other course which I may pursue to become better."

---

*(*A Socratic Dialectic*, E.P. Cubberley, *Readings in the History of Education*, Houghton, Mifflin, 1920.)

2

Education in Cultural Perspecitve

Zakir Hussain wrote that :

> The characteristic mark of an educated man should be a positive attitude towards the goods of culture, that is, towards the ultimate objective values. That attitude should be the cherished product of educational and institutional activity.

Almost every human child is born in a family. Each family, whatever may be its nature, complexions and membership has certain traditions, customs or methods for rearing children and leading a social life. These, the family may acquire from other people in its contact or may get them as transmitted from the previous generation. Whatever may be the source, they form the part of the culture in which the child is brought up. They influence the life of the child from the very beginning and as he grows up form the powerful ingredients of his learning process. Thus to get an insight into the learning process of the child it is almost essential to get an understanding of the culture in which he is born. But what does culture signify? This is the problem which must be examined first of all.

THE DEFINITION OF CULTURE

Very often quoted definition of cultures is given by Taylor. It says:

"Culture is that complex whole which includes knowledge, belief, art, morals, law, custom, and any other capabilities acquired by man as a member of society." In accordance with this definition culture is some thing more than the material wealth of a society. It refers to the capabilities acquired by men.

According to Bantock "the word culture is normally used in two broad senses. It is used by anthrpologists to refer to the total pattern of a society's life........... The other typical use of the word culture however, involves a high degree of selectivity. In the first sense culture refers to the ways in which men cooperate or conflict, their social and political institutions, their customs, rituals and taboos, their methods of rearing children, etc. Taking in this sense culture is revealed by everything in the social life. In the second sense, on the other hand culture something selective. It is concerned with a particular set of skills, ways of understanding and the productions, etc. The use of the term "cultured man" is in this second sense. He is recognized as a sophisticated, well-read, knowledgeable individual who had a long period of education and has developed rationality. In whatever sense we use the word, culture its implication for education are profound. The social living is influenced by education and education itself is governed by social life. The total pattern of a society's life determines education and education moulds the total pattern of society's life. Education produces a cultured man and is also nurtured and nourished by the cultured man. Hence in accepting a meaning of culture which may have relevance for its relations with education we will have to take both the broad as well as narrow view of culture in to consideration.

To get a still better concept of the term 'culture' let us further analyeses the definition given by Taylor. According to Brameld Taylor's definition includes seven more or less distionct components. First of all it refe rs to complex whole.

'The complex whole' indicates that culture possesses some kind of unity. It may have many parts but all parts are intergrated in to a 'whole. This 'whole may give a pattern or design. Second "it embraces an array of psychological achievement that are not so much visible in the form of material objects as they are expressions of emotional and mental life." In the third place it may also include such material-objects those of art or those of marality as manifested in the conduct of visible groups like family. The difinition by Taylor fourthly puts emphasis on customs, capabilities, habits. These refer to a kind of behaviour that manifests a certain regularity and continuity. Fifth Taylor refers to culture as a reality to be viewed objectively and impartially. Sixth, culture is not due to hereduty. It is acquired by man from his surroundings. Seventh, culture is obtained by living in a society. It cannot be acquired individually through only the genius of man.

From the above it seems that Taylor's definition is quite comprehensive. It is because of this fact that this definition is very frequently used even though it is one of the earliest definitions of culture. If we properly extend the implications of Taylor's definition we will find that the terms 'knowledge' and 'belief' imply that culture embraces philosophy, religion, science, as well as folklore and superstitions. Similarly "other capabilities and habits" in Taylor's definition when properly interpreted may imply crafts, skills industry etiquette symbolism instruction, painting, points of view, and goals. This comprehensibility in Taylor's definition might have influenced Fraz Boas to give a more explicit interpretation to the term culture. He says, "Culture embraces all the manifestations of social habits of a community, the reactions of the individual as affected by the habits of the group in which he lives, and the products of human activities as determined by these habits. This definition as also the earlier one, that of Taylor have recognized the importance of the role of both the individual and the society in a culture. Similar ideas are expressed by Malinowski. He says: "culture comprises inherited artifacts, goods. technical processes, ideas, habits and values."

Malinowski considers that man varies in two respects; in physical form and in social heritage or culture. The variations in physical form are due to his heredity. The biologists trace them to the individual's genes combinations. The individual takes the genes from his parents and develops in accordance with them. But the gene combination alone does not determine his life cycle. Once born to particular parents he starts living his life in a social environment. As described above this social environment brings changes in his behaviour pattern and plays a vital role in his developmental process. Also as he develops, he contributes to his social environment. The cultural heritage in which he is born helps him to satisfy his needs. His physiological needs are partly satisfied through his native endowment but to a great extent their satisfaction depends on the cultural environment. For example a child feels hungry. Hunger is a physiological need. The satisfaction of it is food. But food in the form of mother's milk is provided to it in a cultural context. Every human group emphasizes the feeding of the child. In feeding it the mother follows a pattern which she has learnt from others in her social environment. This learning is at the root of the development of a culture. Thus culture develops as a human being gets aid from his associates in the group to satisphy the needs which are born initially out of his own physiological make up or innate urges. The aid which he gets not only satisfies his needs but alos modifies his innate endowment. The child learns slowly not to cry for food but wait for it till the mother; is able to cook and feed him. The giving of aid, which include the object of aid and the process of aid, we may term as culture. Thus food which is given to the child, the way it is cooked and served form the culture of the group in which the child lives. The child learns to modify his behaviour, he learns to surrender his liberty and relishes his obligations due to the demands which others make upon him. This process is also an aspect of culture. Thus we may say with Malinowski, "culture deeply modifies human innate endowment, and in doing this it not only bestows blessings but also imposes obligations and demands the surrender of a great many personal liberties to the common welfare.

To sum up we may say that culture is the creation of man. It includes all that the group conserves for modifying his innate endowments and to meet his innate urges. It emanates from man but is responsible for giving a direction and purpose to his life. It extends the range of individual efficiency and of his power of action. It supplements the man's native endowments and provides him with an additional extension of his anatomical apparatus. It is learned and is thus not the same as biological heredity. It may be called as social heredity.

A term culture pattern is used to describe the ways of behaviour associated with any permanent need or function in the social life. The way the food is eaten in different societies is the pattern of their culture. The Indians eat food, with their hands and fingers. The English use the spoon, fork and knive. These represent the pattern of culture in the two societies. The need is however, the same the food. The emergence of culture is around this need but the patterns which develop are different. Hence we may say that different societies have different cultural patterns. The language, literature, the rearing up of the young, the values in the society the myths customs ideologies beliefs and faiths all are the pattern of culture differ in different societies.

EDUCATION AND CULTURE

The broad - based definition of culture gives us an idea that culture is a complex whole. In this complex whole a child is born. He comes with his physiological endowment but they are not sufficient to let him live peacefully and in harmony with his environment. He has to learn to modify them and to put them to their maximum use in order to satisfy his own needs. This learning means that the society's patterns of culture be transmitted to him. This process of transmission of culture when formally or informally organized refers to the education of the child. Therefore, the transmission of the cultural patterns is one of the important function of education

The definitions of culture given above amply clarify that our culture exercises a profound influence over us. Our way of life is determined to a great extent by it. We learn to see the world as our culture makes us see it. We neither see it in accordance with our pure sensations nor in the light of our own institutions For example, the appreciation of a beautiful flower is not an innate endowment. It is culture in which we are born that guides our ideas towards such an appreciation. Most of those who visit Taj Mahal at Agra appreciate it, and are enamored of its beauty. But there are people born in a had core of Communist society who look towards it not with an eye for beauty but with the notion of the misery caused to the labour in building this gigantic mausoleum. Their love for beauty is clouded with their feelings of misery which a powerful king might have caused to the innocent people who had been treated worse than the beasts of burden. Instances of the influence of culture in moulding our way of thinking can be multiplied. A medieval man saw the world of natural phenomena in a way very different from that seen by us today. Thunder to or medieval man was due to the wrath of gods. Today we understand the natural phenomenon underlying this happening Our feelings, our attitudes, our ideals and beliefs all are the products of our culture. No doubt, we may say that each individual has his own unique way of understanding, of meeting needs and of facing the world, but he is all the time guided by what culture teaches him about life. Since education equips him to understand his environment to learn his course of action in life, to inculcate values and to acquire beliefs and attitudes it cannot proceed without enveloping culture in its orbit.

The above sentence may give an impression that culture is subordinate to education. This will be an erroneous notion. By saying that education envelops culture in its orbit we simply mean that in education culture is an inclusive concept. When we talk of education we are talking of the education of a being who is living in a cultural environment. This being is a product of biological combinations but the biological happening of this birth is in a culture context. The care of the mother during pregnancy when the child is growing up in her womb and which determines its development process is culture oriented. In some cultures the pregnant mother is given utmost care and consideration and in others it is considered as a natural happening and the routine of a pregnant woman is not at all altered. There is a story about the wives of a king. The king went out on an usual and routine round of his kingdom. He found in a hutment in a corner of a town a woman delivering a child without any commotion in the family or near about. The next day the woman was up and working. The king on his return to the capital called his wives and rebuked them, asked them to take their pregnancies lightly and ordered that henceforth they would not be cared for during their pregnancies. The result of this neglect was that many of his dear queens died in child birth. The Vazir who was an intelligent man ordered the gardeners not to tend toe flowers in the garden of the King. After some time the garden started decaying and the atmosphere became dusty. The king was perturded and called the gardeners. The Vazir stood on their behalf and said, "Sir, you have seen the flowers blooming in their full glory in the jungles where no one for them. Why should then these flowers be cared for?" The king was quick in grasping the point and ordered full care for his queens during their pregnancies. The story has a clear meaning. It is the cultural environment which determines the way of life which become ingrained in the people. To prepare the individual for his life the task of education. This task education cannot discharge unless it peeps in to the culture of the people.

Not only that culture provides the data for education but it also provides every shape to education. Education is a part of the cultural pattern. Its nature is determined by the culture in which it is organized. In fact its very existence is determined by the culture of the people. Among people who are living in remote corners of a backward country there is felt no need for a formalized system of education. Whatever patterns are necessary for their modest existence they are transmitted informally from the parents to the offspring. On the other hand, in highly developed technological societies education is also demanded in a highly organized form.

In describing the relationship between culture and education we have emphasized transmission of culture through education. In the previous chapter we have discussed this role in some detail while describing the functions of education. There we have also emphasized another function of education which relates to social change. It may once again be reiterated here that education is not only concerned with the transmission of culture but it also builds new cultural patterns. It brings changes changes a in the existing culture. These changes are necessitated due to the cross-cultural contacts or the buildings of new knowledge which makes the old cultural patterns redundant. The individual is equipped to bring the cultural changes so as to meet his needs in a changing environment and is prepared to adjust his life with the changed cultural life in which he had been born or lived a portion of his life, so that it may be a very major portion. We may say now that (I) education is a product of culture, (II) education functions towards the transmission of culture to the new generation (III) education leads to cultural change (IV) education equips the individual to adjust himself in the changing cultural patterns.

EDUCATION AND INDIAN CULTURE

Spindler says, "the discrepancies and conflicts between intent and outcome, between ideal and real that the teacher transmits to children in any class room must originate in the culture. The culture as we have also described above must form the context in which education is to be provided to the individuals. It is in the cultural context that we can understand the problems and aspirations of education. It is, therefore, necessary that we must make a study of Indian culture before we can discuss the problems and issues in Indian education.

In the first two chapter of this book we have made an attempt to deal with some background factors of Indian social order. We have pointed out the diversities and the need for unity. The diversities as well as the efforts of unity are all parts of our culture. They give a peep into the way of life which has been, moulded in this country due to the cultural heritage and cross cultural impacts, However, these two do not account for all what we consider as Indian culture. They are only small fragments of the culture which we may term an Indian culture.

Let us then first understand as to what specifically we mean by Indian culture.

There is no uniformity in the thinking about Indian culture. The opinions range from denying the existence Indian culture to the inclusion of all that is worthy or unworthy in the human heritage as Indian culture. The denial of Indian culture is often based on a confusion between the culture of a people and the culture of a people of a particular political state. Since India had no political unity in the past it is denied to have any culture. Another source of confusion is inherent in our treating culture and religion as synonyms. Religion is a pattern of culture and much in the cultural heritage of a people might be due to religion. But religion and culture are different. If on the basis of political unity or religion we define culture then we can have no hesitation in saying that there is no such thing like Indian culture. On the other hand if culture is taken in the sense in which we have described it above we will have to admit that there are very sound reasons to believe in the existence of Indian culture.

Indian culture has a long history. Its patterns emerged in the Vedic period. In the course of time they were enriched but only in a few respects they were completely transformed. The belief-system, the values and ideals and the ways of looking at the supernatural had all emanated during the Vedic period and continued till the modern times. The pattern of family life took shape at the same time and with the passage of time except for the addition of more rigidity and orthodoxy no other changes in it took place. The society was divided in 'Varnas' - the Brahmin, the Kshatriya, the Vaishya and the Shudra—and except for the regimentation of it in these 'Varnas' and sub division of 'varnas' in various castes no change in its complexion could take place.

The Muslims, the Christians, the Parsis came to this country. They brought their own culture but that had very little effect on the original residents of this land. In fact they were all absorbed in a biggger cultural milieu of the society. They kept their religion separate and a number of practices which went with their religion but so far as value system, faith in sprituality, ideals of life and the pattern of family life were concerned, they followed the same ways of life as the Hindus. However, on this point there may be some differences of opinion. The two nation theory of Jinnah divided the country. The orthodox of both religions may not believe that there is any intermingling between the cultures. To be at grips with this dilemma let us concentrate towards some of the aspects of Indian culture

Indian Family: The Indian life is concentrated in the family life. Though the marriage customs offer anong different religions, castes and regional groups, yet the structure of an Indian family is not very much different among different groups of the family. The bride comes to the family and in time brings forth her child. The husband, the wife and the child form the nucleus of the family. The husband's relations also stay in the house and give the family a character of joint living. The child is considered as the fulfilment of the cherished desire of a 'grahastha'. A male child is preferred to a female child. As the child grows the family takes over the task of inducting him into social life. In Indian pattern the sanctity of the family life, the birth of a child preferably male; the weaving of the aspirations of the parents around the child and: the influence of the joint family member on the upbringing of the child are some typical aspects which give it a distinctiveness. The child is expected to be obedient and respectful. Mandelbaum describing a family, Jati, village, has come to the conclusion that there are interesting parallels in child rearing between one village Khalapur, some ninety miles north of Delhi and the other Angadi in Calicut district. The children studied, belonged to the caste of Jat in north and of 'Nayars' in the south. It is interesting to note that village Khalapur is within sight of the snow peaks of the Himalayas and Angadi is on the tropical coastal strip of the southernmost state of Kerala. These studies establish the contention that in child rearing practices the cultural patterns are quite similar in whole of the Indian sub-continent.

Stratification: Indian cultural order is very much blamed for its social stratification. The Indian society is divided into different classes, groups and castes which emphasize their own identity and are hostile to no another. Among the most enduring form of social stratification is considered the caste system. The caste system is usually confined to Hindus who form the bulk of population. But it is interesting to note that this type of stratification has also influenced the Muslims and the Christians. The Muslims with their Saiyads and Khan, with their Khojas and Bhoras are also stratified. Though this stratification is not exactly akin to the caste type of stratification of Hindus, their basis being different, is nonetheless a stratification of the same class. No doubt, stratification occurs in each and every culture but the caste-type of stratification is the peculiarity of Indian culture.

There are sociologists who also talk of caste -system in American society. They define caste system in a manner that it includes the stratification of Negro and White in America. Berreman considers that "......the term' caste system' is applicable at the present time in the southern United States...... and......it can be usefully applied to societies with systems of hierarchical, endogamous subdivisions whose membership is hereditary and permanent." But it may be asserted that there are striking local differences between this form of organization and that of India. Harper who made a comparative analysis of caste in the United States and India says, "Although the systems of caste in the United States and in India are similar in great many respects; in two features—the importance of race and the number of castes which compose the respective systems—they differ fundamentally, and from these differences others follow."

In India caste system began as ethnic stratification and continued as social stratification. Caste is unchangeable. It is from birth. There are today attempts to modify the caste system. It is, however, difficult to change it. Caste is a pattern of culture. Culture rests in the minds of men. Till the minds of men are not changed it is difficult to change the caste-system. The peculiarities of Indian caste system may be described as under:

1. One becomes the member of a caste by birth.

2. Caste is unchangeable. It is for life.
3. One marries within his own caste line.
4. Contacts between castes or sub-castes is strictly regulated by the mores.
5. Each castes has its own customs and often its traditional occupation.
6. The castes are governed by a hierarchical order. This is fixed and any changes in it are bitterly resisted.

Besides caste system the other types of stratifications in Indian society are due to religion and economic order. There are Hindus, Muslims, Christians, Parsis etc., having their own way of worship, religious philosophy and religious ideals. There are also very rich and extremely poor people in the country. The poor, however, far outnumber the rich.

Value System: The value system inherent in the Indian cultural order is also worth examination. It has been emphasized in the first chapter that the base of the Indian society is spiritualism. In this society life of spirit is given more importance than the physical life. In ancient India the soul formed the core of Indian thought. Muslim saints did not differ from this line of thought and even the Christian influence was in the same direction. So the Indian value system is woven around the training of the soul. A life of piety, religiousness and worship is considered to be the best life lived which delivers the soul from earthly bondage.

The ideals of respect to elders, cleanliness, physical as well as mental, 'dharma' 'shraddha' and 'karma' are the prominent ones. The forbearance and tolerance are other ideas which have permeated the Indian society. In the modern times the ideals of democracy and secularism are further added to the already existing value system.

There are many other aspects of culture which may be emphasized as the distinctive features of Indian culture but stop over here. In a book on education we have to draw a line on a general discussion of culture. Therefore, even when many other aspect of Indian culture are of great importance in understanding the Indian social and cultural scene we have to stop with the cursory but none-the-less significant glance over the various aspects of Indian culture.

Before we close discussion on Indian culture one aspect of it is worth paying attention to. This is the perennial nature of Indian culture. Radhakrishnan speaking about culture at one occasion has said:

> "The more Indian culture changes, the more it remains the same. The power of the Indian spirit has sustained us through difficult times. It is the intangibles that give a nation its character and vitality."

The Indian culture thus is ancient. It has survived through the ages and is still in a from which can be traced to its ancient origin.

EDUCATION AND INDIAN CULTURE

Education is required to perform the functions of transmission, of fulfilments and enrichment, acceptance and reformulation change and reconstruction. It transmits the culture to the new generation and transforms the outlook of the young towards life in the background of the past, in the context of cross-cultural influences and in the light of the future requirements for the individual and the society. It provides for the fulfilment of the needs of the individuals born out of his being a member of a culturally oriented society. Its function is also to make the life of the individual rich by giving him knowledge of the cultural attainments of the race. Education also helps the individuals in developing a behaviour pattern which makes him acceptable in a cultural milieu and not only this but also equips him for reformulating the cultural milieu with the experiences gained by him by li ving his own life. Culture should never be static. Every moment the man changes and with him the society change. Culture, therefore, also needs a change. Education equips the individual for bringing about cultural changes and for constructing new cultural patterns.

The modern system of education in India is not a system which has evolved out from its own cultural heritage. It has been transplanted from the West and hence many of the functions required of it are not performed. It has been given a shape which emphasizes only bookish knowledge, emorization of facts and the learning of that which can be tested by an elaborate system of examination. It is, therefore, needed that it is re-organized. A large number of Indian philosophers and thinkers of the modern times have preached and propagated for putting it in a proper cultural perspective and for making it a vehicle of change but nothing much has been done about it. It is because or this that an Indian student is neither conversant with the Indian culture nor is prepared to bring about any changes in the cultural patterns. We have said earlier that culture rests in the minds of men and it is to them that an appeal is to be directed so that the educated may imbibe the cultural values and weed out the undesirable patterns of culture. The caste stratification in such a pattern needs an immediate weeding out. But our young men and women have not been properly equipped to attain this change. This is the reason why every time we go to elections the caste plays a major role.

Kothari Commission 1964-66 has emphasized the national and social objectives of education. In Indian thought much is available regarding the changes needed in the country's educational system. But perhaps the perennial nature of culture has entered in our educational system as well. We seem to have established a perennial educational system which resists all changes. The perennial nature of culture has kept our spirit alive but the perennial nature of education is crushing the very spirit which it wants to build. Hence today we need a system of education which lays stress on the transmission of the cultural ideals and values and which also bring cultural changes in keeping with the modern scientific and technological changes.

Enculturation and Education: Mary Goodman uses the

word enculturation to describe the process of transmitting a culture to the young. She quotes R. Pinot to emphasize the need of cultural transmission. Pinot's view is reproduced here:

> Every day society is submitted to a terrible invasion: within it a multitude of small barbarians are born. They would quickly overthrow the whole social order and all the institutions of society, if they were not well disciplined and educated.

This disciplining and educating can proceed through a process of enculturation. But this process of enculturating differs from society to society. It is quite a complex process in a highly developed society. The child comes to the world with his own individual make-up. The process of enculturating him has to keep this individual aspect into consideration.

The enculturating to a great extent takes place through indirect, informal and unconscious processes. It is living in a cultural milieu that the transmission of culture takes place. It is because of this fact that enquiries into the process of enculturating in deferent societies form important part of investigations in cultural anthropology. The child acquires the cultural patterns from his group. A Chinese or an American child or for that matter an Indian is exposed to a different cultural environment and hence due to this, enculturating varies from society to society. Hsu says, "It is no exaggeration to say that while the Chinese glorify their ancestors and the Hindus glorify their gods, the Americans glorify their children." These changes io outlook and similar changes in practice are responsible for variations in enculturating process.

Through education the enculturating process is formalized It is to this aspect that our concern in the present book lies. The transmission of culture should take place in a formal manner. For this the children should be given right type of training. This training, therefore, should be based on

(i) an understanding of the culture of the society,

(ii) an understanding of the individual,

(iii) an understanding of the informal and unconscious

ways by which the child acquires the cultural pattern. Here a study of child-reading practices in the society will be of great help, and

(iv) an understanding of what needs to be transmitted in the light of the present and the future needs of the society.

The last point above brings us to the concept of change. Education is not only concerned with the simple transmission. Its importance lies in preparing the child to meet the needs of the society. Since society is continually changing its needs also go on changing. It is for meeting the changing needs and also for bringing about the desirable changes in the society that education is needed.

3

Sense Realism in Education

Toward the end of the eighteenth century, closely following Rousseau's emphasis on naturalism and individualism in education, and not entirely unconnected with it, came the sense realism (learning by working with the hands) emphasis of Pestalozzi and his two disciples, Herbart and Froebel.

The three men, although differing widely as to aim method, and age of the pupils on which they specialized, nevertheless belong together in their fundamental theory of education. They have had a varying influence on all the systems of education. that were to follow.

HENRI PESTALOZZI (1746 -1827)

The work of Henri Pestalozzi marks the turning point from the old to the new in Western education.

The theories of both the Realists and the Humanists had been weighed and found wanting.

A basis had already been laid by the empiricism of Locke and Rousseau for a scientific approach to education.

Kant was bringing empiricism and rationalism into intellectual harmony.

The times were ripe for the daringly constructive theory of the modest little teacher at Bergdorf.

The caste system of the 18th century everywhere was being questioned.

Napoleon was obliterating national boundaries; the common people were clamoring for liberty and the overthrow of time-honored institutions.

The extravagances of the landholders were being challenged; education in theory was universal, but its methods were crude, and circumscribed by religious traditionalism.

Throughout Europe wages were stabilized at a low level, prices of food were rising, ignorance and vice were rampant, poverty was taken for granted, and living for the poor was austere.

It was definitely a time for a change in pedagogy, and Henri Pestalozzi was the man who offered the magic formula.

Pestalozzi was born in Zurich, of middle class parents, and schooled for the Christian ministry, studied law, and later gave his attention to the science and pursuit of agriculture.

He considered farming "the best means of raising man morally and promoting thereby his comfort and happiness.

His first industrial school at Neuhof was for "beggars," actually children of the very poor.

Dependent upon philanthropic funds, the school failed for lack of support, after six years of the most strenuous effort on the part of its founder.

His second school for orphans at Stanz expired after two years for the same reason.

It was while in his third teaching position as Master of the Common School at Bergdorf, that he elaborated his new theory and method of primary education.

He did not technically become a teacher until he was 51

years of age, but after he started, he continued to teach and write until he died at 81.

The first thirty years of experiments in working with and trying to salvage beggars and orphans, from a business standpoint, was a failure.

These waifs were to be taught to develop thrift and responsibility while they worked, and thus to be made over into good citizens, but his sympathy for them made him an easy taskmaster.

The kindly benefactor was exploited by those who came not to learn but to eat.

The experiment discovered to him that "it is not the improvement of the outward condition of the individual which brings happiness to the community, but his intellectual and moral development."

He undertook to produce a condition in which the happiness of a person would not be affected from without because its source would be from within.

Hence the need of training the young by a new method in order to raise the moral condition of the community.

His educational purpose thus was clear.

Until Pestalozzi's time, education had been largely a matter of hearing about things by verbal process.

He took the ground that real knowledge came through observing things, acquiring an insight into the nature of things rather than through being told about them.

Knowledge, he maintained, comes not through verbal formulas and signs, but by examining with one's senses.

This is something the youth must do for himself.

The teacher must not stand in his way.

Only by skillful, sympathetic direction can he encourage the child's proper exercise of his senses.

In his reaction against the traditional educational methods, and to facilitate the learning process, Pestalozzi even advocated the banishment of books that there might be no stereotyped barrier between the teacher and the child.

Sense perception (anschauung) to Pestalozzi was the basis of all learning; numbers, form, and language its means; and moral, intellectual and physical development in equilibrium its end.

It will be noted that these concepts are very similar to those of Kant; in fact, the philosophy of Kant subtly underlies the practical educational reforms of Pestalozzi.

Pestalozzi's conception of education may be summarized in the following propositions:

1. Education reforms and elevates society
2. Education is the function of the state
3. The child must be educated in society
4. Education involves a natural and harmonious development of all the faculties
5. Education requires an active cooperation between home and school.
6. Education is based on the sensory experience of the child
7. The fundamental principle of instruction is sense impression (anschauung). Under anschauung he includes:
   a. Knowledge obtained through sense impression
   b. Observation, i.e., the act by which knowledge is obtained
   c. The mental faculties by which it is obtained
   d. The objects observed– sense objects

8. The means of instruction are number, form, and language.

Pestaloozi's contribution to education was also influenced by Rousseau, but, unlike Rousseau, Pestalozzi did not stop with the theory of individual freedom.

He rejected the freedom theory after trying it out on his own son.

"Freedom is good", said he, "but so is obedience also".

He advocated expression and restraint in perfect balance and, by testing it through 60 years of experience, proved its worth.

The great innovator had no educational system, but many ideas.

The latter are to be found in his three books: *Leonard and Gertrude, The Evening Hour with a Hermit,* and *How Gertrude Teaches Her Children.*

The first may be used to show how Pestalozzi would have children taught even in the humblest home.

Gertrude was the intelligent mother of a large family.

Her husband, in spite of his good intentions, was a victim of drink.

Gertrude, because of the family's poverty, could not send the children to school, so she undertook to educate them herself.

Every phase of the life of the family is drawn upon to pint up lessons in science, art, music, ethics, hygiene, taste manners, morals, and religion.

Physics comes out of the building of the fire in the fireplace.

It is surprising how many laws of physics–heat, light, draft, air circulation, and control-are illustrated in the simple process of getting the oven ready to bake the biscuits; how many laws of chemistry are illustrated by the mixing of the foods and chemicals to provide the appetizing breakfast; how rules of etiquette, taste, manners are brought to realization as the breakfast proceeds, and so through the whole day's activities.

With intelligent guidance, the family life presents substantially all studies taken up in the schools.

It is the natural laboratory for adventures of head and hand and heart and in their natural sequence.

The following selections from Pestalozzi's writings contain the elements of his theory.

The importance of his influence warrants a rather extended group of his observations.

"The education of men is nothing else than the fitting of every ring of the great chain which cements humanity and makes it a whole."

"The idea of elementary education to which I have devoted my life consists in re-establishing the course of nature, and in developing and improving the tendencies and powers of humanity. It must aim at developing heart, mind, and body in such a way as to bring the flesh into subjection to the spirit."

"Education must consist in a continual benevolent superintendence, with the object of calling forth all the faculties which Providence has implanted."

"Elementary education is nothing else but conformity to nature in the development and perfection to the dispositions and faculties of men."

"The threefold aim of education is to fix the attention, to form the judgment, and to elevate the sentiments."

"A child who knows how to pray, work, and think is already half educated."

"My idea of elementary education was suggested to me by the evils I saw about me; evils resulting from the routine of the ordinary education."

"I wanted to prove by my experiment that if public education is to have any real value it must imitate the methods which make the merit of domestic education."

"The home is the true basis of the education of humanity."

"All human growth and power spring from inborn capabilities."

"Elementary education, then, ought to continue under the master, the mother's work, in the spirit of the mother and in the spirit of Christianity. It should in no way put itself in opposition to the child's former relations of feeling and disposition, but should bring its whole activity into living connection with them."

"The aim of education is the development of man as a whole, with all his moral, physical, and intellectual powers; the particular lines of the development depending upon his position in the world –that is, upon the actual life that awaits him."

"The aim of education is not to turn out soldiers, tailors, tradesmen, or bookmakers that are just good; but to turn out tailors, soldiers, etc., who are, in the highest meaning of the word, men."

"The aim of all education and instruction is and can be no other than the harmonious development of the powers and faculties of human nature."

"The problem or aim of education is to train those practical abilities which are necessary for the fulfillment of the duties of life."

"To be happy in this life, and to become a useful member of society is the destiny of man, and is the aim of the education of children."

"The aim of education is the harmonious development of the powers and faculties of human nature."

"Instruction is the imparting of knowledge subjected to a certain order of succession, the beginning of which must be adapted to the first unfolding of the powers of the child, and the progress kept exactly parallel to that of his development."

"The aim of education is to use the ways and means by which every child may be naturally and easily brought to the talents, sentiments, judgments, and attachments by which he becomes happy in his state of life and a useful member of society."

"Teaching is helping the child to become what he is meant to be."

"You should do for the children what their parents fail to do for them. It is all well and good for them to learn something, but the really important thing is for them to become what they are meant to be, and in becoming which they so often have no guidance at home."

"Oh, if men would only comprehend that the aim of all instruction is and can be nothing but the development of human nature by the harmonious cultivation of its powers and talents and the promotion of manliness of life. Oh, if they would only ask themselves, at every step in their methods of education and instruction, "Does it further this end?"

"All instruction of man is only the art of helping nature to develop in her own way. And this art rests essentially on the relation and harmony between the impressions received by the child and the exact degree of his developed powers."

"Sense perception considered by itself is nothing else than the mere being there of external objects before the senses and the mere stirring of the consciousness of their impressions."

"Object lessons are intended to teach the child to observe and to talk by recounting all the impressions received by surrounding objects."

"The child must (1) recognize objects generally and name each as a unity or an object; (2) become conscious of their characteristics and name these; and (3) by language gain power of more precisely determining characteristics."

"It was my object to arouse the faculties and bring them to bear on the pure and simple circumstances of domestic life, for I was convinced that in this way I should be able to form the hearts and the minds of children almost as I pleased."

"The power of receiving impressions and the power of thinking are separated by a wide gulf which can only be bridged by the power of speaking."

"Words alone cannot give us a knowledge of things; they are useful only for giving expression to what we have in our minds."

"Thus I found in teaching to read the necessity of subordination to the power of talking; and in the endeavor to find the means of teaching children to talk, I came on the principle of joining this art to the sequences by which nature rises from sound to word and from word gradually to language."

"The best elementary exercises for developing the child's power of comparing and judging and thus strengthening his thought are those in number and form."

"The path of nature, which develops the forces of humanity, must be easy and open to all."

"I gave my children very few explanations; I taught them neither morality nor religion."

"The schools hastily substitute an artificial method of words for the true method of nature, which knows no hurry and is ready to wait."

JOHANN FRIEDRICH HERBART (1776-1841)

Herbart and Froebel (whose analysis follows immediately) were both students of Petalozzi.

Although they diverged widely in method, their aims and purposes were the same as those of their master.

Herbart favored firmness, education form without, and believed that the curriculum, method, and lessons should be worked out in detail and standardized.

Froebel leaned toward self-expression, freedom informality, and education from within.

The teacher, to Froebel, was to be an artist, not an artisan.

The views were somewhat complementary.

Both are to be found in Pestalozzi.

The early experience of his two disciples may have been responsible for their wide difference in methodology.

Herbart was the oldest son of a counsellor of the Court of Justice in Oldenburg, Germany.

He was educated in a private school and reached the university of Jena at 18 years of age.

He had a philosophic turn of mind and an interest in physics and mathematics.

In 1797 he became the private tutor of the three children of the Governor of Berne, in Switzerland, visited Pestalozzi in Bergdorf frequently, and became an ardent exponent of the principles underlying the Pestalozzian system.

After two years study of mathematics, natural science, and psychology at Bremen, he was appointed professor of philosophy and pedagogics at Gottengen and later to the chair in Konigsburg formerly held by Kant.

He was a highly popular lecturer.

It is said that the students frequently cheered him in the classroom. It was while in the latter university that he set up the famous pedagogical seminar– a school of practice where his thoughts on education were practically applied.

Classes were never permitted to number more than 13, small enough to permit of close supervision, intensive work, and intimacy of contact.

Herbart begins with the two questions: what are the aims of the future man whose interests are committed to my hands? How can I best prepare my pupil for his future life as an adult?

This can be accomplished by cultivating in the student "manysidedness of interest."

To be interested in a thing means to be in love with it, thus interest develops into desire and ultimately into strong will.

Thus the pupil's interest must be developed and extended so that he will seek knowledge.

Herbart's metaphysical concept of interest is not simple, as the following quotations will indicate:

"The educator ought not to stunt the activity of the future man; consequently he ought not to confine it to a few single points, and just as little weaken it by too much diversity. He ought to allow nothing to be lost, either in intension or extension, which his pupil might afterwards demand back from him."

"Every man must have a love for all activities, each must be a virtuoso in one. But the particular virtuosoship is a matter of choice; on the contrary, the manifold susceptibility which can only grow out of one's own individual efforts, is a matter of education."

"Whoever holds fast to his knowledge, and seeks to extend it, is interested in it."

"It is a well-known pedagogic rule that the teacher must interest his pupils in that which he presents. However, this rule is usually given and understood in the sense as if learning were the aim, the interest only the means. I turn this relation around. The learning shall serve to develop the interest. Learning shall pass away and the interest shall remain, throughout the whole life."

"One cannot expect that all the different classes of interest will unfold themselves equally in every individual; but among a large number of pupils they must all be expected; and the demanded many-sidedness will be all the better cultivated the more even the single individual approaches a mental culture, in which all these interests may stir with equal energy."

According to the Herbart system the steps the teacher must follow in the development of interests are five: (1) preparation, (2) presentation, (3) comparison, (4) generalization, and (5) application. Over this standardized, programmed formula literally hundreds of thousands of lesson outlines have been elaborated for the guidance of young teachers.

It formalized many of the unconscious methods which were inherently in all intelligent teaching of the young.

For example, in a lesson on the adjective, the picture of a man, a pool, and a cave is displayed and on the blackboard a short, terse, essential description was written down.

The pupils are then asked to qualify the objects by adding picture words, indicating what they see.

Under guidance, the picture comes to life, as a thick, slimy, dirty pool, a dark and treacherous cave, and a horrible, monstrous, ugly man.

The lesson follows the fivefold pattern, as do the lessons in all other disciplines.

Herbart may not have done anything new but by organizing it better he made the teacher feel that what he was doing was logical, defensible and scientific.

The methods of building a complex moral personality were to be adjusted to the nature of the individual, his interests, and his facility for reflection.

Reflection could be stimulated by a formal method consisting of four stages: *first*, the clearing up of ideas already in the mind; *second*, the presenting of new ideas; *third*, the association of these new ideas with those already in the mind; and *fourth*, the application of the resulting concepts in practice.

The problem of moral development was one of bringing new ideas into the mind and affecting the will.

The will was to Herbart a kind of referee between conflicting ideas and at the same time a censor of new ideas which might, or might not, fit the system already present.

The modes of combining ideas were regular, ascertainable, and predictable.

In fact, he undertook to work them out in mathematical terms.

The mind, to Herbart, was a mass of ideas with its own characteristic nature.

The old mass tends to welcome ideas which fit in, assimilate and conform, and to reject those which do not fit.

These mind masses are apperceptive, i.e., they give significance to new materials accepted by the mind; in other words, what we learn is new only in terms of the old.

If new ideas are to gain entrance to the mind of the child, the educational program must be arranged to correspond with the growth of the individual child's experience.

Herbart suggests that his growth of experience corresponds in a general way with the experience of the race; so that the curricular presentation in its complexity should follow the culture epocs of history.

It was roughly an application of the recapitulation theory in biology.

Herbart recognized that to be respectable, education would have to be a science, a discipline in its own right, not a series of generalities and naive assumptions; its laws, methods, and procedures would have to be altogether intelligent.

It was to this task that he gave his attention.

In contrast with Locke, whose system was designed to develop conventional gentlemen, and to Rousseau, who emphasized the development of the natural man, Herbart gave himself over to clarifying the aims of education, defining the mind of the person to be educated, and setting up methods for teaching in a scientific and defensible way.

Herbart's system was dignified, orderly, intellectual, philosophically buttressed, and through his efforts for the first time pedagogics acquired recognition and respectability as a college discipline.

Ossian Long has summarized Herbart's peculiar contribution to education in the following sentences:

"Herbart was the first to recognize the true merit of the 'genial, the noble Pestalozzi.' While others based their judgment on observations of the working of the Pestalozzian method of teaching, he sought for the principles underlying it and determined their psychological value."

"Herbart holds that nothing is absolutely good in itself but a good will and bases his system of morality on that famous proposition of Immanuel Kant: 'Nothing can be possibly conceived in the world, or even out of it, which can be called good without qualification except a good will' It must be the aim of education to so develop the will of the child that morality may become the highest aim of his life and the absolute standard of self-criticism. The three educational activities that center in the ethical aim are:

1. Development of right insight into the absolutely binding validity of the moral law or absolute beauty of moral ideal.

2. Training of the will.

3. The bringing about of a permanent harmonious relation between the will and moral insight."

"In order to attain a perfect insight into moral relations, man must know the history and destiny of mankind, himself, his neighbor, society, and God. He must be able to see his place in the universe and how to fill it well. When he has sounded these depths, and has reached the plane of perfect insight, he has attained the preliminary stage of virtue. By making virtue the one supreme end of education, Herbart has not left out anything that is demanded by the aims of morality and of choice, but has simply collected them in an all-embracing unit. Herbart says that he is carrying out the purpose of education if all educational influences that he brings to bear on his pupil tend to excite in his soul a conscious striving for virtue, in moral culture of the will in the broad sense used by Herbart is the essence of all education. That the ideas of the right and good in all their clearness may become the essential objects of the will, that the innermost intrinsic contents of the character–the very heart of the personality–shall determine itself in accordance with these ideas and without regard to any arbitrary impulses–this and nothing less is the aim of moral culture."

FRIEDRICH WILHELM FROEBEL (1782-1852)

As has been indicated, the aim of Froebel was the same as that of Pestalozzi, even though the method was not.

Both were animated by a great love of mankind, a faith in the ideals of humanity, a recognition of truth and beauty, the principles of justice and love, and the possibility of progress.

Froebel was more than a pupil of Pestalozzi; he was "the discoverer of childhood."

His background experience differed from that of Pestalozzi and even more from that of Herbart, which may partially account for the difference between the theories of the two illustrious students of the great teacher.

Friedrich Wilhelm Froebel was born in Oberweissbach, in the Thuringian forest in Germany, and became thoroughly familiar with forest plant and animal life.

His hobby of making models of buildings out of paper and pasteboard, which was later to be put to good use, brought him to the city of Frankfurt to study architecture.

While in Frankfurt he became so interested in

Pestalozzian education that he was made a teacher in the Pestalozzian model school in that city, and a loyal student of the great worker.

After a year in Gottingen, he went to the University of Berlin, where he became "convinced of the demonstrable connection in all cosmic development."

Education thereafter became "the unfolding of a single creative reality."

It was at this point of the fundamental unity of all things that he differed with Pestalozzi.

He says: "All my means of culture I formed from an idea; therefore, I began with a type of unity (the ball). I am in pure contrast with Pestalozzi: he started from the misery of wants and poverty, from external condition; I on the other hand, from the internal, from my own peculiar view of life, hence from an idea."

Froebel's studies were interrupted by a year of military service.

On his return to complete his course, he again taught in the Pestalozzi school in Berlin.

His first full time vocational venture was the teaching of five nephews, a job which allowed him to work out his modification of the Pestalozzi system in his own way.

The experience was formalized in the organization of a small school at Kielheu, which he called The German Institute of Education.

It was founded on three basis principles: self-expression; the development of personality; and social participation.

The pupils were taught to be gardeners and builders, as well as thinkers.

His observations on the working of the plan were published in his first book, *The Education of Man*, which did not meet with general acceptance.

It was as a teacher in Switzerland, shortly afterward, that he elaborated the kindergarten system with which his name has since been identified.

The child was popularly thought of in the Europe of Froebel's day as a little barbarian, inherently destructive, disorderly, measurably depraved, a notion which came out of the Church's doctrine of original sin.

Froebel was the champion of the child.

He was not depraved, but a bundle of potentialities.

If he seems wicked, it is because he has been misled, mishandled, misguided.

To correct unwanted child behavior, it is necessary to locate the "good sources," build up the "good side,"struggle against the bad habit, which is not at all a natural depravity, and the earlier in his life it can be done, the better the results will be.

"The only and infallible remedy for counteracting any shortcoming and even wickedness is to find the originally good source, the originally good side of the human being, that has been repressed, disturbed, or misled into the shortcoming, and then to further build up and properly guide this side. Thus the shortcoming will at last disappear, although it may involve a hard struggle against habit, but not against original depravity in man."

"Selecting our point for illustration, we cannot deny that there is at present among children and boys, little simplicity, little true gentleness, little natural forbearance, brotherly patience, little true religious felling; but on the other hand, much egotism, unfriendliness, particularly rudeness, etc. This is clearly due to the failure of arousing, at an early period, and of subsequently cultivating in the child and boy a common sympathy, but also to the early annihilation of this felling between parents and children."

Froebel has little patience with teachers who assume natural depravity in children and treat them accordingly.

"Such birds of ill omen, especially when they are educators, are the first to bring guilt upon such a child, who, though not wholly innocent is yet without guilt."

He had also to fight against the popular notion that the child had to be pushed into work which was good for him, and restrained from play, which by the same token, was bad for him.

He took the ground that play was highly beneficial for children.

It made education pleasant and effective and was itself educative.

"Play is the highest phase of child development. Play is the purest, most spiritual activity of man at this stage, and at the same time typical of human life as a whole–of inner, hidden natural life in man and all things. It gives, therefore, joy, freedom, and contentment, inner and outer rest, peace with the world. It holds the source of all that is good."

To Froebel, activity, doing things, was the basis of education.

"The starting point of all that appears, of all that exists, and therefore of all the intellectual conception is action. From acting, from action therefore, start true human education, the developed education of man; in action, in acting, it must be rooted and spring up."

Such action initially is self–expression, but it becomes something more.

It becomes creativeness as well.

"Since God created man in his own image, man should create and bring forth, like God."

Learning lies in the recognition of a need, the initiation and carrying out of constructive acts to meet it.

The kindergarten system was worked out in great detail, from the use of the ball in early infancy, the provision of blocks with which to play, familiarizing the child with the various forms in which matter was manifest, to an appreciation of the artistic, the useful, and the spiritual, laying the foundations in the formative years for art, science, occupation, social relations, thought, and belief.

The influence of Pestalozzi on Froebel is seen in the latter's emphasis on the social purpose of education.

The school for young children was not a mere aggregation of persons but a society in itself, a miniature state in which the child should be fitted for dependable citizenship.

He did not even call it a school but rather a children's garden, in order to emphasize his organic concept of early education.

Recognition of Froebel's ideas came slowly.

At first he was ridiculed, persecuted by Church, state, and school, suffered pecuniary losses and estrangement of friends.

However, the name kindergarten and his specialization on young children ultimately made a place for the venture in the staid Prussian system of the first half of the 19th century.

It has had wide adoption in Europe and America and has kept alive the basic purposes of its founder, although many modifications have taken place with its diversified adaptation.

What Herbart did for the secondary school in pointing up and giving rationale to it, that Froebel did for preschool and primary education.

HORACE MANN (1796-1859)

Hitherto we have been discussing educational theory.

Only incidentally has mention been made of administration.

Horace Mann may be called the father of American school administration.

His contribution was not as a teacher but as an educational leader; not as a philosopher but as a framer of legislation; not as a writer, but as a counsellor of school boards and directors of education.

He was America's first entrepreneur in the field of public education, giving to it the type of intelligent management, the know-how for which American industry has become noted.

It was not until he was 40 years old that he was appointed to a position which made it possible for him to change the course of American education and give to our system the peculiar direction which it has since taken.

Mann was born on a farm in Franklin, Massachusetts, in 1796. When he was thirteen, his father died, leaving him a legacy of hard farm work which left little time for education or recreation.

He says he had no more than ten weeks schooling in any year until he was sixteen years of age.

The library and the Calvinistic Church were his diversions from arduous farm labor.

The former he loved and used, spending all the time left over after working on the farm all day and braiding straw hats in the evening.

He distrusted the cold, harsh doctrines of the church and found it necessary to modify them in order to worship God at all.

After six months preparation he entered Brown University in 1816, graduating three years later at the top of his class.

His brilliance gained for him an instructorship in classics at Brown, a post he held for two years.

After a course in law at Litchfield, he was admitted to the bar in 1823 and maintained a law practice for the next fourteen years.

During this period he served six years in the Massachusetts House of Representatives, and four years in the Senate, for two of which he acted as President of that body.

While at Brown University he had been happily married to the daughter of the president of that institution.

Charlotte died within two years of the marriage, an event which profoundly affected his life, throwing him back into the religious conflict of his boyhood– a conflict from which he was never able entirely to free himself.

As a legislator, he was noted particularly for his interest in prison reform, the building of the first American state asylum for the care of mental cases who had formerly been kept in prison, and his revision of the laws of Massachusetts in the interest of consistency.

The latter was an arduous task, added to a growing practice.

He did it conscientiously, although his sympathies were always with the unforunate, handicapped, and ignorant.

In 1837, under a new Massachusetts law, he was appointed by Governor Jerrod Sparks (later president of Harvard) as America's first State Director of Education.

The function of this office was to organize and standardize public education throughout the state, improve teaching, and provide school opportunity for all children within the commonwealth.

It involved visiting schools, consulting with local boards, providing approved textbooks and libraries, training teachers, arranging curricula, even suggesting architectural plans and hygienic facilities.

These projects he carried forward with prodigious energy, but against the widespread inertia of economy-minded legislators.

Against great odds he founded "the first normal school on this side of the Atlantic".

The pathetic beginnings of this school at Lexington, Massachusetts, July 4, 1842, with three students and one instructor, were enough to discourage the most ardent reformer, but that institution became the model for similar institutions throughout the United States and elsewhere in the Americas.

His founding of the *Common School Journal* in 1838 as an organ for those engaged in education, his management of the earliest Teachers' Institutes, helped to establish a basis for the professional teachers' associations which came into being a decade later.

In 1848 after the death of John Quincy Adams who had represented his district in Congress for many years, Mann was elected to replace him in the House of Representatives in Washington.

Here he served until 1853, his interests divided between the question of slavery and the improvement of education on national basis over the pattern he had so studiously and zealously elaborated in Massachusetts.

In 1852 Mann was nominated as the Governor of Massachusetts and offered the first Presidency of Antioch College.

He chose the latter.

It was a small school, in Yellow Springs, Ohio, in which the theory and practice of teaching was to be emphasized.

After a long struggle to regularize the support of the new venture, the promotional difficulties which developed made it necessary for him to carry both the institution's administrative duties and its financial management.

Mann died in 1859.

His statue, erected by friends, stands in front of the State House in Boston.

He left behind him an enormous record of achievement.

As Secretary of the State Board of Education of Massachusetts from 1837-1848, he submitted twelve annual reports, covering not only school statistics but educational topics of vital interest to the country as a whole.

These topics were fresh and show a prophetic range: school economy and equipment, duties of parents, needs of the community, relation of the school to the nation, the preparation and qualifications of the teacher and methods of teaching.

These reports have been American classics in education as they anticipated many of our current ideas, reforms, and laws.

The seventh of the series is devoted to a description of the schools and school systems of England, Ireland, Scotland, Germany, Holland, Belgium, and France, as well as the work being done in normal schools hospitals, asylums, and prisons in those countries.

After his marriage to Mary Peabody in 1843, they had spent a year in observing work in these various European institutions.

The care with which the values of the various systems and their methods are analyzed, compared, and presented has made this widely circulated report a document of the highest national importance.

Mann's educational message is succinctly summarized in his Fourth of July oration in Boston in 1839:

"The great experiment of the capacity of man for self–government is to be tried a new, which wherever it has been tried-in Greece, in Rome, in Italy–has failed through an incapacity in the people to enjoy liberty without abusing it. If in all governments, wisdom and goodness in a ruler are indispensable to the dignity and happiness of the subjects, then in a government like our own - where all are rulers–all must be wise and good or we must suffer the alternative of debasement and misery.

"It is not enough that a bare majority should be intelligent and upright. We need general intelligence and integrity as we need our daily bread. By the vote of a few wicked men, or even of one wicked man, honorable men may be hailed from office, and miscreants elevated to their places; useful offices abolished and sinecures created; the public wealth which has supported industry, squandered upon mercenaries.... If votes come from ignorance and crime, the fire and brimstone that were rained upon Sodom and Gomorrah would be more tolerable.

"Select schools for select children should be discarded. Instead of the old order of nobility, a new order should be created–an order of teachers, wise, benevolent, filled with Christian enthusiasm and rewarded and honored by all."

The following are quotations taken from the journals, lectures, and addresses of Horace Mann:

"I hold it to be one of the laws of God that the talents of man can be developed in the best way and can produce the most beneficial results only when they act in full consonance with all the precepts and the principles of religion. The pursuit of knowledge or science is the pursuit of truth."

"I believe in the existence of a great, immortal, immutable principle of natural law, a principle of divine origin, clearly legible in the ways of Providence – the absolute right to an education of every human being that comes into the world."

"Between religion and science there must be harmony. Truth can never conflict with itself, nor God be the author of contradiction. No work of God can ever come into collision with any word of God."

"Morality consists primarily in the performance of our duties to our fellow men; religion is the performance of our duties to God."

"Moral education is a primal necessity of social existence."

"How true it is that Christianity is made to shrink or expand to fit the intellectual or moral caliber of its disciples."

"We can conceive of a state of existence where we could be happy without knowledge, but it is not in the power of any human being to picture to itself a form of life where we could be happy without virtue."

"Civilization consists in a knowledge and an observance of the laws of God."

"National virtue is as much a product of wise institutions as is national wealth."

"The fortunes of a state depend upon antecedent causes. The future conditions of Massachusetts will be modified and to a great extent determined by the force of causes now put in practice. Enlightened reason discovers the connection between cause and effect."

"To have created such beings as we are and to have placed them in this world without the light of the sun would have been no more cruel than for a government to suffer its laboring classes to grow up without knowledge."

"However loftily the intellect of man may have been gifted, however skillfully it may have been trained, if it be not guided by a sense of justice, a love of mankind, and a devotion to duty, its possessor is only a more splendid as he is a more dangerous barbarian."

"Without understanding any other human agency it may be affirmed that the common school, improved and energized as it can easily be, may become the most effective and benignant of all the forces of civilization."

"Educate your children. Educate them in the great eternal principles of justice and right which underlie the entire length of human existence."

"As the moral tone of the community now is, children have not a fair chance to become moral men."

"All human character and conduct can be referred to two forces –the innate force of the mind acting outwards, and the force of outward things acting upon the mind."

"Education alone can conduct us to that enjoyment which is at once best in quality and infinite in quantity. God has revealed to us by His mighty words what He holds to be invaluable."

"Our means of education are the grand machinery by which the raw material of human nature can be worked up into scientific farmers, into scholars and jurists, into the founders of benevolent institutions, and the great expounders of ethical and theological science."

"As each citizen is to participate in the power of governing others, it is an essential preliminary that he should be imbued with a feeling for the wants and a sense of the rights of those whom he is to govern."

"The great reforms in corporate bodies and in communities will never be achieved until private morals are brought into closer approximation to the standards of the Gospel."

"Nothing but universal education can counterwork the tendency to the domination of character and the servility of labor."

"The annihilation of the sun would no more certainly be followed by darkness than the extinction of human intelligence would plunge the race into the darkness and the helplessness of barbarism."

"We err if we regard the common schools as ends and not as means. A forgetfulness of this distinction would send the mass of our children into the world scantily provided either with the ability or the disposition to perform even the most ordinary duties of life."

"A badly kept school is worse than none."

"All improvements in the school suppose and require a corresponding and simultaneous improvement in public sentiment."

"Whenever we find improvements in the schools it is a gratifying proof that higher views are prevailing in the community."

"We need school committeemen who will scrutinize as carefully the moral character of the proposed teacher and his ability to impart moral instruction as they do his literary attainments and his ability to impart moral instruction as they do his literary attainments and his ability to impart knowledge."

"If none but teachers of pure tastes, of good manners, of exemplary morals, had ever gained admission into our schools, neither school-rooms nor their appurtenances would have been polluted as some of them now are."

"Every teacher ought to have some notion of the beings confided to his hands. The character of children is always forming."

"Preparation for teaching involves a knowledge of the whole being to be taught, and of the precise manner in which every possible application will affect it."

"It should never be forgotten that the highest duty of the teacher is to produce the greatest quantity and purest quality of moral action."

"One of the highest and most valuable objects to which the influence of the school can be made conducive consists in training our children to self-government."

"Aptness to teach involves the power of perceiving how far the scholar understands the subject matter to be learned – what, in the natural order, is the next step he is to take. It involves the power of discovering and of solving at the same time the exact difficulty by which the learner is embarrassed."

"The greater accumulation of facts until the comparing and foreseeing faculties have acted upon them is as useless as a telescope or a watch would be in the hands of a savage."

"Single ideas may be transferred from an author to a reader, but the habits of thinking are intransferable; they must be formed within the reader's own mind if they are to exist there."

"In every intellectual department there must be accurate observation in collecting the elementary ideas, which ideas must be compared, arranged, and methodized in the mind so that they may stand ready to be reproduced and to be embodied in any outward fabric or institution which their possessor may afterwards with to construct."

"The ability to acquire, and the ability to impart are wholly different talents. The former may exist in the most liberal measure without the latter."

"No one is so poor in resources for difficult emergencies as they may arise as he whose knowledge of methods is limited to the one by which he happened to be instructed."

"We arrive at knowledge in two ways: first, by our own observation of phenomena without; and second, by our own consciousness of what goes on within us. And we seek words aptly to designate whatever has been observed, whether material or mental."

"The pupil may do something by intuition, but generally there must be a conscious effort on his part. He must do more than admit or welcome; he must reach out and grasp and bring home. It is the duty of the teacher to bring knowledge within the reach of the pupil, but the final appropriating task must be the learner's."

"Until a desire to learn exists within the child, some foreign force must constantly be supplied to keep him going ; but from the moment that a desire is excited, he is self-motivated and goes alone."

WILLIAM HOLMES McGUFFEY (1800-1873)

What Horace Mann was doing for the organization of schools, making provision for them by legislation, seeing that they were adequately staffed with qualified teachers, william McGuffey was doing in providing proper textbooks for use in the schools.

Their work was contemporary, their aims alike, and their methods not incompatible.

Each in his own way had a singular impact on American educational life.

It was mainly through the McGuffey Readers that the ideas of the great thinkers of the 18th and 19th centuries reached the American public.

These books had wide use from 1836 to 1906, particularly in the West and South.

They were carefully read and analyzed.

Of all the books sold in America, the McGuffey Readers were exceeded only by the Holy Bible.

The selection of materials for inclusion over the 70 years of their popularity undoubtedly reflected the bias of their authors.

Their frequent revisions reflect the trend of American literary taste and criticism, for the readers were a commercial venture, and textbook adoptions depend upon popularity, reputation, and the absence of fundamental criticism.

They were more than aids in the proper use of the English language, more than instruments used to develop an appreciation of poetry.

The books were compilations of excerpts from the writings of great statesmen and politicians, well known moralists and outstanding religionists of the previous century.

They reflected the great schisms, political, religious, and moral issues of the period.

They emphasized the identity of the moral and natural law, defined the Christian fundamentals from which sprang the social virtues of truthfulness, temperance, modesty, kindness, and tolerance.

They assumed the Fatherhood of God, the brotherhood

of man, the wickedness of war, crime, and inhumanity, and above all, they buttressed the concept of the sacredness of property and bulwarked the position of the middle class in society.

An explanation of the aptness of the McGuffey Readers, their timeliness and vast popularity is to be found in the life, experience, professional pride, religious affiliations, and friends of the author himself.

William Holmes McGuffey was born of Scotch-American parents in Pennsylvania in 1800, but at the age of two his parents moved to Trumbull County in Ohio.

Due to his place in a large family and the necessary work on the pioneer farm, he received no formal education until he was 18 years of age.

After a brief academy training, alternately tutoring, teaching, and attending Washington College, he graduated from the latter institution in 1824.

In the same year he was appointed professor of ancient languages at Miami University at Oxford, Ohio, and after being ordained as a Presbyterian minister, was transferred to the Miami chair in mental philosophy.

Four years later he accepted the presidency of Cincinnati University; in 1839 the presidency of Ohio University at Athens; and in 1845 his final appointment as professor of moral philosophy at the University of Virginia.

Here he remained until his death in 1873.

It was while he was teaching moral philosophy at Miami that he prepared the manuscript for the first and second readers, testing them out on a small group of school children whom he taught to read in his own house.

As one of the most competent teachers in the region, he had been commissioned by a Cincinnati publishing firm to prepare them for publication.

The first two were published in 1836; the third and fourth the following year.

The four volumes constituted the original series of eclectic readings which, through various revisions, bore his name for the remainder of the century.

The books were put out in green cardboard covers, containing 72, 164, 165 and 324 pages respectively.

To the series of readers in 1844 there was added a fifth volume, *McGuffey's Rhetorical Guide*.

The latter was arranged by a younger brother, a lawyer in Cincinnati, at the request of the publishers, and was elaborated in 1855 into a sixth reader, making the series complete.

The latter two volumes, from the standpoint of the selections included, the taste and style displayed, the political and religious standards, and the conservatism throughout, show so close a similarity to the 3rd and 4th readers as to approach identity of authorship.

In his little book *Making the American Mind* (King's Crown Press, New York, 1947), Richard P. Mosier has analyzed the selections in the readers, both prose and poetry, original and revised, in an attempt to discover the impact of these texts on the minds of young Americans in the fields of patriotism, religion, morality, and the social virtues.

He also shows how the strong bias of the authors finds expression in the selection of materials for inclusion and how the materials align with "the body of belief and ideas which has come to be recorded as traditionally American."

He concludes, this "pattern of ideas in the McGuffey readers is a part of that larger pattern which is the context of American culture."

Henry H. Vail, a member of the firm which published the revised readers after 1873, says (H.H.Vail, *A History of the McGuffey Readers*, 1910, page 65, also 69) in explanation of their popularity:

"The books in their first form were strongly religious in their teaching without being denominational. If a selection taught a moral lesson this was stated in formal words at the close. The pill was not sugared. Thus at the close of a lesson narrating the results of disobedience, he represents the three little girls as 'talking about how happy it made them to keep the Fifth Commandment.'

There was in the books much direct teaching of moral principles with *thou shalt* and *thou shalt not*. In the latter revisions this gradually disappeared. The moral teaching was less direct but more effective. The pupil was left to make his own deduction.

.... The author and the publishers were fully justified in their belief that the American people are a moral people and that they have a strong desire that their children be taught to become brave, patriotic, honest, self-reliant, temperate, and virtuous citizens."

In answer to a question as to what earned for the readers such wide and constant use for three-quarters of a century, Mr. Vail says:

"Their greatest value consisted in the choice of masterpieces in literature which by their contents taught morality and patriotism, and by their beauty served as a gateway to pure literature–thousands of men and women owe their wholesome views of life as well as whatever success they may have attained to the wholesome maxims and precepts found on every page of these valuable books. The seed they scattered has yielded a million fold."

A wise man wrote: " I care not who writes their laws if I might write their songs."

McGuffey's influence in America was probably subtly greater than that of any single law–maker America has produced.

4

The Children

The proper up-bringing of children has exercised the mental powers of some of the greatest thinkers. Strict instructions as to the training that should be given to the Brahmacharis were issued by Manu and other rishis of Ancient India.

The Republic of Plato enunciated a theory of education based on a psychological analysis of the child. Comenius, the greatest of modern educators, in his great book "Didactic Magna" and Rousseau, one of the most dynamic names in modern European thought, in his "Emile" both propounded systematic and comprehensive theories of child education.

Pestalozzi, Froebel, Herbart and others developed and systematised the ideals and methods of early education. In our own days early education has witnessed a remarkable revolution in Europe through the successful efforts of Madame Montessori. In India, experiments of a highly interesting nature in this all-important field were carried on with great success by the Poet Rabindra Nath Tagore at Bolepur and by a section of the Arya Samaj at Kangri Hardwar.

It would not be denied that this is a problem on the

successful solution of which the very existence of nations as civilised communities depends. The proper upbringing and training children, a sound system of primary and secondary education, the existence of easily accessible centres of culture and intellectual activity, these form the main educational problems of every nation.

Of these, the education of the child is the crux of the whole. A part from the two remarkable experiments alluded to before, child education has been till now grossly neglected in India. We are but slowly awakening to the fundamental fact that the most important period in the development of the human mind is when the child is receiving its first intelligent impressions of the world and is acquiring for himself the fundamentals of knowledge.

The training that a child receives during this period remains more or less unalterable and is carried down to the very grave. It may be kept down by a later training. It may even disappear temporarily in a foreign and unsympathetic atmosphere. But it is always there, deep down in the heart and this great fact makes child-training the greatest responsibility for the educationist.

The conditions of child education in India are very peculiar. The problem is complicated by the peculiarities of our social institutions and the artificial character of status relationship that they involve. The fact that India is not self-governing and that her educational ideals are consequently dominated by foreign tradition should also be taken into consideration.

Social institutions all over the world have a most important and very intimate bearing on child education. The family is the first school and perhaps the most important one. We speak of principles imbued with one's mother's milk and apart form questions of heredity and inherited tendencies the phrase implies the essential fact that the fundamentals of morality and knowledge gained at that age persist through life. Everywhere, therefore, the family is the most important of calculable influences, natural gifts apart, which go to make a man. If a child has a healthy home, one in which his body, his mind and his sensibilities get proper food and training, he grows up to be a properly developed man.

It is an obvious truism to say that every educational system should have as its ideal the development in full of the potentialities of each human being. The physical, mental and aesthetic qualities of each individual should be so developed that each generation may benefit by a full use of its powers. Maximum utilisation and minimum wastage ought to be the first principles for our guidance. Child education should therefore give equal importance to physical, intellectual and aesthetic development. Undue emphasis on one at the expense of the other is found to have very serious effects in the long run. Physical development cannot be neglected in favour of intellectual training because the future of the race is dependent on physical vitality. An intellectual education without proper aesthetic training would mean a mind devoid of the imagination and knowledge without culture. Indeed the three are so intertwined that a purely onesided development is impossible and the duty of the educationist consists in the mere adjustment of the right proportion in which these factors should stand to each other.

Whether this ideal is best and most effectively realised by what Rousseau called negative education meaning the "preparation of reason by the exercise of senses" is the great problem in child-training. He called the education positive which tends to form the mind before the age and to give the child the knowledge of the duties of man. Everybody is agreed that education should be graduated, progressive and suited to the intellectual faculties of the age of the child. There is also an almost general agreement that prxemature intellectual training leads merely to pedantry and verbalism. But in the matter of physical and aesthetic training, even Rousseau, the great prophet of 'negative education', does not deny the necessity for devoting attention very early in life. For the culture of the body and imagination a wasted childhood means a wasted life. Men may educate themselves intellectually at a very late period in life but a child neglected physically in his early days very seldom regains the vigour of his body. In the case of imagination and sense-training too, this is equally true. A child brought up in ugly surroundings without either intelligent appreciation or natural enjoyment of the beautiful in nature can never become truly cultured.

It is the most deplorable fact with regard to the up-bringing of the great majority of Indian children that the surroundings in which they live are such as do not give proper chance for physical development. Unwholesome food, insanitary surroundings, lack of proper medical care together no doubt with such pernicious social customs as early marriage render Indian children physically much weaker than children in other civilised countries. It has been calculated that 60 out of the 320 millions of India are too poor to have one full meal a day; a much greater number has to be content with a much lower standard of comfort than the poorest class in Europe can get. This phenomenal poverty has made Indian manhood a matter of contempt for all nations. The physical deterioration of the race operates in a vicious circle, weak men rearing up weak children and weak children growing up weak men. The reform here has to begin at the bottom and the physical training of children in their early youth should be carefully attended to by parents and school authorities.

There are two considerations which should not be ignored in this connection. The Hindu family system, the chief characteristic of which is the joint residence of more than one family (often three or four) in the same house under the chaperonage of a common mother-in-law restricts to a very great extent the free movement of children. Accommodation in an ordinary Hindu home is neither very comfortable nor very convenient. Proper housing is an elementary but essential consideration of physical well-being especially in the case of children and in the case of the vast majority of Indians this is very imperfectly looked after. A study of that rapidly increasing literature on the economic conditions of rural India will disclose this one fact, which seems to be of universal applicability in our country, that Indian houses from the brick-built *kotis* of the well-to-do middle classes down to the mud huts of the poorest Pariah are more of store houses than habitations for human beings. This state of affairs is certainly changing with the rising material standards of the country, but the statement will remain true in a broad sense for many more years to come.

That the growth and training of children should be entirely spontaneous and as little restrictive as possible will be admitted on all hands. But does our present system give them a chance? An ordinary Hindu home contains so many children of different parents that even in well-to-do families proper nursery arrangements do not exist. Their health is not taken particular care of ; witness the very high percentage of child mortality in India.

In the school it is the same. Long and uninterrupted periods of premature intellectual work enervate the children. Physical education is grossly neglected and the hours for recreation are few. Nourished on bad and insufficient food, forced to a premature intellectual education, with their bodily development utterly uncared for, both by the parents and by the teachers, Indian school-going children present a most heart-rending sight to all patriotic sons of India. For the first of this, the only remedy lies in a wider diffusion of education among our women. For the second, a thorough reconstruction of our elementary education is necessary. The indivisibility of the three factors, physical aesthetic and intellectual, of education should be recognised not only in theory but in practice and emphasis during the early years should be laid entirely on physical education.

"The greatest, the most important, the most useful rule of education, that of losing time instead of saving it" - the great gospel of Rousseau- should find more place in our educational system. Juvenile movements meant for "hardening" children and training them physically, like the Boy Scouts organisation, should find greater encouragement and support of our educationists and public men. And finally the idea should be abandoned once for ever that the great thing in education is a race for time, a crowding of vast information during early years.

The training of imagination has been equally neglected among Indian children. Our young ones even now grow up in surroundings that are by no means conducive to the growth of a healthy imagination. It is not that Mother India is less beautiful; not that *vasanta* is less bewitching here than elsewhere, not that our flowers are less glorious and our scenery less magnificent. In fact nowhere is landscape more varied, natural beauty more effective, than in India. Nowhere the mountains higher, the snowclad peaks more sublime, the slow running rivers more majestic and the primeval forests more terrible. But unfortunately our children are not brought up to appreciate this. The system of old Indian pilgrimages has become an empty form. The spirit of complete unison with nature which one feels during a tour in the mountains of Switzerland has for us only a very faint echo on a pilgrimage to Hardwar at the foot of the Himalayas, or to Cape Comorin where the waters of two seas mingle. We have lost our artistic sense.

The surroundings of our childhood are not of a kind that develops the imaginative faculty. The walls of our houses are bare except occasionally for the horrible reprints of Ravi Varma's mythological pictures. The magnificent designs that we see on the walls of the Mughul buildings no longer adorn our mansions. Palaces and cottages alike proclaim our lack of artistic sense. The Maharajah of Kapurthala builds a palace in the French style of the Regency. The Nawab of Murshidabad prefers a Louis Seize mansion to one built in the old style. The same is the case with the middle classes. They have so utterly lost their sense of artistic beauty that it is a very rare thing to see a beautiful Indian house furnished in an artistic manner.

Children growing up in these surroundings can hardly be expected to show any very great development of the artistic sense in later life. We must remember that a beautiful house is a necessity, not a luxury. The idea that gardens, flowers, pictures, in fact all things that appeal to one's imagination, are luxuries that only the rich need bother about is a dangerous fallacy. It is quite true that poor people cannot afford to have an ornamental garden or a collection of pictures. Then it becomes the duty of the community to lay out public gardens, to collect works of art in galleries and museums, to erect public buildings with an eye not only to material utility but aesthetic beauty. The Mughal Emperors who built beautiful palaces, who laid out gardens in their chief cities, who made Chandni Chowk of those days a wonder, and raised "dreams in marble" to the memory of their queens were not merely revelling in personal glory and "pagan pomp."

But in India those days are gone. Our children have no galleries to visit and study, no public gardens except in big towns, no modern building which expresses an idea or exemplifies an original style. Even our temples and mosques which have been for so long a time the main field of artistic expression have become mere copies of old designs. This decay of artistic sense has begun to tell terribly on the proper development of our genius. One of the main ideals to be kept constantly in mind in the reform of our educational policy is the necessity of recovering this lost sense of aesthetic enjoyment.

Aesthetic education can only begin at home. It is during the days of childhood that the mind grasps essential differences more easily. If the home in which the child grows up is full of beautiful things, suggestive of beautiful thought, the eye and the mind get accustomed to them and feel repulsion at ugly and unedifying objects. The value of music, "of all arts the most inspiring and divine and the most synthetic and most evolutionary", in the development of emotional and imaginative faculties should be recognised and care must be taken for training the ear to musical masterpieces. The ideal of Indian boyhood, let us not forget, is the Eternal Child with the flute. The image most popular to the mind of the great majority of India's population is *Muralidhara Gopala;* the Cowherd with the flute. Children must regain that ideal and let it be remembered that it is the special power of music "to arouse to discipline and to express deep feeling and vital emotion."

It is this lack of aesthetic training that should account for the deplorably small percentage of people who really benefit by our educational system. The narrowness of outlook, the meanness of ordinary ambition, the absence of fellow feelling, these characteristics that mark out the so called educated community in India, are due to the continued neglect of this important side of education and of the unnecessary emphasis placed on the training of intelligence. An educated sense of beauty, a regulated faculty of imagination, these are the most disinterested forms of culture in man and they are the best guarantee of the greatness of his soul and the generosity of his impulses.

The training of intelligence is what generally goes by the name of education. The system to which one is subjected at school is mainly, if not entirely, devoted to it. The courses in our educational institutions, for children, boys, or youngmen, are avowedly meant for such a purpose. Education has come to mean for the ordinary man ability to remember a few things or at the most to discourse consistently on a topic. Even among those who pose as leaders of thought, the value of a man has come to be measured, in the words of Le Bon, by the quantity of things he is able to repeat. The extent of one's instruction has become the measure of one's intelligence.

This tendency, though universal, is especially emphasised in India. Here education and instruction have become synonymous, owing to the fact that the medium used is not the mother tongue. Hence the process has become mechanical and education has not been for us the realisation of fundamental values and the recognition of universal principles. It has been merely an accumulation of facts which are treated merely as such without any reference to living conditions. The principles which are studied and of which one reads in text books are considered different to those which are implied in social institutions.

In fact, conviction and knowledge have remained different in the English-educated Indian mind. This is the result of a premature training of intelligence without the co-ordinate development of body and imagination.

The grand secret of child-education, "that of losing time instead of gaining it," is not recognised in India. It is a temptation everywhere to put the child early to school so that he may become a "boy bachelor" like Wolsey. In India, where the motive of education is government appointment, the temptation is absolutely irresistible. The child is hurried through a course of instruction, carried on mainly through the medium of a foreign language, where his powers of memorising come to be developed at the expense of his understanding, so that he may be matriculated at the minimum age and pass out of the university by the age that an English boy leaves his public school. Need we be surprised that the results have been so deplorable?

The premature intellectualisation of our child-training, without recognising that in the early years the training of body and imagination is more important, is the main defect that vitiates the whole system of Indian education. We should now recognise that premature "education" is not only useless but thoroughly harmful, that it destroys the understanding and merely develops a plausible verbalism at best and a mere parrot-like memory at worst. We should remember that in child-training an indulgence of our own personal ambition, whim and fancy would be disastrous to the future of the child and detrimental to the community. The interests of the child and the nation ought to be the only factors in deciding the course of instruction and his early training should be entirely negative and meant to keep his instincts and nature free from vice.

The great reform that is required in the training of Indian children is, so to say, a de-intellectualisation of the present system. Education should be integral. The training of all human faculties should be attended to. They are all so intertwined that it is impossible to neglect any one of them without affecting detrimentally the others. A perfect education consists in a just equilibrium of these factors. In child education this is more important because the child itself is not able to express its desires and alter the instruction to its tastes. And no mistake is greater in education than the one which considers the mind of the child as a *tabula rasa*, a clean slate, for the teacher to draw what he pleases. In these days, when inherited tendencies and child psychology are subjects studied and popularised by scientists, such an attitude would have no justification. We should recognise and utilise diversity and our educational ideal ought never to be uniformity of method or standardisation of intelligence. In the case of children especially, each should be *studied* and taught as a separate unit. This is where child education differs from school and collegiate course and, unless proper attention is devoted to it, no solution of the educational problem can ever have any permanent value.

5

Primary Education

In almost every Western European country without exception, however, this primary education– or elementary education as it was so often called-was a kind of mass education,intended solely for the working class, and it was kept quit separate and distinct from the kind of primary education received by the boy or girl of non-working class parents which usually started in the primary department of a grammar school (or *lycee)* and so led naturally and easily into the main fields of academic work. The boy or girl educated in the elementary school moved rarely (and then with great difficulty and often inadequately prepared) to the secondary school. The elementry school, in effect, led nowhere. Once a child's education had been completed in it there was little or no further full-time education for him, unless he elected to train as an elementary school teacher. Only gradually, throughout the first decades of the twentieth century, was the way made easier for the elementary school child to transfer to the secondary school, And only in this present postwar period have the rigid barriers of the dual system of deucation been finally lowered.

"Open a school and close a jail" became the nineteenth century slogan, and the elementary school was expected to produce not only a more literate and capable workman, but also to discipline him and shape him both morally and socially for his lowly task. The three R's-reading, writing and arithmetic were the basic tools needed by the future employee in industry, and it was genetally held that the methods employed in teaching the three R's (the dance's cap and the twitching cane) were salutory. An intellectual and moral discipline was expected to result from the effort require at learning by rote and from constant repetitive drilling. Order and method was the watchword. Flushed by victory over the French in 1870, the Prussians felt that the qualities the German army sergeant had showr during the campaign should not be wasted, and they therefore recruited such men to teach in their elementary schools. And most other European countries–if less openly and usually to a lesser degree–followed suit through the strict regimentation they imposed on the training of the elementary school teacher eithser at pupil teacher centres or in teacher-training colleges. There was one undeviating way of doing things. The "fold-your -arms school,"as it has been often called, was not interested in the child but in the techniques involved in teaching children *en masse.* Good figuring, well-kept exercise books, copper-plate handwriting, were essential parts of the drilling of the child, and the copy book used by the child gave him a whole series of moral maxims to be copied laboriously many time, and therefore (if indirectly) fixed for all time in his mind: Knowledge is power. Honesty is the best policy. We reap what we sow. Look before you leap. A stitch in time saves nine"– and so on.

It was only at the very end of the nineteenth century that new subjects crept into the curriculm in the shape of history, geography, elementary science, and what came to be called "object lesson"– usually some simple form of nature study. Even then, however, the emphasis was still on imparting skill and informatrion : a child would be shown a sticky bud and brought to study its growth and development day by day–but he also had to draw what he saw (and what the teacher made him see) with exactitude and meticulous detail. He had to learn by heart the names and dates, in strict chronological order, of kings and queens and decisive battles. He could chant like a litany the names of bays, capes, promontories and great rivers around his native country.

The shift in emphasis from the teaching of a subject to the education of the child came in the first place, of course, through the pioneer efforts of those educationalists whom we have discussed in Chapter Four, and from all the new information on the child that came pouring in from the psychologists. Men of calibre like the Englishman Herbert Spencer who dared to ask the question: "What knowledge is of most worth?:" also had their inflience. Herbartian psychology became fashionable in Germany and America, and later in England. But education for living, as we have called it in Chapter Four, became only a reality in proportion as the varioues countries were in a position, economically, to make enforcement of their laws on compulsory primary education really effective. A gradual reduction in hours of labour, thus making for more leisure time for all, was also a prerequisite. To make the teaching child-entred and to give each child the individual attention he needed demanded a much longer period of schooling. These are important points that are often overlooked.

Again if the child was to be given "new things to love and admire," as Sir Michael Sadler put it, then radical changes had to be effected in the attitudes adopted towards teacher training. Economical and technological reasons might demand that the teacher should be really skilled and well versed in the subjects he taught. But it had to go much further than that. Beauty and truth (aesthetic, moral and scientific) are in the eye and brain of the beholder. Then the teacher must be trained to perceive, and in consequence given an education that taught him to see so that he might bring others to see. It is at this point that the philosophical ideas of Henri Bergson have a particular relevance. Similarly, it was necessary that the elementary and primary schools should cease to be grim barrack- like buildings, and should be transformed– if they could not entirely be abandoned–into something gayer and freer and that really would help to open the windows of the mind.

But none of this–as I have said–was possible until compulsory primary education for all became a reality and until the school-leaving age could be extended to give the child at least eight full years of education. It is significant to note that the school-leaving age was raised to 14 in Belgium in 1914, in England in 1918, in France in 1936, and that not even to-day can Italy (particularly in Calabria) compel full attendance much beyond the years of primary education (5 to11). Even in America it was not until 1920 that Mississippi came into line with the other states by making its primary education at long last compulsory for all. On the other hand, America has been the pioneer for the gradual raising of the school–leaving age, and the ultimate aim has been the education of all to the age of 18. It is nowadays rare for an American child to leave school as early as 14, and most children stay on until their junior high school course at least is completed. America, therefore, is the obvious starting–point for our survey of variant aims and practises in the starting–point for our survey of variant aims and practices in the practises (elementary) school.

U.S.A. If the American public school is to be considered the foundation of American democracy, then the elementary school– which is a common school attended by over 90 per cent of American children–is looked upon as the keystone of the whole educational structure. In most states compulsory schooling begins at the age of 6, and, whilst the length of time devoted to elementry education may vary from state to state (and even withing one state), two main practises exist : either an eight years' elementay education followed by a four-year high school course, or a six years' elementary education followed by six years to be spent in the high school– usually divided into the junior high school and the senior high school.

The elementary school is looked upon as the place in which the child gains the fundamental knowledge, skills, habits, and ideals of thought, feeling and action which are considered necessary for all American citizens regardless of social status, vocation or sex. Obviously, the work of John Dewey has much influenced the pattern of work in the elementary school and equally obviously the elementary school has been used for educational experiments of all kinds–not always with fortunate results. Indeed, one main criticism levelled at the schools to day from within the U.S.A. is that the children have been too much considred as guinea pigs and too little as human beings, and that a kind of spurious science of education has been erected which ignores humanistic values and the great cultural heritage of the Amercan nation. Teaching is as much an art as it is a science, and in any case deals with a different kind of material than that with which the scientist deals in the fastness of his laboratories.

The Dewey approach was a revolt against the formalism in education which favoured the establishment iof the "fold-your–arms" type of school of which we have spoken. It led to the establishment of the one-time fashionable "child-centred" school which in its turn has been criticized as much too individualistic and concentrating to exclusively on the immediate needs and interests of the pupil to the detriments of the community's interests. Nowadays thes fashionable catchword is "the community-centred school" which is defined as aiming at giving the child an appreciation and understanding of his environment, a sense of civic and social responsibility, and a feeling of loyalty to the American democratic ideal. There is also another outlook–that of the "essentialists" as they are sometimes called–which claims that the prime function of education is that of transmitting the cultural heritage of the American people. Though the "essentialists" are attacked as being primarily concerned with the content of education, they start none the less from the principle that the teacher should base his work on the interests of the child, whilst insisting that through those interest the child must be prepared for community living as a free and responsible citizen, and that this can only properly be brought about through making him conscious of his heritage. In any case, in all three groups of thought-child-centred, community-centred and "essentialist" the emophasis tends to be on group-learning and co-opetrative effort; topics for study (rather than subjects) are selected at local, national and world community levels; and all have to agree that the basic skill of reading, writing and arithmetic must first be taught.

In all state-maintained schools there is a complete absence of any general religious instruction or school worship, but on the other hand all kinds of means (direct and indirect) are used to inspire the work of the school with moral and spiritual values. Slogans on the walls–such as "Don't make excuses, make good!" –abound, and every effrort is made through literature, music and the arts generally to develop standards of good tastse and appreciation. In literature the twelve-year-old will have read the usual myths and folklore (including stories from the Bible) which have an appeal for children, and he should know how to use reference books to extend his knowled on a basis of his interests, and how to set about using libraries to widen his reading. In history, he should know something of the biography of outstanding historical charactres and the stories of a few of the more important historical events, present and past. In the liberal and practical arts he should be able to sing and draw and should be showing the beginnings of an interest in some of the best music, pictures and other forms of art. He should possess information in nature study, and, if possible, have a definite interest in some phase of nature study as a scientific pursuit that will help in the proper utilization of his leisure. He should possess the ability to do simple constructive work and be able to make some of the things he is interest in. He should know something of the several industries that are the concern of the locality in which he lives both through visitation and through participation of a limited scale wherever possible.

The promotion of good physical and mental health is also a major concern of the primary school, and in a sound progressive school the child of 12 should have had training in the fundamental habits of exercise, cleanliness, eating and sleeping; he will play several games and belong to one or more societies, as for example the Boy Scouts.

Finally, it should be noted that the still prevalent European custom of class examinations held at the end of the academic year in order to decide who shall be promoted to the next class have in America long since been discarded almost everywhere. For this traditional type of examination, what are called achievement tests are substituted, and much energy has gone into the compilation of such tests which are of the true/ false kind, or of the completion kind, or of the multiple kind, all calling usually of one-word answers. It is interesting to note that such methods of testing have crept into the kind of "intelligence" test set in England at the elevern plus examination for admission to some form of secondary education, and that the some criticisms are now being levelled at achievement test in both America and England; that for mere factual information and cut-and-dried instances of right and wrong such test have their place, but it is a strictly limited one; for the more subtle kinds of discrimination and evaluation they are a danger in that they lead the pupil to over-simplify and do not train him to think in sentences or to develop a simple logical argument. The value of the achievement test, of course, in a large country like America, is that they set up comparable standards of achievement in the teaching of a given subject throughout the whole country, and they also help teachers to discover the weaknesses in their own methods of instruction as well as the difficulties the chidren are likely to encounter. It should also be noted that it is important in America to discover and isolate such weaknesses because of the general marked reluctance to keep a pupil down in a class to repeat the work all over again if it can possibly be helped. Discouragement, frustration and a sense of failure are at all times to be avoided. All well and good. But the cumulative effects of this policy repeatedly make themselves felt at the high school level and prove often embarrassing of not disastrous. On the other hand, we must admit that the common school principle behind American education which makes it automatic of every boy and girl to pass from the primary school to some form of secondary education in the high school frees both parents and children from the anxiety neuroses which abound in Europe wherever the kind of secondary education a child shall have is determined by some kind of examination hurdle at the completion of the primary school course.

The sum up, the American public schools cater for all who come. They aim at least to interest and carry along the dullest and give them a useful preparation for life. They do not aim at preparing bright boys for college of professional life. Everything is made as easy and as attractive for the pupil as possible. Knowledge is absorbed in the smallest of doses, and there is no grind or drill. What is taught is what is considered suitable as a broad preparation for life and citizenship of the great American continent. It is at school that the American learns his characteristic attitudes to life, to his fellows, to his country, and in school that he is introduced to sociery in which it is the proud boast that the lines of demarcation between classes are very indistict. None the less, about 10 percent of the total population of America can be classified as not having received an adequate primary school education. Most of these are Negroes from the Southern States in which problems of racial descrimination amply aboud.

Scandinavia. The principle of a common primary school, with well over 90 percent, of the total child population in attendance, is equally characteristic of the Scandinavian countries, though each of these counties differs in reaching a decision as to how much time shall be spent in this school. Norway, for example, is extremely proud of its "people's" school which covers the entire period of compulsory attendance from the age of 7 to 14 years, and on which all the secondary education to follow is based. In the towns of Norway the percentage of pupils who apply for further schooling is large, and every effort is made to encourage children from the remote country areas to do the same, particularly as distances between town and country are increasingly diminished through the new electrification of the railways. It is to be noted in passing that nursery schools and kindergartens (as in America) have so far not played great role in the Norwegian school system. The need for schools of this kind is more urgent in the highly industrialized areas which have less favourable conditions for education at home.

The "people's" school is a public institution run by the municipality under the supervision of the State. All parents are under an obligaton to send their children to school, and are liable to pubishment if they fail to do so. There are a very few private schools, but these are generally frowned upon as it is held to be of great importance in a democratic country to have *one* school which caters for *all* children from the different from the different social strata. The school is free for everyone, and so are text-book, stationery and materials used in handicrafts, gardening, etc. At most schools the children are given a free breakfast. The programme of study in the school is carefully laid down so that fixed standards are guaranteed in each subject on which the higher schools may safely base their teaching. To this end also the school boards, in consultation with the teaching staff, decide the kind of text-book that are to be used in the various subjects. All text-books chosen have further to be autorized by the Ministry of Education.

The range of subjects taught in this "people's" school might at first sight appear too large, but it is to be remembered that there are children who will receive no further schooling beyond the age of 14, and it is the aim to give such children an elementary grounding in all the main subjects as well as to prepare the other children adequately to cope with the secondary education they will later receive. Instruction is given in scripture, Norwegian history, geography, arithmetic, natural history, physical training, drawing, singing, handicrafts (for boys) and needlework (for girls). For girls domestic science is generally compulsory in town schools and the boys may also do gardening. In the last two years of the curriculum, English is taught as a compulasory subject on a basis of five lessons a week.

Activity methods are the basis of all teaching beacuse it is considered more important to give children inquiring minds and to teach them to find out things for themselves. Indeed, the principle of freedom of thought, belief and action is the basis on which all Norwegian schools are founded;

Here is the surest way of abtaining a free, healthy-minded generation of men and women who will be able to gain an independent outlook on the problems of their time and yet be able to find their place in society, to realize that they do not live alone in the world but must adapt their lives and their actions so as to serve the good of the whole community-first in the small community of the family, then in the larger community which comprises all the peoples of the earth.

In Denmark, the principle of education in the home has become so deeply rooted in the traditions of the country that even to-day a parent is not obliged to send this child to school provided he is willing and able to secure the necessary instruction for his child in other ways. None the less, Frederick VI of Denmark was well in advance of all other contries when in 1814 he made schooling compulsory for three days a week between the ages of 7 and 14, and insisted that every township must have its elementary school. In 1849, compulsory schooling was extended to cover a full sixday week.

The period of compulsory attendance in Denmark is still from 7 to 14. There are nursery schools for children under the age of 7, but most of these are privately run institution, and fee-paying. A child may enter the tree State primary school at the age of 6, and he must be there not later than 8. Thus, the primary school proper in Denmark starts at any age from 6 to 8 and (in contrast to Norway) ends at the age of 11. There is in the school, as in Norway, the same stress on educating the child for co-operation and common responsibility, and to independence of thought and action, and the same basic activity approach is to be noted. The subjects on the curriculum are the same as for Norway, with the exception that English is not taught at this early age. The study of history and geography become serious time-table subjects only in the last two years, the study of science only in the last year.

Compulsory education in Sweden, as in Denmark, dates back to the early nineteenth century and until relatively recently it was thought of as extending from 7 to 14 years of age with the possibility of some form of secondary education at about the age of 12. The position still holds, but much experimentation has gone on in recent years, In 1921 the idea of comprehensive school was first mooted, and after much careful thought and palnning between 1940 and 1952 a school law was finally passed (not yet in full operation) creating what is called a unitary school. It is intended that the child should enter the lowest form of the unitary school at the age of 7 and in his first three years be taught by a fully trained woman infant school teacher. The next three years are to be considred the elementary school proper, in which the teaching will be done by either a man or woman trained elementary school teacher. In these first six years the child is to be taught all subjects by the same teacher. In the seventh and eighth years there is a common core of subjects of all children, but those showing some academic ability can opt to learn a seond language, English being compulsory in these two grades and German being the option. Other children can have additional course in Swedish, whilst still another group will starts on some vocational course. In these last two grades it is intended that the children shall be taught by teachers who are specialists in two or three subjects. At Grade 9 streaming is to begin. One group will follow the academic four year *gymnasium* course, another group will take a one year modein shtudies course, a third group will pursue vocational studies, usually in collaboration with local firms and businesses. Thus, for all but the academically gifted, compulsory attendance is designed to end at 16 plus after nine years' continuous schooling.

Curriculum and methods of teaching are in general respects similar to those found in Norway and Denmark. It is intersting to note the differences that exist between the Scandinavian and the American conception of the role of the common school. There is in Scandinavia no desire to be other than selective of the academic elite at a given point in the child's school career, though opinions differ as to the age best age for effecting the selective process. Scandinvia feels that it nees this educated elite and makes no bones about education for it within a truly democaratic framework. Thus the curriculum in the primary school is a very full one, even by English standards, and whilst the activity principle may be said generally to apply, there is no intention that work of a serious nature shall not be done by all. "There is no better baggage on a journey than much of knowledge."

U.S.S.R. Naturally, the idea of a unitary school is part of the whole way of life and thinking of the Russian people, and all children--irrespective of sex, nationality, social origin or religion -are required to attend this common school for a minimum period of seven years, it being understood that from 1955 onwards the period of obligatory schooling will be gradually extended throughout the whole Union to ten years. Thus, compulsory schooling starts at the age of 7 and ends at the age of 14 or 17. Unlike the other countries which we have so far discussed and which favour the unitary school principle, however, Russia is laying increasing stress on the necessity for sound pre-school care and education and is conviced that indoctrination cannot begin too early. Train up a child in the way he should go, and when he is older he will not depart from it. Parents, therefore, an opt if they so desire--and many working -class parents are bound to do so-- to send their children first of all to baby creches which care for the child between the ages of 1 and 3, and then to the kindegarten proper which keeps the child from the age of a 3 to the age of 7. The creche depends on the Ministry of Public Health, the kindergarten of the Ministry of Education. Both establishment are open the whole year round, and the chilren may stay there between nine and twelve hours of each day. The young women who undertake this specialized kind of child care and teaching receive a very thorough training lasting four years after completion of a ten-year school course. Many of these pre-school institutions charge fees commensurate to the ability of the parents to pay, and quite a number of them are run by the firms of factories of collective farms empoyling the parents.

The avowed aim in the primary school proper- which, of course, is free - is to bring every child to complete satisfactorily his school course, and the teacher is held responsible for arousing the interests of the child and stimulating his will to learn. All children are deemed educable, though there are naturally special schools for educationally subnormal children and special schools classes in the ordinary school and outside the school for children retarded in some branch of their work for some specific reason. There are no exminations until the child has completed the first four years of study, the curriculum for which consists of Russian (or the native language), geography, history of the U.S.S.R., arithemetic, nature study, singing, drawing and physical training. To move into the fifth year the pupil must pass written examinations in native language and arithmentic. In the three remaining years of the seven-year school course, botany, ancient history and a foreign language and added to the original curriculum (for Grade 5) and later (for Gradeds 6 and 7) algebra, geometry, zoology, physices, chemistry, and the constitution of the U.S.S.R.

School only takes place in the morning for six days of the week, and during the afternoons the pupils seek their leisure in the pioneer palaces, in all kinds of pupils'clubs and societies, always strictly followed and strictly guided to think, work and play along approved lines. In effect, no one–parsent, teacher or pupil–is in any doubt as to what is expected. As one leading Soviet statesman put it in 1946: "Soviet Youth must be brought to consolidate what has already been won by our Soviet socialist system, to increase our standards of living and to widen and deepen, our culture. To accomplish these gigantic tasks, our youth must receive a sound and thorough education that teacher them to be bold and enterprising in overcoming the many obstacles in their way. Our people must be educated to the full in their cultural and moral obligations. They must be fired with zeal for the Soviet regime and must selflessly devote themselves constantly to improving the lot of the masses of the people."

Germany. The organization of education throughout the German Federal Republilc favours the common primary school (*the Grundschule*) but leaves each individual *Land* to control and direct as it best thinks fit. The post -war organization has stated quite badly in article 7 of the Basic Law that:

1. The intire education system shall be under the supervision of the *Land*.
2. Religious instruction shall form part of the curriculm in State school, though those entitled to bring up children shall have the right to decide whether their children shall participate in it.

3. Private schools must have a state licence, and this will only be granted if the state is satisfied that (*a*) the curriculum conforms to the basic minimum required in State schools; (*b*) the academic staff is competent and qualified by state standards; (*c*) the wealth of parents is not made a criterion for entry to such schools.

The aim, of course, is to ensure that the *Grundschule* becomes the foundation for all instruction for all classes, and to try to make education in some measure compulsory between the ages of 6 and 18. The idea of the *Grundschule* is no new one. As early as 1920 the Weimar Republic, in its campaigning for the *einheitschule* (comprehensivse school), decreed that there should be a basic and compulsory four years' schooling in an elementary school before any child be allowed to pass on to any form of secondary education, and to further this aim it discontinued all preparatory schools attached to the grammar school proper. To-day there is a distinct divergence of opinion throught Germany as to how long the period of common schooling should last. Many *Lander* are in favour of the original four-year school, but Hamburg in particular has advocated a six-year school on the grounds that four years of elementary education is too short when it is remembered that 90 per cent of the population of the *Grundschule* will be passing on to some form of further education that is not academic; it is folly to sacrifice the mass of the German people for the doubtful benefit of pushing further forward a mere 10 percent elite who will attend the academic grammar school. Upholders of the four year *Grundschule* argue that six years of primary education dangerously shortens, in this age of acute specialization, the period of secondary education and holds back unnecessarily the gifted child.

In any case, it is generally held that the function of the *Grundschule* is to recognize, cultivate and develop a child's natural gifts and to give him a thorough instruction in the basic essentials of a good general education. These essentials are variously listed as : confident oral and written use of the mother tongue; assurance with figures, familiarity with the objects and workings of nature, appreciation of poetry (and the arts in general); a sound religious grounding, a knowledge of history that will gear itself closely to the study of the workings of a democratic society. And all this time the school will be on the watch to distinguish as well as possible between what the Hamburg system defines as the practical, the technical and the academic talents of its individual pupils. Free tuition for all pupils following a course of elementary instruction has been common usage in all schools for at least seventy years. It has now been extended in all *Lander* to cover the part-time vocational schools.

Switzerland. The Swiss also attach great importance to the basic training given in a common primary school, also called the *Grundschule* and in which all children receive instruction in the common core of subjects necessary before any kind of secondary education is attempted. Enormous differences of opinion exist, however, from canton to canton, as to what shall be the length of this essential primary school course, and whilst the majority of cantons practise a six-year *Grundschule* some others work to only a four- or five-year course. The schools are free, excellently organized (even in the remote and more inaccessible places where schooling is only possible for six months of the year); and in consequence private schools–except in some parts of Romance Switzerland where the hold of Catholicism is strong–are to all intents and purposses non-existent. Compulsory schooling begins at the age of 6 or 7 and lasts eight or nine years. In addition there are kindergarten schools, some of which take children from 2 years of age, though the majority have age ranges of between 4 and 6 years. Attendance at such schools is not compulsory and in the industrial areas is often free.

The range of subjects covered and the standard of work demanded in the Swiss schools is very much the same as in Scandinavia or Germany, and much insistence is placed on a thorough grounding in essential subjects.

France. Within the framework of the highly centralized system of education that hold in France, the primary school has an important part to play, and despite post-war reforms the French remain adamant in stressing continually the two fold aim of the primary school to form conscientious and loyal citizens who shall perpetuate the glory that is France, and to give the pupil a fund of practical knowledge that will be necessary for him inthe performance of his daily task as a worker. In other words, It is still held that the majority of pupils passing through the state primary schools will become manual or agricultural workers. It is a realist view. Existence for the Frenchman has always been a serious matter, and he has always insiste (and will continue to insist) on the necessity for a sound intellectual training at all levels in the school system from the nursery school upwards. Thus, if pre-war reforms in education eased the way for the transfer of the working class boy or girl of ability to the *lycee* (grammer scbool) and post war reforms have created on entirely new range of possibilities for secondary and an technical education for all, the over-all effect of this has been to focus attention still more actualy on the best way to organize the primary school meet the challenge presented by the changing conditions elsewhere.

Compulsory schooling in France now begins at the age of 6 and ends at 14, and the examination for the *certificat d'etudes primaires* (the primary school leaving certificate) which could formerly be taken at the age of 12 is now no longer sat until a pupil is in his last statutory year at school. It is also important to remember that primary education covers nursery and infant school attendance as well. Private schools are allowed to exist side by side with the state school system, provided they can give guarantees of offering the same basic training and that the teachers employed hold the necessary qualifications as stipulated by the Ministry of Education, but these are not necessarily free. Most of them are Catholic schools, and there are a few Protestant ones. It is to be remembered that state schools are non-denominational and give no religious whatsoever the schools being closed every. Thursday to enable pupils to receive whatever kind of religious instruction their parents may desire. Traditionally and here we can trace the prevailing Catholics influence throughtout the country–boys and girls must be educated separately from the age of 6 onwards wherever the population of a locality exceeds 500. Permission to conduct a mixed school, even of an experimental nature, must always be sought from the Ministry.

The *ecoles maternelles* (nursery schools for the voluntary attendance of children between the ages of 2 and 6) have had a long and glorious history extending as far back as 1837, and are justifiably proud of the role they have played (and continue to play) as a social force in caring for children of working-class parents. Because of the unique part they have played in the life of the country, though they fall directly under the control of the Ministry of Education, they have acquired to themselves special privileges and a special inspectorate and are consequently permitted a much greater freedom for experimentation and initiative than is normally allowed other state-controlled educational institutions. Their aim is two–fold : child care and child welfare (which includes instructing the mother in the correct upbringing of her child), and to lay a sound basis for the primary education to follow by creating an atmosphere in which children can develop their interests, with particular reference to physical development and sense training. In other words, all the most modern ideas of nursery education are in use with particular stress laid on the psychological and philosophical principles of Decroly, Piaget, Claparede and Ferriere. One important aim towards the end of the nursery school course is to initiate the child to the mysteries of reading, writing and arithmetic; The schools are open six hours a day– three in the morning and three in afternoon– and there is a growing tendency to use them as *garderies* until six o'clock until the working parent can find time to reassume her full responsibilities as a mother. It is estimated that about 60 percent of the children of France between the ages of 2 and 6 are now cared for in such nursery schools, and it has become an avowed aim of the Ministy of education to extend still further facilities offered.

The primary school is now faithfully striving to pick up

the threads where the nursery school leaves off, and the work done in this school is divided into five grades : a preparatory section for children between the ages of 6 and 7; an elementary section for children from 7 to 9 years; a middle section for children from 9 to 11 years; an upper section for children between the ages of 11 and 12; and a final section, leading to the primary school leaving certificate, for children between the age of 12 and 14. The children attend school six hours a day for five days of the week, Thursday and Sundays being whole day holidays, but extra supervised study takes place each day after school for those pupils who are ambitious to do extra well or to improve in their weaker subjects. The curriculum comprises reading, writing, arithmetic, the history and geography of France and her possessions (as well as the geography of the greater powers), moral and civic education, the element of science, drawing, singing, manual work, physical education, and guided activities and recreation.

Between the two wars the curriculum to the primary school was repeatedly attacked as bring too academic and remote from life, too bookish and too much devoted to the amassing of encyclopaedic (and often useless) knowledge. Directives issued in 1945 urged the schools to bring thier work closer to life and to introduce a "bath of realism." It was also hoped that the food work being done in the nursery schools would have its own salutory effects at least in the earlier years of the primary school course. Important changes that have resulted include the introduction of the Decroly global method of teaching to read and to write, creative writing, group work and local studies, and the delivery of lecturettes by individual pupils to the rest of the class designed to encourage individual children to develop some particular and personal interests. None the less, there is to be no"playing at working", and all pupils are constantly aware that important examinations that concern their future lie ahead of them.

The first of these is the eleven plus examination which will decide to what kind of secondary education the pupil will go. This will be discussed in detail later in our next chapter on secondary education. Those pupils who do not leave the primary schools at the age of 11 or 12 for some kind of secondary education will then spend the rest of their time preparing for the primary school leaving certificate, taken at the age of 14. This examination falls into two distinct parts : first. there is a dictation together with a few simple comprehension questions, the writing of a composition to test the pupil's not to maul" the French language, and a number of arithmetical problems to be solved; then follows an oral examination including reading aloud, recitation, questions on history, geography, science, and possibly singing and drawing. It is a searching test, and a comprehensive one. On the other hand, only pupils who seem reasonably sure of passing the examination are entered (just ovser half the number in the final year of study) and about 80 per cent of these are usually successful.

Belgium. Like the Frenchman, the Belgian is no woolly-headed idealist, and his education means much to him. Belgian independence was achieved mainly because of a struggle over scholastic issues, and the whole tumultuous history of the country between 1830 and the present day throws again and again into sharp relief the importance of education along practical, democratic lines to a small country that has to contend not only with threatened domination from abroad (both economic and military), but also with ceaseless internal conflict over religious and linguistic problems. Hence the importance attached constantly to the historic clause in the original Declaration of Independence of 1830:"Education is free; no attempt shall be made to prevent anyone from educating his child as he so wishes." Hence also the present avowed policy of bringing coharmony, cohesion and simplicity into the school system; of achieving parallel classes of study that make for easy change from one type of education to another; of improving further the already well-establilshed systems of child and vocational guidance; of replacing the workshop apprenticeship system by vocational education that does not neglect the cultural aspect; of ensuring that every child, without distinction, may easily find the type of education as well as full preparation for the career for which he is manifestly most suited.

It was in 1936 that the Minister for Education, Bovesse, put forward his plan for the complete reform of education, but events postponed the full implementation of the Bovesse Plan until after 1945. The three primary aims of this plan may be said to be : to furnish mind– to give all children that knowledge which is considered the indispensable minimum if they are to enter fully into social living; to enable all children to acquire the basic techniques and the tool subjects; to exercise the mind and to form character, which implies the development of a sense of values, the stimulation of spontaneous interests, and the fostering of a growing ability to look, to observe, and to experiment sanely.

Thus, education proper starts with the infant school, open to both boys and girls between the ages of 3 and 6. Such infant school education is, of course not compulsory, and the various communes are free to organize such schools though they may not be compelled to open a school if there are less than thirty children seeking admission. The avowed aim of the school is to prepare children to enjoy their primary school education without encroaching in any way on the work that will be done in the primary school. Thus, the school seeks to develop in the child power of observation, to correct and improve his speech, and to give him a sense of discipline. A sense of taste and manual dexterity are also developed by simple handicrafts, paper cutting, clay modelling, and so on. All infant schools are run on sound, progressive Froebel lines, and Decroly's influence is everywhere evident.

Usually, only infant schools maintained entirely by the state are free. As with the primary schools, it is possible to have schools run by *(a)* the communes; *(b)* the provinces; *(c)* the state; *(d)* private persons; *(e)* outside bodies– usually the Catholic Church–whose schools are recognized by the State and subsidized, or which are maintained by the local authourity. At the primary school level all the schools are free except those very few run by private persons.

Primary school education is therefore compulsory between the ages of 6 and 12, after which every pupil must pass to some form of secondary or technical education for a minimum period of two years, making the school leaving age 14. Co-education is frequent in village but not in towns. The primary school programme is divided into four cycles of two years each, and it is on the completion of the third cycle that the pupil now normally closes his primary school career. The fourth cycle (ages 12-14), which was instituted when the school leaving age was raised to 14 in 1914, was intended to round off the primary school course by "nurturing a man and a citizen who would have a highly developed sense of community." In its present form, and because of the increased facilities for entry to some form of secondary or technical education at the age of 12, this fourth cycle is becoming increasingly redundant and the aim is to kill it completely.

All teaching in the primary school is based on Decroly principles, suitably adapted, and the avowed aims of the school are : (*a*) to give all children a strong and sound basis to enable them to prepare for future life; (*b*) to enable them to speak their mother tongue (French or Dutch) simply, clearly and correctly, to read and understand what they read, to write and reckon correctly; (*c*) to develop in the children powers of observation, of altruism, and a sense of fair play–in other words, to enable them to grow into responsible citizen types. The curriculum includes religion or ethics, the mother tongue, elementary arithmetic, some notions of another language than the mother tongue(Dutch on French), geography, naturalhistory, drawing hygiene, singing, physical training, some basic notions of the natural sciences. There is also needlework for girl, and in rural areas gardening for boys.

Holland. The schools of Holland are the people's schools, and when the Dutch Minister for Education surveyed in 1946 the havoc caused by the war years and tried to bring the Dutch people to face the realities of a post-war situation that had thrown the previous delicately balanced economy of the country permanently out of alignment, he made a special plea to the people of Holland and stressed that "new thoughts must come from the people." In a little less than a hundred years the population of the country had increased threefold; it was becoming increasingly and vitally necessary to secure the transformation of the Netherlands into a highly industrialized country; and there must be increase opportunities for specialization, open to all, with the schools still more closely geared to the imoportant task of forming high-grade technicians, yet not neglecting in so doing the equally important duty of safeguarding Dutch liberty of thought and conscience and of attempting to reconcile, as always, the claims of the State and those of the parent.

Education in Holland is compulsory from the age of 6 or 7, and one of the first concerns of post-war educational reconstruction, in view of the changed and changing economy the country, has been to extend the duration of the elementary school course proper to eight full years–this by a law which became effective in January, 1950. In addition, parents are being encouraged to make an increased use of the growing facilities for non-compulsory nursery and infant school education between the ages of 3 and 6. About two-thirds of the children within this age range are now in such schools. Not unnaturally, in a country where so many of the schools belong to private trusts, to towns, communes, or religious bodies, and where the state control is limited to general inspection, standards vary considerably from school to school. On the whole, however, the approach is as modern and progressive as in other countries, and the influence of Decroly and Montessori is much in evidence.

The primary school course proper lasts for six years, sometime seven, and all but the Roman Catholic schools are co-educational. The pupils are taught reading, writing and arithmetic; they learn the Dutch language, Dutch history (including the element of political institutions), geography, natural history (including swimming) and (for girls) needlework. Religion is optional, but it is of course taught in the denominational schools. The few pupils from the primary school (about 9 per cent of those in the top two classes) who intend to proceed to some kind of clearly defind secondary education are allowed to follow private classes, outside school hours, in which a foreign language (usually French) is taught.

Bearing in mind the employment difficulties which present themselves in a country that in 1930 had a population of just over 6,000,000 and in 1954 more than 10,250,000, much attention is paid not only to thoroughness in training at the primary school level, but also (and particularly so) to what is done for the mass of the children who do not enter the secondary streams. Thus there is what is termed a continued elementary school course of two years' duration, usually attached to the elementary school proper, which caters for those children who go neither to the secondary schools, nor to what is termed an advanced elementary school. Instruction at this school "must be practical and simple social instruction, and must in no way compete with technical instruction." It is intended as preparation for leading a fuller and more useful life, and the two years are intended as an orientation period to enable the child to discover for what employment he is ultimately best suited. Woodwork and metalwork for boys, domestic science and homecrafts for girls, together with an elementary course in English for both, are considered indispensable, along with study in greater depth of the run of subjects studies earlier in the primary school.

It is hoped that the children leaving this course may then at least be encouraged to follow day courses of instruction for at least eight hours per week until they reach the age of 18, thus perfecting themselves in their chosen *metier*. The more ambitious will naturally pass to some form of technical training in one of the many technical and professional schools that abound, and of which the Dutch are justly proud.

The advanced elementary school course is of four years' duration and it recruits about one-third of the pupils who have satisfactorily completed the sixth class of the primary school. In addition to continued study of the basic subjects, the curriculum includes at least three of the following: French, English, German, mathematics, commercial training. In the final year, opportunity is given for specialization in a mathematics-physics section in preparation for entry to a secondary technical school. The majority of pupils, however, on completion of the advanced school course embark on some kind of office work. A few pass to a teacher's training college.

Italy. It is often said that the structure of Italian education has not changed in any significant way for about a century, since the Casati law was adopted in 1859, or at any rate the Coppino act of 1877; and the most usual explanation given is the poverty of the country. There is still, it is true, widespread illiteracy, particularly in Southern Italy, and although from the turn of the century the State programme has aimed at a minimum of five years' free schooling for everyone, even the more prosperous and industrialized northern provinces have often achieved no more than three. It is also true that the rival claims of Church and State to control the education of the young have not always made for advance; and that the Gentile reforms of the Mussolini regime, which could in theory have achieved so much, foundered because they were applied as a protest against the ideals of democratic government. Similarly, the Bottai reforms of 1939 became in reality a most reliable instrument of Fascist policy, for while they gave a more stable organization to the schools of the working class, they ensured that the way was blocked for any kind of liberal secondary education at the people's level.

The first post-war need in Italy, therefore, was to awaken the people to a recognition of their cultural heritage; the second, and perhaps in many respects the more important, was for the planners to recognize that the reconstruction of the Italian school, to be successful, had to be undertaken by the Italian people themselves. In consequence, when the Minister for Education, Gonella, put forward his tentative scheme for reform in 1947 he sent out detailed questionnaires to all concerned with education and then encouraged parts of his plan to be tried out by a few enlightened people. It is generally felt still too early for the plan as a whole to be put into effect. Like the French and the Belgians, the Italians want to be sure where they are going, and are moving slowly. The immediate objectives, however, are to overcome illiteracy, to make good the glaring deficiencies in school buildings and equipment, to provide equality of educational opportunity, to meet the demands for technical education at all levels, and finally to educate the teachers and general public to understand the principles of the new education and to honour the work done in this field by successive generations of their own countrymen.

At present, primary education is in theory compulsory from the age of 6 to 14; in fact, particularly in the poorer south, children often leave school at II. For children between the ages of 3 and 6 there is ample nursery school accommodation in the larger and wealthier towns and communes. The teaching is modern and bears comparison with the best done in France or Belgium, and close on one million children are at present in such schools. Only a few of these schools (mainly those attached to teacher-training establishments) are State-controlled; the remainder are run by private, civic or religious bodies. They provide free lunches and free medical treatment for the children of all poor parents, and the importance of their work is recognized by the urgent recommendation in the Gonella plan to extend it to the poorer and more remote areas of Italy by making it compulsory for all communes to establish such schools, where they are needed, with financial aid from the State.

As is natural, the primary schools have received most attention since the war. The primary school proper extends only to the age of II, and is concerned with the basic subjects together with an emphasis on religious, civic and moral training. In the rural districts tremendous efforts have been made, despite financial stringencies, to ensure this adequate basic schooling for all, and also, particularly in the southern povinces, to overcome illiteracy among the adult peasant population. The war years also caused appalling havoc in family life, and many young children were for left wandering, homeless and uncared for, or in entirely unsuitable homes, in a state often bordering on extreme delinquency. State and Curch alike– though the majority of primary schools are State–controlled –took the matter in hand, and some extremely interesting experimental village school communities have since developed, notable amongst which is the Pestalozzi City School of Florence, situated in one of the poorest and most densely populated (and sordid) parts of the town.

A general dissatisfaction with the old traditional methods of instruction is gradually making room for more modern acivity methods and among the younger teachers there is at least the desire, not only to see that every school draws from its environment "the cultural and practical motives which constitute its very life," but also that every child is imbued with"a serene desire for work and service to the fatherland with honesty of purpose." There are new emphases on self-expression through drawing, painting and singing and the importance of *lavoro* ("work") is continually stressed. "Work" is not to be interpreted in the narrow sense of manual instruction, or handicrafts, or domestic science and needle-work, but rather as a form of honourable productive activity. Again, there is a faint link with Decroly principle here. Briefly, the theory is that in school children should acquire the ground work for either artisan, agricultural or "feminine" pursuits and should also visit work "on location." Thus, in school, they will repair chairs, doors, desks, cultivate plants and (if girls) not only do cookery and domestic science but also economics of balancing the household budget, shopping, bathing the baby, and so on. It is stressed that town boys should have their gardens to cultivate and on which to raise saleable vegetables. The general policy behind all this, of course, is to remember that Italian labour exports itself the world over; that the dignity of labour must not be traduced; and that a stable economy in the present age of automation depends on the workman recognizing that his is an honourable calling.

Conclusion. It is to be noted that in almost all these countries with which we have been concerned considerable attention is now being paid to pre-school education, at the nursery and kindergarten level. With the possible exception of America (which in any case has not many nursery schools) it can be said that the policy is one of "indoctrination" allied to a conviction (proved by experience) that you cannot start too young in educating the child in the way you would have it go.

Nursery schools started, of course, almost everywhere as institutions for children whose home conditions were unsatisfactory or whose mothers had to go out to work. Nowadays, however, it is recognized that they have an important physical, social and educational part to play. In Russia the process is frankly that of indoctrinating as early as possible to the accepted Russian way of life, and showing the parents how the young Russian child is to be handled. In France they educate the working-class parent in child care, they prepare the child most carefully for entry to the primary school proper, they act as a spearhead for constantly "freeing" the curriculum in the primary school, and they stress the importance of the child's heritage. In Belgium and Holland they make for proper child care and "indoctrinate" for individualism and personal competence. In Italy they are an important element of educational reconstruction. Only the Scandinavian countries, which have enjoyed the blessing of local self-government for so long, feel little need for nursery schools. And where nursery schools do exist in America they are much more laboratories for psychological study and observation than anything else.

Much importance is now also attached to the primary school proper to ensure that it really does become a *Grundschule* and provide a sound basic training from which the child may draw strength to embark with confidence on some form of post-primary education.The curriculum, and the approach to the presentation of the curriculum, is determined by the kind of post-primary education it is proposed to offer. At the same time, it is recognized that a well-informed, inquiring mind is much more necessary to the nation than one that is passively stocked with information. Hence the prominence generally of techniques derived from the "new" education and the gradual abandonment of teaching in mass in favour of individual attention. One point, however, is still much debated at teachers' conferences everywhere in Europe": Can freedom in the primary school go too far in the wrong direction and lead to lack of real discipline in the use of the basic tool subjects ?" The general opinion (for what it is worth) is that America provides an important example of what not to do. In England there seems to be a move to check too much of a drift in the American direction. France sublimely goes its own way with its own unchanged objectives constantly in mind. And Norway, Sweden and Russia all prove that you can have a unitary school system and still train your elite, if you pay close attention to the work done in the *Grundschule*.

Finally there is the controversial question as to the age at which the child's primary education should end. In America, Norway, Sweden and Russia there is no problem–yet if their systems are closely examined it will be found that in practice there are divisions: 6 to 12, 12 to 15, 15 to 18 and onwards, roughly speaking. Most other countries make an end to primary education at about the age of 12, in effect, and many are advocating an intermediate school from the age of 12 to 15.

6

Secondary Education

The breakdown of social barriers that started with the Industrial Revolution and which gained increasing impetus as the nineteenth century drew to its close inevitable threw up all kinds of problems in the field of post–primary and secondary education that left most European countries (as we shall see) bewildered and uncertain about the right solution to seek. In the first place, there came a challenge to the traditional concept of what was meant by the term "secondary" as applied to education.

For centuries, it had been assumed that secondary education was education that befitted a gentleman, and that gave some training for the learned professions, and for offices of government, very much according to the pattern established by John Locke in his *Thoughts on Education*. There was a governing elite, and tradition decreed that the basis of the curriculum for the formation of this elite should be the Latin and Greek tongues, ancient history, and some philosophical training usually arising as a by-product from a thorough grounding in the classical languages.

Only towards the end of the nineteenth century did a study of foreign languages grudgingly find a place in the curriculum, along with mathematics, and finally the sciences. Even then, however, it was still held (as in not a few public schools in England to-day) that the study of foreign modern languages and the sciences should become easier options for the less able pupil. That traditional outlook still persists almost every–where in Europe despite the post–war reforms that have taken place.

The second problem arose from the prevailing idea that only those of wealth and a certain social status were fit to govern and to form an intellectual elite. The children of such parents had a pre-emptive right to profit from the kind of education given in what we will call the classical secondary school, and to this end all classical secondary schools established their preparatory departments through which it became almost imperative for a child to pass before gaining entrance to the main school at the age of 11 or 12. Thus, two clearly-defined and distinct types of primary education established themselves : the one for the masses of the people that led nowhere except to some kind of job at between the ages of 12 and 14 , the other which was a careful preparation for an advanced academic training up to the age of 18 or beyond. So did what we have already called the dual system of education come into existence. Until the nineteenth century, however, education throughout the ages had been for a select few. Now, the masses had to be and were being educated. An increasing demand for a still more highly educated person in science, industry and trade focused attention on the anomalies in this dual system of education, forced the classical secondary school to open its doors more widely to include more and more scholarship children from among the working classes and to give constantly increasing importance in its curriculum to modern subjects like foreign languages, history and geography, and led to the creation of the creation of new types of school to rival and old classical secondary school and so call for an entirely new assessment of what was meant by secondary education.

But all this brought still a third problem. Tradition dies hard, and as more and more pupils came to profit from an increasingly liberal but still highly classical kind of secondary education such an education became a sort of *cachet* and was looked upon as a necessary preliminary to a wide variety of black-coated jobs. The former matriculation certificate in England, for example, became necessary for entry to an insurance firm, to a bank, to a commercial business house as a clerk, and to minor civil service appointments such as a post office. An army of black-coated workers arose, side by side with the itellectual elite, and work of a practical or technical nature came to be despised by the very people most notably suited for it and at a time when the demand was increasing for highly trained technical skill.

Finally, as increasing prosperity due to technological advances in industry and higher standard of living made it possible to raise the compulsory school leaving age still higher, so again did the question of what kind of post-primary education to offer become acute, and so did the cry of equality of educational opportunity for all make itself heard. It needed none the less the serious challenges to the by then accepted ideals of democracy that came from the totalitarian states, allied to insistent demands for better and better trained workers in science and technology, to make most countries in the immediate post-war period recast their whole way of thinking and re-form their school systems drastically at the post-primary level. It is in particular with such re-formation that we shall be concerned in this chapter, though we shall relegate the whole complicated and vexing question of what kind of technical training is offered to a chapter on its own. In other words, we are by implication defining secondary education to-day as that kind of post-primary education which is not directly concerned with man and machines but rather with a kind of broad, modern and humanistic culture that it is hoped will enable man to release to the full his potentialities and so direct his towards the kind of employment for which he realzes himself he is most especially suited.

As the American approach to education has been one which requires education for the masses first and education for the most talented second, so have the Americans anticipated practice every-where in Europe both in recognizing the need for a kind of secondary education suitable for those not going on to institues of higher education and in developing a wide range of courses supplementary and alternative to those offered by the traditional classical curriculum. All this has, of course, been made possible by the phenomenal increase in the wealth of the U.S.A. which has both kept adolescents off the labour market and made more money available for the building of more and more high schools. We must not forget also, however, the strong egalitarian feelings of the American people which have caused them to move more freely and naturally towards the idea of equality of educational opportunity. Thus America once again becomes a starting-point for this particular survey of practice and changes in education at the post-primary secondary level.

U. S. A. We have already noted that the break between primary and secondary education comes either at the age of 14, when normally there is a four-year high school course to be followed, or at the age of 12, after which three years are spent in a junior high school to be followed by a further three years in the senior high school. This latter plan (popularly known as the 6–3–3 system) has gained favour because of the opportunities it offers for the better guidance and counselling of pupils and for providing exploratory courses to discover a pupil's abilities and interests. It is this aspect of the work in the junior high school which has caught the attention particulary in Western Europe and caused countries which had no clearly defined middle school system in operation to implement one when they carried out their post-war reforms at the secondary level.

Because the American sytem of education is dominated by the idea of the comprehensive school, all pupils, whether gifted, average or backward, are expected to attend the same school, and this policy – if in practice it is not extended to work in the senior high school– certainly holds as far as the junior high school. In consequence, all high school education is free and text-books are also provided free of cost. There are incidental fees for games and certain clubs, and parents must naturally bear the cost of clothes, transport and maintenance of the pupil. It thus is not unknown for pupils to engage on wage-earning activities either before or after school in order either to obtain pocket money or to contribute in some degree to their support at home. Again, because the schools are considered the parents' school and because the cdhildren are expected to stay ideally the whole of the high school course, all kinds of vocational subjects have crept into the curriculum, and the academic traditions holding in Europe are strongly criticized as being no longer suited to the needs and abilities of the mass of the pupils who now fill the high schools? A close study over a number of years of the in take of the high schools reveals that there are roughly 20 percent suited to academic subjects, 20 percent. to vocational subjects, and 60 percent for whom entirely diferent curriculam must be devised.

The curriculum of any given high school is therefore not easy to describe. As time goes on, and as social demands change, new subjects are incorporated displacing those that are outmoded. The fundamental "core" subjects taught in both junior and senior high school are : English, history, mathematics and science. In addition, a number of " elective" subjects are studied, these being chosen by the pupil after consultation with his teacher counsellor, who, because of the wide range of abilities that exists amongst the pupils he has to help, fulfils a very important role in the high school system. A pupil, after counselling, may elect to do a subject for one or two terms, and then drop it in favour of something else.

The senior high school, designed to complete secondary education, must make provision for a more or less complete training in the fieilds of study chosen as a sesult of the work in the junior high school. Diffferentiated curricula are provided by means of which each pupil will be able to pursure, once his decision is reached, work systematically planned with reference to his needs as an individual and as a member of society. The main lines of work found in the senior high school are: college preparatory, business and commercial, industrial arts, agriculture, home economics (domestic science, etc.), and special subjects such as music and art. Defferentiatrion can also exist within these special curricula. The college preparatory programme, for example, can subdivide for entrance into liberal arts colleges, schools of engineerings, schools of medicine and dentistry; a commercial course can provide for salesmen, secretary typists, buyers and business managers; the agriculture course can have grain-growing, dairying, fruit-growing and livestock-raising subdivisions. How far the ramifications extend depends on the size and resources of the school, and the Americans favour large comprehensive schools in order to be able to provide as many "elections" as possible. Certain large cities will have special-type high schools, as for exampale a commercial high school or a technical high school.

Those pupils who graduate from high school on the college preparatory programme can then normally pass to what is termed the junior college which supplies two years of training beyond the standard high school course. The junior college may be the first two years of a fully organized university, or it may be a separate institution. Such a course represents either the preliminary training to the reading for a university degree proper, or the preprofessional requirements of schools of medicine, dentistry, etc., or the requisite two-year course to qualify in pharmacy.

One marked feature of the American high school is the emphasis placed on extra-curricular and out-of-school activities, these being regarded as increasingly important in the development of charater and in teaching the young adolescent the correct use of his leisure time. Games and athletics loom large in such programmes, of course, but they form in reality only one small part of the whole. There are schools at which something is going on every night, and on Saturdays as well, organized by the pupils on an often expremely elaborate scale. The fact that most of the drive behind these activities comes from the pupils themselves is evidence that they are genuinely interested. The initiative is left to them, but teachers naturally supervise generally and proffer advice and help as required. As is to be expected there is a wide variety of activities ranging from pupil government of the school and student councils to movie clubs, school bands, rodeos (in the far West), broadcasting stations, running their own cafeteria, organizing their own bus services, down to the more humdrum European idea of out-of –school activities such as dramatic societies, dance clubs, language clubs, debating societies, producing the school magazine, and so on.

On paper, it is all very fine indeed, but in actual practice discerning Americans find much to criticize. The idea of a comprehensive school running ito hundreds of pupils of both sexes is all very well, but the close personal contact between teacher and taught that can hold in a European school of smaller size is lost. The school becomes a depersonalized machine, and the teachers automata for enabling children to make their grades and amass the necessary credits required for the graduation ceremony. All these extra-curricular activities which make the school the pupils school day and night mean that increasingly the home and home influences recede into the background. Again, is the gradual cowding out of academic subjects in favour of an increasingly widening range of vocational subjects going too far? Does not each country need as large an academic elite as it can muster? Has not the American's inherited belief that all men are created equal led to the conception that all school children have the same potentialities, and is not America confusing equality of opportunity with identity of opportunity?

U.S.S.R. Russia at any rate, though it has embraced firmly the idea of the unitary school system, has not fallen into this error, and at the secondary level every attempt is made to sort out pupils of ability and to encourage them to go as far as they can. Similarly, there has been a marked reaction against early experiments in freedom and with new education techniques in favour of a reintroduction of the examination system and of a firmly disciplined approach to work. Co-education has been abolished in the large cities (that is to say, wherever it is economical and practical to do so) because it is now felt that the needs of boys and girls in adolescence differ considerably, not only psychologically speaking, but also with particular reference to intellectual interests and occupational pursuits. Finally, it has been decided to reintroduce fees for all children attending the upper secodary school as well as all places for higher education.

We have already noted that the first examination a Russian child takes is that which passes him from the fourth grade (the end of the primary school proper) into the fifth grade where secondary education properly begins. At the end of the seventh grade he sits still another examination, this time in eight subjects: Russian lanaguage and literature, algebra or arithmetic, geometry, history, geography, physics, and constitution of the U.S.S.R. This terminates the seven years' school course, the last three years constituting what is called the "incomplete" secondary school. Though this has not yet been achieved everywhere, the ultimate aim is to make the seven years' school compulsory for everyone.

The "complete" secondary schools, which are the ten-year schools, are to be found only in the large cities and industrial centres, and pupils who pass succesfully from the "incomplete" secondary school (the seven years' school) are therefore obliged to attend the last three classes of full secondary education away from home. It will be obvious that pupils who are fortunate enough to live in an area which has the ten-year school, and can therefore move up year by year in the same buildings and social atmosphere, are at an advantage over the country boy who comes to a strange town and has to board, or live with relatives if he has any conveniently placed. Again, the ten-year school is more luxuriously equipped, can offer greater facilities for extended study, and commands the services of the best teachers.

The same subjects studied in the "incomplete" secondary school are continued but special emphasis is now placed on the teaching of chemistry and physics, trigonometry is introduced, and the emphasis in foreign language teaching shifts from language to literature. In the last two years a course in philosophy is introduced, and this is divided into two distinct parts: in the first year psychology is studied, in the second year, logic. Quite a number of ten-year schools have also introduced Latin (previously postponed to the university courses) in the last years of study.

At the end of the ten-year school course the pupil sits a final maturity examination (introduced for the first time in 1944). There are written tests in Russian language and literature, mathematics (geometry and trigonometry). There is an oral examination in the same subjects and also in algebra, chemistry, physics, history and foreign languages. Pupils in non-Russian speaking areas also have an oral examination in their native language and literature. A candidate who receives a distiction in this maturity examination (and he must receive the award of "excellent" in all subjects to do this) is automatically given admission to the university and other institutes of higher education. Others must sit an examination on a strictly competitive basis for the few places that are left over when these distinction awards have been made.

Scandinavia: The principle of the unitary school in Norway has been achieved by building the secondary school on to a common seven-year primary school. Secondary schools have existed in Norway as far back as 1150, when they were attached to episcopal sees and were termed "Latin" schools and had the sole function of preparing for university entrance. In the 1850's the curriculum was modernized to introduce modern languages and science, and again in 1896, when three distinct streams came to be recognized: a Latin, stream a modern stream (with particular exphasis on the teaching of English and history), and a mathematics-physics stream. In 1935 came the last reform which recognized two distinct types of secondary school: the traditional academic grammar school (*the gymnasium*) preparing for university entrance, and the "modern" or realskole, designed to give a general education and also to prepare pupils for other kinds of post-primary education. A small tuition fee is payable in both schools, but needy pupils always get adequate financial aid.

Usually, the course at the *realskole* lasts for three years, though in towns and urban districts it is often only a two-year school and in country districts can be extended to four years. The *gymnasium* course lasts for five years. The curriculum for both schools is the same for the first two years, thus making transfer from one school to the other a practical possibility. In addition, there is a four-year *gymnasium* and a two-year *realskole* for pupils who have attended for one or two years at a continuation school or youth school. These are usually State boarding schools and they are designed to ensure that no pupil of promise, however remotely he may be compelled to live from the hub of urban activity, or however late a developer he may have proved to be, is denied a fitting secondary school education. There is no country in the world, including America and Russia, which so carefully provides for equality of educational opportunity.

The general curriculum of the *gymnasium* and the *realskole* includes religious instruction, Norwegian (with Old Norse), English, German, French, history, geography, citizenship, mathematics, science, art, gymnastics, and needlework for girls and wood-work for boys. Specialization in groups of particular subjects begins in the *gymnasium* after the first two years of the course. There is an annual and uniform State examination for passing out from these schools controlled by a special council of secondary education, members of which also inspect the school. At the *gymnasium* level this examination is taken usually at the age of 19 and is called the *examen artium* (note the, medieval flavour). In the *realskole* the examination is known as the *realskoleeksamen* and is usually taken at the age of 17.

Though every effort is made to encourage as many pupils as possible to pass from the primary school to one or other of these two schools, it has to be recognized that there are some children who could not readily benefit from such an advanced type of education. The Norwegians, however, are loth to turn a boy or girl loose at the age of 14. Thus, continuation and youth schools have become prominent as providing some form of post-primary education beyond the compulsory school leaving age. The continuation school is the responsibility of the local authorities who are left to decide whether they shall make attendance at such schools optional or compulsory. In these post-war years it is increasinly felt that the continuation school has an important part to play in rising the standard of general education still higher and preparing for further specialized education. To this end, therefore, there is a move to make the school everywhere compulsory and to make changes in the curriculum. There are at present two types of continuation school: one chiefly theoretical, with Norwegian, mathematics, history, hygiene and citizenship as the principal subjects; one which is purely vocational. Proposed changes in the curriculum would compel at least one-third of the time in the theoretical school to be devoted to practical subjects, and a third in the vocational courses to the study of Norwegian, history and citizenship.

Instruction in the continuation school is free, and the actual courses can be of short duration, varying in length from three to six months, or they can be spread over a period of two or three years with part-time attendance.

Youth schools are either folk high schools, Christian youth schools, or county schools, the first two being privately owned. Intended primarily for advanced pupils, they should in theory admit only pupils of 17 years of age or over. In practce, they overlap with the work of the continuation school, and projected reforms envisage clearing up the anomaly by taking over from the youth schools those subjects which are peculiarly the province of the under-seventeens, adding them to the curriculum of the continuation school and so raising its status. Youth schools are usually boarding schools, and are increasingly becoming "preparatory" schools for young people between the ages of 17 and 20 who wish to complete their secondary education (missed for one reason or another at 14 plus) in order to be able to study at teachers' colleges, agricultural schools, etc. Originally, of course, they were designed like the Danish folk high schools to make for a happy and contented democracy imbued with a love of the fatherland, and they still mainly pursue this original aim. Attendance is voluntary, the teaching is free, and needy pupils can obtain financial assistance from the state to cover part expenses for board and lodging.

The unitary school system of Sweden, as we have already seen in discussing primary education and the 1952 Swedish school law, aims at securing a common core of primary and secondary education for all children to 15 plus, when streaming begins. Thus the intermediate, or *realskole*, will diappear. All tuition in State primary and secondary schools is free. The curriculum is much the same as in Norwegian and Danish schools.

The attempt to make a unity of Danish schools and to coordinate the work of both the primary and secondary schools began in 1903, and the Education Act of 1937 made secondary education for all a reality. the peculiarity of the Danish system (as we have noted) is that a clear break is made at II plus. All children then pass to one of two types of intermediate school. The one is termed the "examination middle school" because at the end of the course there is an external examination to be passed. The other is called the "non-examination middle school," and the student's progress is measured by internal assessments. Both courses last four years. The decision as to which of these two schools a child shall attend is determined partly by the parents' wishes, partly by the general school report, and partly by a simple examination in the basic primary school subjects. Roughly 40 percent, of the pupils go to "examination" middle school.

Both middle schools offer a general education, but the non-examination school stresses the practical application of basic subjects. One foreign language (English or German) is normally included in the curriculum. Pupils from the non-examination school leave at 15 plus, and then proceed to vocational or technical schools, to youth schools, or (compulsorily) to evening schools whilst being in daytime employment. Pupils in the examination school sit the State leaving examination at 15 plus, and if successful may either stay on for another year to take the State *realeksamen* or pass to the *gymnasium* for a further three years and prepare for the *studenteraksamen* necessary for university entrance. The *gymnasium* offers three distinct lines of study: classical languages, modern languages, and mathematics and natural sciences. Tuition is free throughout the whole school system except for children of wealthy parents when tuition fees are charged proportionate to the parents's income. One final interesting feature to be noted is that since the passing of the 1937 Education Act, for reasons mainly of economy multilateral schools have come into existence comprising the primary school, the two middle schools, and the final year leading to the *realeksamen*.

In addition, it is to be noted that the Danes have paid particular attention to the organization of education in villages and remote districts where it is not feasible to run a multilateral school such as we have described. there is a special village school which has classes covering the whole range of compulsory education from 7 to 14. There is no leaving examination, and whilst most pupils will continue their education on a full-time or part-time basis at youth schools or vocational and technical schools, many regularly pass to the *gymnasium*. Further, if the parents demand it and if there are at least fifteen children between the ages of 14 to 18, then the local authority must establish afternoon or evening classes for pupils to prepare for the *realeksamen*, or combine suitably with other local authorities towards the same end.

Germany: Just as Germany (or more accurately Prussia)

was the first modern State to create a comprehensive national system of education and to recognize the importance of education amid the changing economic and social conditions heralded by the Industrial Revolution, so has Western Germany in this present post-war period been farsighted enough to introduce into the reformed school system sufficient elasticity to allow children who have been misdirected into the wrong school, or who develop late, to change in time. Similarly, the preparation of an intellectual elite to hold all the really responsible posts has in no way been neglected, though elasticity in seeding out the elite has been encouraged. This again, however, is no new departure, for as early as 1901 the classical *gymnasium* saw the birth of its rivals in the *realgymnasium* (which taught Latin but not Greek) and the *Oberrealschule* (which taught neither Latin nor Greek), both of which were empowered to prepare their pupils for the Abitur (school leaving examination) and so for entry to the Hochschulen (higher institutes of learning - including the universities). To-day the *Realgymnasium,* which emphasizes the teaching of Latin and one foreign language (usually English) together with more instruction in mathematics and the natural sciences than the classical *gymnasium*, is easily the most popular school. Next comes the *Oberrealschule* with two modern languages (English and French) and emphasis on the sciences and mathematics.

Only relatively few children, of course, pass from the *Grund-schule* to one or other of the *gymnasien* to follow an intensive academic course lasting eight or nine years where the *Grundschule* has been a four-year school, six or seven years where the *Grund-schule* has been of six years' duration as in Hamburg. Much thought has been given, and continues to be given, as to how best the *gymnasium* can fulfil its task of educating the future leading personalities of the intellectual life of the country and yet continue to act as the people's school that will meet the requirements of every type of talent and promote intelligence in every way. It is to-day felt that whilst the *gymnasium* must aim at a substantial widening of the intellectual horizons of its pupils, and at the creation of a mind capable of discriminating judgment, it must also give as full and complete an introduction as possible to the various categories of scientific and scholastic thought prevailing, and that in consequence the traditions of devotion to high academic endeavour must constantly be maintained. The entrance examination to the *gymnasium* is therefor a searching one, and a number of *Lander* have gone so far as to require intending pupils to spend a trial fortnight in the school under direct observation.

An attempt to be just to all children deserving some kind of academic education is being made by using the *Mittelschulen* increasingly to take those pupils who show promise and are yet not amongst the cream recruited to the *gymnasium. Mittelschulen* were first established in 1894, and the course they offered was of six years', duration, its avowed aim being that of giving "general education, the aims and objectives of which go beyond those of the elementary schools. A "To-day, they recruit their children in the main from amongst those who wish to be skilled craftmen minor civil servants, employees in trade, industry or commerce. One, and usually two foreign languages figure on the curriculum, and the schools are already performing (and could increasingly perform) the useful service of education along Western European democratic lines that amorphous "middle-man" upon whose actions, in any form of democracy, so much ultimately depends. According to the time spent in the *Grundschule* the course now lasts four to six years, and it is possible in a few *Lander* for the pupil who betrays outstanding promise as a late develper to transfer to the *gymnasium.* Generally speaking, however, the *Mittelshule* has a character of its own, and its curriculum is not designed to link up with the *gymnasium.* Pupils having satisfactorily completed the course gain their school leaving certificate and then either take up some business employment or follow some further period of full-time or part-time vocational or technical training.

A still further type of secondary education is offered in

the *Aufbauschule* which gives children from the country who have not had a secondary school within easy reach the opportunity to start out on a secondary school career after completion of six years of primary education. This, of course, is often a boarding school. It runs a seven-year course along the lines of the *Realgymnasium*, with English as the first foreign language, and Latin. In Bavaria, however, this type of school has become so popular and so much in demand that since 1950 *Aufbauschulen* have been instituted representing all types of *gymnasium*, and adding one additional type with the emphasis on art and music. It should be noted in passing that art and music are increasingly figuring on the curicula of *gymnasien* throughout the whole of Germany.

One factor determining also the kind of secondary education offered in Germany is that–unlike all the other countries we have so far discussed–Germany looks upon co-education as a practice of expediency rather than one based upon principle. Small rural schools of necessity instruct boys and girls together, and seondary schools for boys will admit girls if no girls' school of a similar type exists in the vicinity. On the whole, however, there is determined separation of the sexes. In point of fact, it was not until 1872 that Prussia made secondary education for girls a possibility, and it is from these early beginnings that the present *Frauenoberschule* originated. It is a three-year course based on a ten-years, school for girls (lyceum) and it combines education along academic, scientific and artistic lines with a study of the domestic sciences. The school leaving certificate, however, is not recognized for university entrance, though graduates from such a school may enter a teachers' training college. In consequence, the *Frauenoberschule* is steadily failing to attract girls, who obviously prefer in these days of equality of the sexes to attend in their own right their own *gymnasien*.

A relatively recent creation is the economics high school which runs a three-year course leading to university-level schools of business administration and also to studies in the economics department of universities. Pupils are admitted to this economics high school either on satisfactory completion of the middle school course, or from the *gymnasium* at the age of 16 plus.

No one can deny that the organization of education at the secondary level throughout Germany is thorough, enterprising and forward-looking. It is highly specialized and it seeks constantly to provide an appropriate elite at all levels of public endeavour : academic, commercial and technical. It still holds fast to a belief in dual streaming, though it strives conscientiously to give every child of promise a chance. To this end, most *Lander* have made all education free, and those *Lander* which make a charge at the secondary level do not allow the very nominal fees usually asked to deter the poorest child from attending school. Of course, the majority of children do not have the necesary intellectual capacity to profit from any of the kinds of secondary education we have been discussing. These children go on to the *Oberstufe* on completion of their primary school training. This is an advanced elementary school which takes the child at either 10 or 12 years of age and keeps him in full-time attendance for a further two or four years. A few *Lander* have added still an extra year, making this period of further elementary education last until 15 plus. There then follows compulsory full-or part-time attendance at vocational or technical schools until the age of 18. We shall discuss this in greater detail in our next chapter.

Holland: The Dutch have had to be equally enterprising and thorough as the Germans in arranging a secondary system of education that will enable them to compete at a high industrial and commercial level with other countries, and in practice the solution they have found to their own particular problems is not dissimilar from that of the Germans. Like the Germans, they have through their continued elementary and advanced elementary school courses perpetuated a kind of dual system of education, but they have also produced a secondary system that is bewilderingly diverse in the types of education it has to offer. Admission to these schools usually takes place after the pupil has passed an entrance examination set by the teachers in the appropriate schools, and on the production of a satisfactory report from the head teacher of the last school the child attended. The average age for admission is 13. Fees are payable, based on the parent's income, but no one of ability is denied secondary education through poverty.

By far the oldest (the *Gymnasium Erasmianum* of Rotterdam was probably founded in 1328) and most traditional type of secondary school is the *gymnasium*, which has a six-year course of studies based on the classics. Dutch, French, German and English are also compulsory (as in all secondary schools.) After the fourth year of study (this since 1976) a pupil may opt to go on the science side, but the study of Latin and Greek must still continue. On the satisfactory completion of this gruelling course of pupil is awarded his diploma (by his own teachers) which gives him right of entry to a university or some other place of higher education.

A much more flexible type of secondary school, and one which has been willing to show adaptability to changing circumstances and to experiment more freely, is the *Hogere Burgerschool*, first established as long ago as 1867 to cope with the then growing commercial and economic enterprise of the nineteenth century. The school course generally comprised five years of study, the main subjects being : mathematics, physics, chemistry, geology, botany, zoology, cosmography, geography, economics and statistics, history and commercial subjects (with the four modern languages already mentioned). There are two distinct types of school, the one having a scientific basis, the other a literary-economic basis. The programme of the former is taken up largely with the exact and natural sciences, that ot the latter has in view, above all, the preparation of its pupils for a commercial carrer, though naturally pupils are prepared for jobs in all walks of life as well as for university entrance.

The *lyzeum* is interesting in that it has no legal basis proper to itself, being a combination of the *gymnasium* and the

Hogere Burgerschool. The object in view when establishing this school was to defer the choice between the *gymnasium* and the *Hogere Burgerschool* for at last two years. Thus, for at least two years, the same curriculum (without Latin or Greek) is followed by all pupils. There then follows either a four-year specialized study of the classics, or of mathematices and science, or of social subjects. The *lyzeum* is proving increasingly popular in these post-war years and is cautiously experimenting to meet constantly changing and modern demands.

Other forms of purely secondary education deserving of note in the light of post-war economic developments are the *lyzeum* for girls only, comprising usually five years of study of the usual secondary school subjects with the emphasis on domestic and economic science; day commercial schools offering three to four years of study, and with the emphasis on political economy, commercial law, political institutions, the history of commodities, the organization and the technique of commerce–along with a study of the French, English, German and Dutch languages; evening commercial schools with three, four, or five-year courses, taking young people between the ages of 14 and 20 who have already had some experience in the commercial and business fields. All these schools award State-recognized diplomas to successful students, and these diplomas are a guarantee to employers of the ability and competence of the holder.

Switzerland: The Swiss are faced with similar problems to those of the Germans and the Dutch, and they also have felt the necessity for prolonging education beyond the *Grundschule* proper to at least nine full years of schooling for those children who are not to follow some course of secondary education, and to prepare them more adequately for entry to a society which is becoming increasingly speacialized. Thus, project methods, practical work and "learning by doing" are much to the fore in their contiuned elementary schools.

Pupils who show any ability to profit from some form of secondary education, however, are encouraged to attend a kind of intermediate school (variously called the *Realschule*, or the *Handelschule*, or the *Progymnasium*, or the district school) where the education is entirely free of cost. Like the German *Mittelschulen*, these schools aim at giving a sound general education, but they also do prepare pupils to enter the higher forms of the secondary grammer school. The courses are usually of two or three years' duration and stress the teaching of mathematics, science and modern language (for a German-speaking pupil, for example, French and English or Italian- are compulsory). Most pupils on completion of this school course, enter on some form of apprenticeship or continue their studies at commercial and technical institutions.

The secondary grammer school has a function similar to that of the German *Gymnasium,* but is rather confusingly referred to as the *Mittelschule.* All pupils are expected to be capable of taking the State school leaving examination which gives entry to the universities and higher institutes, and there is therefore a searching test for entry to such a school, intellectual ability and not the parent's social position being the sole criterion. This academic secondary education is not left entirely to the cantons, though they have so much freedom in running and organizing their schools as they will. Ultimately, however, because the State lays down exactly what shall be tested at the State-leaving examination, and what standards shall be attained, the schools must conform closely to a "type" curriculum.

The duration of the school course varies from *canton* to *canton*, and is usually from six to eight years. Fees are payable in this *Mittelschule*, but again they tend often to be nominal and no child of ability is denied an academic education through poverty. There are three distinct types of school, as in Germany, preparing for university entrance : the *gymnasium*, concentrating on Latin and Greek; the *realgymnasium* concentrating on Latin and two modern languages; the *Oberrealschule*, without Latin but concentrating on mathematics and the natural sciences.

Belgium: The Belgian system makes a real attempt to

cover every possibility and to see to it that none shall be deprived of that kind of secondary education they most justly merit. We have already dealt with the work done in the fourth cycle of primary studies and the reasons why a determined effort is now being made to make this fourth cycle redundant. We shall leave the manifold provisions made for technical education to the next chapter, and here concentrate on the two types of purely secondary education offered. As a child completes his primary school course the parents are invited to state what they now want for their child and they are guided as skilfully as possible to make the right choice in view of school performance and general school reports on the child's proved aptitude so far. The options in the field of pure secondary education are either the *ecole mayenne* (middle school), which is either mixed or run separately for boys or girls, and the *athenee* (for boys only) or the *lycee* (for girls only). Secondary schools run by religious orders are usually called *colleges*.

If, on the satisfactory completion of his primary school course, a child enters the *ecole moyenne*, he now follows a course of study over a period of three years which is so skilfully planned that it offers both a Greek and Latin, and a general section, exactly parallel with the work done the three lowest forms of the *athenee* or *lycee,* as well as what is termed a pre-professional section in which girls have domestic and homecraft courses (as well as the usual commercial and secretarial work), and boys do general crafts and agricultural and industrial training, with technical streams in wood and metal work. A further skilful arrangement of the time tables makes it possible within the *ecole moyenne* for a child to change at almost any time during his three years of study from one to the other of the three sections if it is found desirable for him to do so. Thus, the final and irrevocable choice of specialized study is postponed until the age of 15, when the work of the *ecole moyenne* ceases. It is also at the age of 15 that children are increasingly seeking and profiting by guidance given by one of the psycho-medical centres that are becoming an important distinctive feature (there are thirteen large centres operating at present) of the Belgian educational system.

A variety of possibilities are open to pupils who satisfactory complete their studies in the *ecole moyenne.* Some may enter an *ecole normale primarire* to train as primary school teachers. Others will transfer to a technical school, there joining up with those pupils who, instead of going to an *ecole moyenne,* either went direct to the technical school where the first three years of study of the cultural subjects are again parallel to the first three years in the *athenee* or *ecole moyenne,* or came to the technical school at 14 plus after two years in the *quatrieme degre.* Others will pass to the three upper and specialist forms of the *athenee* or *lycee.* It should be noted in this connexion that not a few *ecoles moyennes* have been empowered to offer a full six-year course to university entrance standard, and thus rank as *athenees* or *lycees* in all but name. These circumstances usually hold when no *athenee* or *lycee* is conveniently placed to cater for the pure academic streams from the *ecole moyenne.*

The three lowest forms of the *athenee (lycee)* have a programme parallel to that of the *ecole moyenne,* and, in the basic cultural subjects (i.e. not Latin and Greek), not dissimilar from that in the 12 to 15 year range of the technical school. Naturally– as in the French *lycee–* Latin and Greek are the core subjects (if not the only important ones) in an *athenee* which seeks to give a sound, modern academic discipline and expects from its pupils a constantly high standard of work and achievement. From the fourth year onwards specialization begins, and five possibilities are open to the pupil to meet as far as possible both desire and aptitude.

The traditional Greek-Latin section still draws to it some of the ablest pupils in the school, and normally only those who started their secondary school career in the lowest forms of the *athenee (lycee)* will opt for this. The remaining four sections are: Latin-mathematics, Latin-science, pure science and economic-commercial studies. All these later modifications came about in 1948. All pupils will have courses in at least one modern language (English of German) and all have now to learn the opposing mother–tongue–French or Dutch. On the completion of a full six-year course a pupil presents himself for a passing-out examination that is controlled by a special jury to ensure uniformly high standards throughout the country, and this leaving certificate confers on him the right, should he so wish, to enter a university or higher institute of learning.

Many *athenees, lycees* and *colleges* run a boarding side to the school and a number of parents form the habit of sending their children away to the *athenee* to board rather than have them attend as day pupils in the *athenee* in their home town. The boarding houses, of course, cater also for those children form country districts too remotely placed for them to attened easily as day pupils. There are fees payable for all forms of secondary education, but these are again low. The 12 to 15 age group pays an average of £4 per annum, the rest pay £ 6 per annum. Fees payable can be much higher in the Catholic colleges, but in neither case is a pupil of ability debarred from having a full secondary education through poverty. Boarders, of course, must pay an extra boarding fee.

France: The four most important influences in the development of education in France have been the Catholic Church, the Revolution, Napoleon, and the development of industry in a country that, like Germany, has been primarily (and mostly still remains) agrarian in outlook. The destruction of the Church control of education by the Revolution and the introduction of Napoleon's highly centralized system of educational administration of Napoleon's highly centralized system of educational administration that none the less eventually recognized the Church and Church's influence led to the nineteenth-century struggle between Church and State. The final outcome has been the recognition of a seprate Church system of education, parallel to the secular State system, and with State subsidies eventually granted to Church-maintained educational institutions. The Church runs its school as it will, but as it must prepare its pupils for the State *baccalaureat,* it has to conform very closely in respect of curricula. None the less, the strong Republican element in France is repeatedly alarmed at the high proportion of children seeking to be educated in Catholic schools, some 40 percent. Again, the pedominant influence in French secondary education being that of the Jesuits, the classical ideal in education has repeatedly shown remarkable resilience in resisting the encroachment of more modren subjects, and, whilst a variety of solutions have been, and are still being tried, the classical hold is still strong and Frenchmen as a nation remain peculiarly conservative whenever any proposed reform seems to attack the general principles of *une culture generale* and *preparation d'un elite.* In other words, the dual system of education as the best possible means of maintaining the acknowledged historical superiority of French culture over that of her neighbours maintains itself in spite of the many attempts made throughout the twentieth century to secure equality of educational opportunity for all.

It was in 1926 when Herriot arranged that certain higher elementary schools (*ecoles primaires superieures)* and technical schools should be attached to neighbouring *lycees* under the same teachers for common "core" subjects such as French, modern languages, history, geography and science. In 1927, as a further incentive, fees were abolished in the three lowest forms of the *lycees* where this arrangement held. And in 1930, fees were abolished in all secondary schools, starting with the *sixieme* (the lowest form in the school). In 1937 the minister Jean Zay started his famous series of orientation classes in an attempt to discover what kind of education best suited each individual pupil and then to secure for him that education. The experiment came to an untimely and inconclusive end with the outbreak of war.

During the dark days of occupation much thought was given to the whole question of reform on a basis of effectively killing the dual system, and after the liberation a commission was set up under the presidency of the distinguished physicist, Paul Langevin, radically to examine the structure of the whole educational system and to make proposals for reform. The Langevin Plan that resulted can briefly be summarized as follows: a common school for all, compulsory to the age of 18; primary school education to cease at the age of 11 plus; the years 11 to 15 to be devoted to obtaining a *culture generale,* the first two years of this four-year course being an observation period, the last two years being years in which the pupil should opt to try out those branches of instruction for which he seemed most fitted; the years 15 to 18 to be devoted to specialized instruction in those subjects finally chosen by the pupil; finally, those pupil wishing to pass on to some form of higher education would do so after a trial period to make certain that they were fitted for study at a really advanced level.

It was a bold and sweeping plan which (for reasons which will be obvious to the reader) no Frenchman in practice could fully accept though he could not seriously quarrel with the main principles that gave it its inspirational drive : equality of educational opportunity for all; extended development of technical and scientific studies; the idea of education as being for the whole man *(l'eleve est l'artisan de sa propre culture);* the increasing importance to be attached to the individual, with the idea of the superiority of the child to the adult as the fundamental point of departure, thus leading to a child-centred approach. The real trouble has been that the plan made for an over-exaggerated and impetuous application of these principles that look no consideration of the prevailing culture pattern, that tried to force the peace of change and was in consequence in danger of getting out of step with the national character and the national outlook.

None the less, "new" classes were started in October, 1945, in the *sixieme* of the *lycee,* on an experimental basis some 200 schools (this beyond all expectations at the time) volunteering for the experiment. The exuberance of the early pioneers caught on and led to the rapid expansion of *Sixiemes Nouvelles* and– in conformity with the suggestions of the Langevin Plan–to the extension of the scheme to the *cinquieme, quatrieme and troisieme,* the latter class being roughly the equivalent of the pre-certificate form in an English grammer school. But here a halt has been called. The middle–aged *professeur agrege* had always been opposed to the scheme, even if he half-heartedly attempted to conform, and his words of warning to the effect that intelligence and clear, precise, and logical reasoning, based on a sound humanistic culture, were the pride and strength–the very–essence-of the French nation as a nation bore fruit. It has now been decreed that all *classes nouvelles* shall be closed down with the exception of those running in four "pilot" *lycees* (Sevres, Montgeron, Toulouse, Marseilles) which are intended to act as a spearhead towards any further projected reforms.

The experiment, however, has been both popular and successful, and a total of about *800 classes nouvelles,* with about 200,000 pupils in them, have proved themselves over a number of years important focal points for experimentation and new developments. What is perhaps most important is that the insistence in these *classes nouvelles* on activity methods, on correlation of subjects, on child study, on a prominent place being given to handicrafts, music and games, has resulted generally in a considerable leaving of the over-intellectual and bookish approach that tradition has dictated shall be the lot of the pupil in the *lycee or college* from the moment he crossed its portals even at the tender age of 9 or 10. Greater freedom of choice in the subjects studied has also resulted and much greater emphasis has been placed on the child, as an individual, to discover a method of his own that does not conform to a framework arbitrarily laid down by the teacher.

It is now time to turn to the actual reforms that have been fully implemented and to see what, according to present practice, happens to the boy or girl who at 11 plus embarks on some form of secondary education. The method of pupil selection is one devised not unduly to influence parents. A parent desirous that his child shall follow some kind of post-primary education must make application before May 15th in the year in which he wishes to enter his child for the autumn term. The child must not be less than 11 and not more than 12 years of age in that given calendar year. The parent must state whether he wishes his child to enter a *lycee*, a *college moderne*, a *college technique* or a *cours complementaire*, and he will be invited to place all possibilities open to him in order of preference. The child will then be submitted to an entrance test comprising: (a) a dictation of about ten lines in length; (b) three questions designed to test understanding of the passage dictated, vocabulary range, word function; (c) the summarizing, in about ten lines, of a narrative of two printed pages in length that is read twice to the candidates; (d) one or two questions on this passage designed to test the child's judgment, imaginative powers, feeling for style; (e) two arithmetical problems, one designed to test facility in calculation and the other to test power of reasoning. Sections (a) and (b) together take forty minutes, excluding the time taken up by dictations; sections (c) and (d) together take forty minutes; section (e) similarly. In addition, careful attention is paid to the primary school reports and to the child's record of home circumstances, interests, actual achievements and potentialities. Wherever possible, a parent's wishes for his child are respected, though in practice, since the teaching staffs of the primary schools are coming into ever closer contact with parents, they are increasingly advising on and deciding the choice parents, they are increasingly advising on and deciding the choice made. In any case, whether the child goes to the *lycee*, the *college moderne*, or the *cours complementaires*, the first years of the curriculum are roughly parallel and transfer from one to the other is at all times possible. The deliberate aim in all three establishments is clearly defined by ministeril decree as that of providing in the four lowest classes *un premier cycle de formation generale et d' orientation.*

The *cours complementaires* are in a somewhat anomalous position in that they still remain under the direction and control of the primary school inspectorate, and in effect tend to fulfil their original task (when they were two-year schools annexed to the primary school proper) of providing some kind of post-primary education for those pupils not intellectually capable of attaining the academic level required in the *lyucee*. They now offer a four year course mainly to pupils intending to take up a commercial or technical career, but they follow closely a curriculum on the lines of that holding in the first four years of the *college moderne*. One young eleven-year –old in the *sixieme* of a *cours complementaire* in Paris writes: "We have a lot mathematics, French and English (five periods a week). In history we are studying ancient times. In science we study the animal world (the dog, horse, cow, pigeon, rabbit). We spend two hours each week in the workshops. In geography we learn about French and other explores. We have a lot of homework and each week we have to write an essay." It should be noted that *cours complementaires* in towns tend always to give thiis general course of instruction such as described by the French boy. In the country districts, however, there is an agricultural bias, and in some areas an industrial bias according to the kind of work a child is later expected to seek.

At 15 plus the pupil can present himself for a general first school certificate exanunation, and can then be transferred according to his performance to some suitable further education course. Often this will be to *the college moderne* where he can pursue his studies to a deep and advanced level culmination at the age of 18 plus in the acquisition of the *baccalaureat*. He may also enter an *ecole normale primaire* to train as a future primary school teacher. He may transfer to a *college technique*. Or, of course, he may leave school and enter on some suitable form of employment for which his leaving certificate indicates he is in some measure prepared. Latest figures available from the French Ministry of Education (1955) indicate that a general course is given in 87 percent of the *cours complementaires*, comercial courses mainly in 8 percent.,vocational (trade) courses in 4 percent, and agricultural and domestic science courses in I per cent.

The *college moderne* came into existence only in 1946, though the *ecoles primaires superieures* were closed down in 1941 to pave the way for such a change. It had become increasingly obvious in the early 1930's that the traditional course of study offered in the *lycee* or *college* classique was not providing a basic training sufficient to cope with industrial needs and with the new and rapid advances that were taking place in the field of scientific investigation and research. Secondary education had become an essentially bourgeois education that pinned its faith on the supreme value of the study of the classics and that made every effort to maintain classical scholarship as the essential qualification for administrative posts of all kinds. When the modern studies tried to gain a footing in secondary education, they were looked upon unfavourably by both teachers and parents as being suitable only for the less gifted and less ambitious students. A more practical schooling was necessary, and there must be a better adaptation of the school to the needs of the individual child and to the complex needs of a modern society. In consequence, it was the obvious step for the Algerian Commission of 1944 to take when it advocated the immediate post-war establishment of a new kind of secondary school that would still aim at producing an elite but which would make modern studies the core of its curriculum and realize their essential disciplinary and humanistic values. The Langevin Commission endorsed these proposals, post-war legislation did the rest, and so was the *college moderne* born.

The *college moderne* offers a seven-year course, the first four years being devoted to a basic culture generale, as in the cours complementaires and the *lycee*. There is no Latin-Greek section as in the lycee, however. Some few *colleges modernes* offer only a four-year course to the first school certificate examination, and pupils who wish to continue their studies further must then transfer to a *lycee* or to a neighbouring *college moderne*. Obviously, the *college moderne* would not wish to prepare its pupils for the oldtype *baccalaureat* sat by the *lycee.* So, among the post-war changes came new types of *baccalaureat.* The technical *baccalaureat* came into existence in 1946 to meet the demands of the technical schools. In 1951 four new sections of specialized work were approved to meet better the demands of the *college moderne*, to prepare the way for a commercial *baccalaureat* (created in 1953), and to widen still more the programme for the pupil in the classical stream of the *lycee.* Thus, in the two years of study leading to the first part of the *baccalaureat* the pupil in the *college moderne* has three possibilities open to him:

1. Two modern languages (7 hours), 4 hours mathematics, 4½ hours natural science;
2. Two modern languages of which one is optional

(3 hours and 2 hours), 4 hours mathematics, 4½ hours natural science, 3 hours biological sciences;

3. Two modern languages (6½ hours), 4 hours mathematics, 2¾ hours natural science, 2 hours special geography-cum-history.

Option (2) has been specially created for those pupils who come to the *college moderne* from the *cours complementaires*. In addition, everybody has 4 hours French, 2 hours history, 1½ hours geography, 2 hours physical education, I hour art. There are optional extra courses, of I hour's duration each, in music and manual work for everybody; I hour's optional work in each of shorthand and typewriting for those taking option (3) above. In the second year of study, those taking option (3), which is geared towards the commercial *bacalaureat*, will add 1½ hours economics and I hour commercial geography.

The second part of the *baccalaureat* requires a further year of study in what are called the *classes terminales*. All these sixth forms (for that is what they really are) teach philosophy but subdivide into *Philosophie*, *Sciences Experimentales* and *Mathematiques* sections. The time-table is devised as follows:

Subject	Philosophie Hrs.	Sci. Exp. Hrs.	Math Hrs.
Philosophy	9	5	3
Mod. Language	1½	1½	1.5
Mod.Language optional	1½	1½	1½
History	2	2	2
Geography	2	2	2
Mathematics	1½	4	9
Nat. Sci.	2	5	5½
Biol. Sci.	2	4	2
Phys. Edu.	2	2	2

A *lycee* pupil is generally fitted to present himself for any of three possibilities. The pupil in the *college moderne* will normally choose between the last two.

Thus, the *college moderne* is in many respects for France a unique institution that stands midway between the old classical disciplines and the newer technical and commercial schools. It meets the challenge of modern times and makes room for any pupil of proved ability, no matter what his origin and how late a developer he may be. It recruits primarily from among the lower middle and the working classes, but it also sets out resolutely to prove to the bourgeoisie that modern studies can provide just as rigorous and as useful a training, for a new kind of elite, as the classical studies of the *lycee*. It keeps a sympathetic eye on the technical college and the various purely commercial subsections of the technical college, and is geared to open its doors to all whom at any stage it can usefully serve. More particularly, it is proud to draw regularly on the *cours complementaires*.

Indeed, the desire to serve more faithfully the needs of many students from the *cours complementaires* has led to a projected reform whereby a newer kind of *baccalaureat* is envisaged, not leading to university studies or their equivalent, but rather designed to work as the former English Matriculation Certificate worked and show prospective employers that, whilst the student is not of university calibre, he has received a sound, general education practically suited to the immediate necessities and complexities of modern existence. Such a *baccalaureat* would be taken after one year's study only in the *classe de seconde* of a *college moderne*. "We cannot afford, says the official circular," to waste the hidden talents of those countless children who are the life-blood of France: the children of the artisan and the working classes. We must prepare our country for a future worthy of its past and in keeping with the demands of the age in which we live."

Having discussed the *college moderne* at such length, we can now dismiss work in the *lycee* or *college classique* relatively briefly. Entry is at II plus, and the course lasts seven years. The former proparatory schools attached to all lycees no longer exist except in so far as they give the standard primary school course. The first four years are a general course, but Latin and Greek is then started. On the other hand, the effect of introducing new kinds of *baccalaureat* has made for greater elasticity in programmes of study, and all lyceens can sit for *baccalaureats* offered in the *college modrne* as well as for five distinct categories of their own:

1. Latin, Greek, one modern language, science and mathematics;
2. Latin, Greek, one modern language, but extra science and maths.;
3. Latin, two modern languages, and maths and science as (1) above;
4. Latin, one modern language, a second (optional) modern language, and maths. and science as (2) above;
5. Latin, one modern language, maths and science as (2) above, and biological sciences.

Successful completion of both parts of the *baccalaureat* entitled the student in pre-war days to entry to the university. Following the recommendations of the Langevin Commission, this is no longer the case. A preparatory year is now required of each intending undergraduate for him to prove that he is fit to proftit and benefit from a university course. It is in effect another examination hurdle, but it also serves a useful present purpose of keeping down overcrowding of all university courses. It should also be remembered that most *lycees* and *colleges classiques* run additional advanced courses for pupils preparing for entry on a competitive basis to teacher training, for preparation for the higher grades of the civil service, and to army, industrial, engineering, and commercial schools of the top rank —the *Grandes Ecoles,* as they are called.

As in Belgium, most *lycees* and *colleges classiques* have

a strong boarding side, the Catholic *colleges* in particular favouring this.

It is finally interesting to note that latest official figures available show that throughout France there are 238 *lycees* and 659 *colleges*, of which 365 are *colleges modernes*. Thus, there are 532 State secondary schools following the old academic traditions as opposed to 365 schools given over to strictly modern studies. Catholic *colleges* are to the number of 1,700, but they vary considerably in importance and performance.

Italy: Here, on the completion of his primary school course at the age of II plus, a pupil may pass (according to ability, aptitude and desire) either to a vocational training school or to an intermediate comprehensive school, the latter being our immediate concern in this chapter. The course in this intermediate school lasts three years, at the end of which the pupil takes a school leaving examination. Success in this entitles him to enter one of the several types of schools of advanced academic education. The curriculum in the middle school comprises: Italian language and literature, history, geography, mathematics, natural sciences, drawing, singing, *lavoro*, Latin, and one foreign language. This *scuola media*, as it is called, came into existence only in 1940, and its present curriculum dates only form 1945. Its aim is obvious: that of providing a terminal education with an academic bias; that of giving teachers and pupils can opportunity to postpone the final decision of choice of vocation until 14 plus; that of providing ample time for guiding and counselling the pupil. It is to be noted that the curriculum in the vocational school is exactly like that in the *scuola media* except for Latin and one foreign language.

Pupils in possession of the school leaving certificate from the *scuola media* may pass either to the *liceo classico*, or the *liceo scientifico*, or to the *istituto magistrale* (*primary teachers*' training college), or to the *istituto tecnico*. Those pupils who enter the two licei are traditionally considered the intellectual elite and are normally expected to reach the university. The *liceo classico* divides itself into two cycles of study : the *ginnasio superiore* which offers a general introductory course lating two years and at the end of which course there is an examination bar, and then the main course proper lasting three years and which prepares the pupil or the classical maturity examination which, like the *baccalaureat,* is State imposed and controlled and also grants the right to attend all lectures in the various faculties of the university. The curriculum of the *liceo classico* comprises: Italian language and literature, Latin, Greek, history, geography, natural sciences, mathematics, one foreign language, philosophy, and the history of art.

The *liceo scientifico* was founded in 1923 "to develop and intensify the education of students who aspire to university studies in medicine and science, with particular emphasis on scientific culture." Originally a four-year course, it was extended to five years after the last war. In its curriculum the study of Greek is replaced by double the time spent on a foreign language, and the syllabuses for mathematics and the natural sciences are considerably widened. The maturity diploma awarded at the end of this course entitles the holder to attend classes in the university in all faculties *except* Letters and Law.

Secondary education is not free, but the State actively intervenes to assure that no deserving pupil is in need. Thus it regulates the fees that the private Catholic schools are allowed to charge and it compels each *commune* to set up its own patronage fund for the needy pupils of the *commune.* In addition, it controls forty schools of its own which provide an entirely free education for those pupils who gain scholarship places for each year's list of vacancies.

Conclusion: Perhaps the most striking common factor emerging from all these various systems of secondary education is that, no matter what the system and no matter how centralized or decentralized the machinery of control, there is a determined attempt made everywhere to educate all children on a common "core" curriculum up to about the age of 14, and so postpone as late as possible the final choice of vocation and further studies in view of that choice.

Thus the middle school assumes an increasing importance as being the obvious place in which that common "core" curriculum shall hold. In almost every country the middle school or its equivalent) shows flexibility and takes into consideration the needs of local economy. It offers, generally speaking, the same subjects that are found in the academic grammar school, but it mannages to cut away from a too academic approach at too early an age and gives a sound, broad, cultural and yet practical education. Many observers of continental practice have in my view been too prone to assume that the work done in these middle schools (and particularly in the *cours complementaires* in France) is roughly parallel to what is achieved in the secondary modern school in England. Nothing could be farther from the truth, at least as far as my experience goes in visiting schools not only in capital but also in small provincial towns. the middle school is not despised by parents abroad but admired. It is admired because leads somewhere and is given its own individual *cachet*. It strives to keep the child to at least 15 plus and all the time it stretches him intellectually to his fullest capacity. If there is any criticism to be made it is the one that it can drive the intellectually weak child too hard. Let us not, however, exaggerate this. There is a perpetual outcry against *surmenage scolaire* on the continent, but no one does much about this grievance (real or imagined) but talk.

Finally, we should note that in almost every country in Western Europe, except England, the parent is always carefully consulted as to the type of secondary education he would like for his child and his wishes are as scrupulously respected as possible. The parent's responsibility for his child's secondary education is not entirely abrogated, and this is constantly before him in countries where fees are payable.

7

School and Socialisation Process

Victor Hugo : He who opens a school, closes a prison.

The society establishes schools for the provision of education for its members. In ancient times when the society was simple and the knowledge had not advanced much, education was usually given by the family and religious institutions. As the society grew complex and its store of knowledge enhanced, the need of a formal agency like school was felt. With the development of writing and arithmetic in Egypt, China, India, Rome and Babylon, the schools were organised. But even when the schools were established in the ancient and also medieval times the agencies of education for an average citizen remained mostly informal. Education in the schools was given only to the children of those who had high prestige in the society or to only the issues of religious leaders. In the modern times, this situation has changed. The school education is now considered essential for the children of all the citizens of a nation whether they are rich or poor, high or low in status or in birth-order.

Now the school is considered as one of the most important agencies of education. The knowledge has grown tremendously and cultural needs have grown so much that it is almost impossible to provide proper education without the help of the school. Today the society has been rapidly industrialized, the sciences have grown tremendously and the data on history and social studies have grown rich. The result of all this is that the importance of school has increased manifold.

From the point of view of educational sociologists the school is an agency to conserve and transmit culture. When cultural heritage had grown so much that it was not possible to transmit it through primary agencies like family, the schools were established in China, Egypt, Babylon and in other ancient countries. Thus school can be described as an institution of the society with specific functions.

The School as an Social Institution

As is evident from above, the school is a social institution which fulfils the special needs of the society. Social institutions as summarized by Hertzler are "purposive, regulatory, and consequently primary cultural configurations, formed, unconsciously and/or deliberately, to satisfy individual wants and social needs bound up with the efficient operation of any plurality of persons." He further says that "they evidence themselves socially and in standardized and uniform practices and observances......" A school is described as a social institution because: (*i*) it is a cultural configuration, (*ii*) it is formed deliberately to satisfy individual wants and social needs, and (*iii*) it embodies norms and has its own standardized way of solving societal problems.

The school trains and socializes the individual and thus serves the societal needs. But it is to be remembered here that the societal needs differ in different societies. The societal needs in a society wedded to democracy are different than those to be found in a totalitarian or a communist society. Similarly the societal needs of a developing society will be different from an affluent and developed society. Hence the type of educational institutions in different types of society will be different; also the socialization task faced by the school will vary with the needs and demands of the different societies. The Indian society has different demands than those of the western society and, therefore, its schools will have to be organized differently. For example Indian society is backward and tradition bound; its needs are mordenisation and enlightenment. Its schools will have to be organized in such a manner that these needs are met. It is unfortunate that in India the schools are as yet oblivious of social needs.

Though the tasks of socialisation in different cultures may be different yet there is no denial of this fact that schools'' major function is socialisation. Let us now examine the functions of a school.

Functions of the School

Since the school is a social agency it has many responsibilities. It helps in social progress. It inculcates the ideals of equality, liberty, fraternity and justice. It is the duty of the school to contribute as much as possible to the raising of the society to a higher standard. This responsibility is much bigger in a democratic country. In a democracy the schools are expected to provide new definitions and new meaning to the social ideals. Democracy is a dynamic concept. Therefore, in a democratic society, new viewpoints are necessarily sought to be developed. The school can greatly help in this process.

The school is not only concerned with the social progress but also with the individual development. One of its important duties is to prepare the individuals to lead a happy and rich life. It recognises the capacity of each child and tries to develop it fully. It seeks to increase the work efficiency of the individuals. In short it socialises the child.

Here we will now try to explain more clearly as to what we mean by socialisation process and how a school performs this function.

Socialisation Process

Guskin and Guskin define socialisation as "the process

by which an individual learns the behaviours, the values, and the expectations of others that enable him to take on particular roles in society." They thus define socialisation in terms of learning of the behaviours, values and expectations. These are learned so that one can play his particular role in the society. An individual does not come to this world with his role clearly defined. He learns his role by living in the society. For example the role of the mother or father or son is learnt by living in the society. The individual learns what is expected of him as father or son. He grasps the values involved in the role prescribed to him and takes up that role. The process by which the individual comes to learn his prescribed role and is prepared to take that role is known as socialisation.

In simple words we can say that "socialisation refers to the process by which persons acquire the knowledge, skills and dispositions that make them able member of their society." A person becomes the able member of his society when he is able to take on particular role in the society. Each individual has to meet the requirements laid down by other members of society for his behaviour in a variety of situations. These requirements may be arising out of his being a husband, a son, an employee, etc., which means that requirements are attached to some recognised positions or statuses in the society. The husband or son or employee has a position or status distinct from the other. Being in this position it is expected of him that he will behave in a particular manner. The son will be obedient or the husband will protect his wife. The behaviour which is required of a person in a given position can be defined as *prescribed role* and whatever are the requirements they themselves may be called as *role prescriptions*. Socialisation is thus a process through which the individual learns role prescriptions and role behaviour. Also though this process he understands the recognized statuses in the traditional positions in his society. He learns about the positions or statuses of father, son, employee and others in the society and is able to locate other individuals in the social structure as well as is able to identify himself. Thus we may say that socialisation performs the function of transforming human raw material of society into good working members." Through this process an individual is led to understand the society's status, structure and the role prescriptions and behaviour associated with different positions in this structure.

School and Socialisation Process

Durkheim has said, "Education consists of a methodical socialization of the young generation." Durkheim uses the words methodical socialization which seem to indicate that he is making a distinction between the socialisation that takes place in and out of school. Socialisation outside the school tends to be unmethodical because of the informal and spontaneous manner in which it takes place. For example, in a family the child learns about the statuses and positions in an incidental manner. On the other hand it is school where in a methodical manner the efforts are made for socialisation. School learning is planned, organized and scheduled. It is methodical socialisation with which we have a concern in this chapter. However, we cannot completly isolate the methodical from unmethodical. Whatever is exprienced out of the school has a profound influence on school learning.A student's out of school socialization conditions his in-school learning. A child who has learned about roles, statuses and positions in the family feels difficulty when school puts something else in the form of role prescriptions.

According to Brembech there are three pre-conditions for socialisation: (1) certain biological endowments, (2) an ongoing society, and (3) an oppurtunity for the person to interact with the society.

The native endowment is the most fundamental equipment of an individual. Every child comes to this world with certain hereditary traits. These traits are modified due to the influence of the society. Each individual is influenced by the society in which he develops. Thus an ongoing society is the second pre-condition. For socialisation not only the presence of the native endowments and the society are required but also there must be oppourtunities for the individual to come in contact with the other members of the society and to be influenced by them. This influence then is the stage where socialisation process becomes active. An example may clarify these three pre-conditions. A child is weeping. The mother rushes to him. The child continues to weep. The mother becomes anxious, calls the doctor, provides the child with medicine, soothes him and puts him to sleep. In this process the child has felt pain due to native endowment of sensation. He has a mother in his social sphere who runs and provides him with comfort. This feeling of mother playing the role of protector, the doctor, a person who gives cure develops in the child an understanding of their roles and thus his socialisation takes place. Here is may be seen, all the three pre-conditions have existed. If there is no mother or no interaction, the socialisation will not take place. This is however, an example of unmethodical socialisation. In schools situations are created systematically for interactions within a group and between the groups and hence socialisation is achieved in a systematic manner.

In the schools the teacher can be an important socializing agent. The teacher can put the socializing influence on his pupils. This he can do by (a) motivating the students to engage in intellectual activities, (b) providing a student with feed back about his behaviour and offering him suggestions about desirable ways of behaving, (c) presenting his own example to the student to follow so far as role prescriptions and role taking are concerned, (d) forming close interpersonal relationship with student and encouraging him to re-examine his attitudes or support his present attitudes or support his present attitude and (e) giving him knowledge of various positions or statuses in the society and preparing him for role-behaviour.

The teacher can help in socialisation if there is positive and meanigful contact between the faculty members and their students. A stumbling block in the teacher's efforts for socialisation may be the lack of congruence between the intellectual and academic demands of the faculty and the pressures of the student's peer group. In the present situation this lack of congruence is very much evident. The students today go on strikes, cheat in examinations and are as a whole, not very respectful to the knowledge which is being imparted by the teachers. We will deal with this problem of lack of congruence in another chapter in this section.

School and Social Change

School as we have said earlier is not only an agency for socialisation but it also concerned with conservation of culture and social progress. Let us discuss these :

1. Conservative Function of the School: Most of the social philosophers are of the opinion that the main function of the school is to promote the conservation of the present culture.

2. Progressive Function of the School: When the school does not accept the old ideals but gives education so that the progressive elements in the society might become acceptable the function of the school becomes constructive rather than conservative. In doing so the school acts in accordance with a different principle of social organization. That principle relates to the school taking steps towards social progress and owning responsbility for bringing progressive reforms in the society. The proponents of this principle express their opinions in two ways. They are that : (a) the school should criticize freely the present condition of the society but the social developments through the school should take place indirectly. It means that the school should not directly try to bring about social progress but encourage it through the critical education provided in it, and (b)the school should plan a framework of progressive society and with all the power at its command make effort to construct it.

Those thinkers who have this opinion that the school should be in the forefront of social progress are the strong supporters of progressive education. But it is very difficult for the school to bring about social progress because of the following reasons: (*i*) For bringing about the social progress the school and the society are required to formulate a definite plan. The progressive education fails in putting up such a plan. (*ii*) The teachers are expected to be the forerunners of social progress. But in that case they lose the security which they get as tradionalists and are very badly criticised. (*iii*) The school by itself cannot achieve any success in this tremendous task of social progress. It has seek to aid of other agencies like family, church, etc. (*iv*) Every teacher cannot be adequately trained that he may develop the capability of becoming the leader of the society. (*v*) If the society rejects the progressive programmes organized by the school then there will arise serious problems of adjustment to a large section of student population. The students will be prepared for a progressive society but they will be forced to live in a society which will have an orthodox outlook. The result will be that they will find themselves as misfits in the society. (*vi*) In a democratic society it is the right of adult members that they determine the type of social order which should be encouraged in the school but the school functioning just in reverse manner stabs the society in the back. (*vii*) The mainspring of social changes is not the school but the other strong forces like economic condition, political agitation and religious view-point.

The above criticisms of the role of the school in bringing reforms in the society are not entirely against the progressive function of the school. In spite of these criticisms it is accepted that the function of the school is to bring a fulfilment in the social organization and to work for the acceptance of social change. These criticisms only point out that the school is a follower of social change and not its initiator.

Some educationists believe in the principle that the school should not take sides in any controversial social problem. It should keep itself aloof from social conflicts. But this is not possible because the school is a social agency and when there are going on changes in the society it cannot keep itself aloof from them.

Therefore, we can say that there is an intimate relationship between the school and the society. The school is responsible for the progress in the society and the society for the development of the school. We have discussed above the difficulties which are faced when the social progress is sought through the school. But it is also true that without the co-operation of the school it is not possible that there can be brought about wholesome progress in the society. Thus the school organization is considered most superior which makes it the centre of social life.

The Indian Schools and their Defects

In general, the pattern of the Indian schools had been determined by the English rulers. It had been based on the culture of the West. But because of their organizational set up of the schools instead of merits of Western education the defects of Western education had more dominated. Organized as such they had naturally failed to discharge their functions adequately.

An ordinary Indian school has failed to develop good habits among the students. It has failed to bring out the good latent in their nature. It has failed to direct their creative urges in the constructive channels. In Indian schools the knowledge of text books has only been given importance. Efforts has been directed chiefly towards this end that the minds of individuals are stuffed with knowledge. Importance is excessively given to memory. The schools glorify the achievement of a degree or diploma and preach that there is no other end of education except to pass the examination. The feelings of liberty, happiness, love towards work are emphasized as subsidiary goals. This situation is entirely different from that situation which is found in some advanced countries. There the schools work ceaselessly towards the good of the society as well as the individual.

Unless we think seriously about the defects in our educational system and pay attention towards the proper organization of the schools it is not possible to purge out the evils from our society. As we have said above education is responsible for bringing about both the individual and social progress. Our schools have failed to achieve any of these.

The organization of our schools is so defective that it has become very difficult that proper individual or social development can take place. The obstacles in the path of individual development may be summarized as follows:

1. Unchangeable form of Methods of Teaching: In our schools the same methods of teaching are followed with each and every type of individual. No change in the methods or way of handling is permitted either with is gifted, problem or backward child. The uniformity in the pattern of handling children of various capacities and capabilities has bought about a sort of rigidity in the educational effort in Indian schools. This course has resulted in the failure if individual development.

2. Stability of curriculum: In our schools the curriculum is usually quite rigid. It is set by the education departments of the State Governments or by the examining bodies. The schools are required to follow it without any sort of flexibility with the result that the teachers are left with no freedom to bring about any amendments in it. The curriculum usually is framed without paying any attention to the differences in the intellectual capabilities of different children.

(3) No consideration to individual differences: Psychology has shown that every individual is different from the other. Every child has is own interests, attitudes, aptitudes, motivations, etc. Therefore, his education should be in accordance with these. But in our schools no attention is paid to the individual differences. All the children are treated alike so far as the teaching methods and the curriculum are concerned. Thus education completly fails to develop the individuality. It, on the other hand, promotes repressions and encourages maladjustments.

(4) Booking knowledge and no playway: Our schools give more importance to uninteresting bookish knowledge. They do not give any importance to the education through playway. In them education starts with the reading of the books and ends with it.

(5) Absence of constructive activities: Our schools also fail to promote the constructive and creative activities of the students. In them very few such activities find place which give proper oppourtinities for creative work. This very often results in constructive and creative tendencies of the children dying without getting any chances of expression.

(6) Disregard of curiosity tendency: In our schools the curiosity tendency is disregarded. No answer is given to the children's questions. If a child asks questions again and again he is rebuked. Thus his curiosity for knowledge is repressed violently.

Our schools also fail to discharge their responsibilities towards social progress. There are two main reasons for it.

1. Our school are not society-centred. In fact there is found an absence of all types of social and corporate life in them. More or less they have artificially. Those schools which have accepted the formal ways of social life in the form of student's unions and student's societies, are none the better. At many places these societies instead of contributing to the progress in social life have resulted in its degeneration and have created some very though problems for the teachers. The mass indisciplines organized by the union societies of a good number of institutions are posing serious threats to the stability of the institutions themselves and to the larger socities outside the institutions.

2. Our institutions have not undertaken any solid steps towards social progress. In the field of education, everything is topsyturvy. The majority of the schools are ignorant about their important functions. They have no idea that they can be the initiators of social progress.

Thus we see that out institutions are full of defects and they are not discharging their functions properly.

Suggestions for Reorganization of the Indian Schools

To remove the above evils it is necessary that in India

new schools on novel patterns are established and the old ones are re-modelled. In the past few years, many experiments have been conducted which are helpful in the establishment of good schools. But a majority of the schools are very successful in defying all the attempts for their re-organisation.

There is a need that the new schools are orgainized in such a way that they may ensure both individual and social progress. Keeping the individual outlook in the forefront, Nunn says, "The school must be thought of primarily not as a place of learning where certain knowledge is learnt but a place where certain forms of activities-namely, those that are of the greatest and most permanent significance in the wider world are performed."

For Dewey school is a "special environment where a certain quality of life and certain types of activities and occupations are provided with the object of securing child's development along desirable lines." He points out three main characteristics as regards the environment in the school. They are:

1. It presents a simple environment.
2. The school environment removes all that is bad in social life and images only that which is valuable and educable so that the children can be made acquainted with a good and pure society.
3. The school brings a harmony between the various co-ordinative elements and factors in the social atmosphere.

It creates co-operation between different types of people and establishes a co-ordination between the interests of youths and children which often pull in different directions.

On the basis of out discussion above we can point out certain desirable characteristics of a progressive school in India as follows :

1. It organizes different types of activities for its

children and gives more importance to happiness and fullness in life than the mere acquiring of knowledge as a personal refinement.

2. It meets the specific needs of the society through re-orienting its educational programmes.
3. It prepares the students for social change by introducing in the school an environment of free discussion and uninhabited expression.
4. It seeks to establish ideal social life in the school.
5. It acquaints the child directly with the truths of life and also acquaints him with the most precious characteristics of life which are presented in such a simple manner that every child can take an interest in them.
6. By organizing and evaluating properly its activities it creates an uniformity in children's point of view and establishes a co-ordination in their personality.
7. It utilizes the native and acquired tendencies of the child for his education. It believes in giving liberal as well as utilitarian education.
8. Education is centred around such vocational activities which are in keeping with the interests of the children.
9. The most novel characteristic of these schools is that in them the greatest importance is given to the free development of the child. For the child such activities are planned which put no impediments in securing his complete individual development.

In the end, we can say that our schools can perform the functions required of them in a democracy, only when the defects in their organization are removed and they are able to incorporate the characteristics mentioned as above.

8

Teaching

It may be helpful to begin our examination of 'teaching by looking at the implications of the grammar of ordinary talk about teaching.

(i) In grammar, 'teaching' is an active verb and a transitive one, suggesting that teaching is an active process, which it is, and that something is being taught. Sir John Adams, as is well known, extended and illuminated this by pointing out that the verb 'to teach' had a double accusative. In his example, you not only teach Latin, you teach John: you teach John Latin.

This is all right as far as it goes. But ordinary grammatical use can, we know, conceal philosophical conceptions or misconceptions; ordinary speech expresses ordinary common -sense ideas which may require investigation: so it is here. Ordinary language about teaching says one thing simply, and for practical purposes; a teacher does teach subjects, and he children. But if we are too much dominated by ordinary grammatical use, a wrong idea may become fixed which is difficult to unfix. The picture here is of the teacher doing something active to children, or even at them, talking actively and pointing at them. He is not only doing this, but in his teaching of a subject is presenting them — on a plate as it were, in a parcel of samples, on a blackboard, in books, with a 'subject', knowledge, 'fact'....If one were to draw a picture of this simple -minded grammatical idea of teaching, it might show the pupil sitting receptively at his desk, and the teacher standing on a platform (a raised platform, for he is the important person), one hand pointing, in the other a plate extended to the pupil.

(ii) Against this view there has been, as everyone knows, a strong reaction. It may be helpful to think, to begin with, of the development of the idea of teaching in a rough dialectical way–thesis, antithesis, synthesis (which becomes a thesis with a further antithesis, and so on). This formal technique is crude and over- simple, but it may serve to elicit at the outset contrasting views clearly and to show how, dialectically, they build up into a complex picture—soon too complex by far to be expressed in dry logical terms. Let us therefore use the form for what it is worth, dropping it quietly overboard when it becomes too awkward. This will happen very soon—and the reasons for this will be quite illuminating.

The first thesis then (crudely) is: Teacher does, and gives, All to the pupil, who ony receives. The formal antithesis is a very extreme imaginary caricature of 'activity' theory. In which the children's activity is all and the teacher's nothing. In the first picture the child looks, attentive and receptive. But of course his mind may be wandering, or he may be simply copying the words of the teacher or of a book. The teacher may be 'teaching' in the grammatical sense and yet be doing very little teaching in a more important sense, for a child may not be learning, or if he is, may be learning only pre-digested material which may fail to develop his growing organism. As against this, it is said that education and learning can only take place through the pupil's self- activity. St. Thomas Aquinas (who is not an extremist says that it is the pupil's own intellectual self-activity which is the 'efficient cause' of the pupil's learning, of his being educated. St. Thomas (I repeat) was not an extremist; but there have occasionally been extremists–few and far between, and usually only at moments—who have in effect preached the abdication of the teacher. It is only through his own activity that a child learns, so, they say, leave him alone and let him learn in his own way. This extreme view—the antithesis—might be pictured as ***Learning Springings Spontaneously***, as the jack— in— the– box seems to be the sole initiator of his own springing up.

(iii) But no one has affirmed this for long, or consistently. There is, I think, little trace of it in John Dewey, though some of his extremist disciples have gone in that direction. Every sober educationist had taken the part of the teacher seriously. (In dialectical terms, they have wanted a synthesis of functions of teacher and children.) Admitting that the pupil's self -activity is that without which no learning can take place, the teacher is always admitted as having much to do with the induction of the activity and generally with its direction. Although for St. Thomas it is the pupil's own intellectual self—activity which is the efficient cause of his learning, the teacher has a function, which is that of an 'extrinsic proximate agent. The active intellect of the child is helped by the external ministrations of the teacher rather as the return to health is helped by the doctor and in a different way by drugs. The child possesses the 'potency'; the teacher is one factor in the change from 'potency' to 'fulfilments'. In a more up-to-date analogy, the teacher is sometimes called a 'catalyst'.

But these views, although they correct the one-sidedness of their extreme opposites, do not provide an adequate image of teaching. The term 'extrinsic proximate agenty', which is based on Aristotle, needs to be interpreted in the light of the Aristotelian assumption that (in the words of the late A. E. Taylor) 'the efficient cause and that on which it exercises its efficiency are *en rapport*'. The idea of *rapport* introduces a new idea. Learning does not take place just through the' external ministrations of the teacher'. There has to be rapport too. Indeed, learning takes place through complicated interactions in relation to a teacher, to a subject matter and to oneself, the learner.

The teacher may be an 'extrinsic proximate agent', but he does not merely set going processes which unfold from within. This terminology does no justice to the internal relations between teacher and pupil or to the complexity of the teacher's function. The term 'catalyst' is likewise inadequate for something like the same reasons. One small part of the teacher's function may be 'catalytic' but in itself the analogy is inadequate and misleading. (Formally, this synthesis, Teacher-Pupil in External *Relation*, is again a one-sided thesis needing to be complemented by an antithesis which affirms a unique sort of internality of relationship of teacher and pupil. Here formal dialectic becomes too, too artificial, and is now dropped overboard. The dialectic, which works up to a point with things or logical ideas, breaks down in the human situation, where the relations are personal and interpersonal rather than material or logical. 'Dialectics' to give place to Dialogue, and much more.)

Material and Selection of Material

The account so far has mainly discussed the teacher's function with little reference to the part played by the subject matter or material (though in the first imaginary picture there is a filled plate). The presence of material in itself is a stimulus to learning. In the case of young children it may be enough to give them sand, water, tins etc, and leave them to it. Earlier still, the baby is continuously learning in his waking hours by his own unaided experimentation with himself and the world around him. In other words, play with materials is the earliest kind of education; and it is an education which can go on for a considerable time without any teacher. (Here the half-drowned Dialectic bobs up gasping, '*Materials Without Teacher*'.)

(i) But this is only true of the early stages. After the early beginings the teacher is urgently needed to select appropriate 'materials' as well as to Present them in a suitabe way. She selects stories for reading, she perhaps tells them. She selects the problems to be solved, prepares lessons in history, biology, poetry.... . The teacher does not simply leave the children with unarranged materials, saying, 'Do what you like with that'. She (or he) shows them selected material in a certain way for their attention and for learning in certain directions. (with the last drowning gasp the cry comes, '*Teacher Selects Material*'.)

(ii) Why does the teacher select and arrange as he does? The answer to this to be adequate would have to be long. Briefly, he selects in the light of slowly acquired knowledge of his subject matter. He selects it, too, in the light of his knowledge of the children he is teaching, some of it scientific knowledge, some of it personal. From his knowledge of the psychology of development, he is helped to choose what is appropriate to his particular age-group. From his knowledge of social conditions and the children's background he is able to adapt to their interests and abilities. But behind all this (and much more) he chooses, in so far as he is a free agent, because he is making 'philosophical' assumptions of different kinds. As we have amply seen, his sense of values determines at every point what he teaches and the emphasis he lays on this or that. His decisions express them.

The teacher's assumption about the nature of knowledge and learning are involved too. The old-fashioned teacher may still unwittingly assume a *tabula rasa* view of the mind as a tablet to be written upon, or alternatively as a kind of mirror. The disciple of Dewey will regard ideas as essentially activities, and learning as taking place through active participation, experimental enterprise. The teacher's metaphysical assumptions, we have seen, also affect what he does and the way he does it. Is he acting under the authority of

God, or only under human authority? Is he preparing his children finally for the life of society in this world, or for this world, and a world to come? What are his assumptions about the person? Is the pupil something to be conditioned by the teacher? What does he assume about the relation of symbols to experience? In teaching biology, for instance, does he use symbols in place of, or before experience, insisting on the learning of names of plants or animals or their parts before seeing and handling actual specimens in their colour and three-dimensional vividness, and with all their aesthetic impact? Does the name and the concept, instead of arising out of a total experience and abstracted from it, become a dry substitute merely to be one more item stored in an over burdened memory, reproduced correctly in the examination?

Involvement of Teacher and Pupil in Teaching and Learning

(i) But the teacher does not only teach selected material in a particular way. The 'material' he offers is not really separable from him. It is not just objective 'stuff' it is material mixed with the teacher's mind and not with his intellect only, but with his will and character. Geography, History, English, Mathematices Physics ... they are, no doubt, subject, carefully planned and chosen, selectively presented. This is an intellectual conception. But there is so much more, than that; what is offered by the about the 'discipline of the subject's. This is, in part at leat, what happens to character through a tussle with the subject; the intellect submits itself to the subject's demands, and the person through this dialogue grows in integrity. When a teacher teaches his subject in a living way, these effects upon him can be seen and felt by the pupils, who themselves come to participate in it through contact with him. His love for the subject, his excitement in it, is directly conveyed, and this is not a mere emotional infection but an intellectual passion which is the pupils' very active education. In the earlier stages of education, his pupils are very dependent on the personality of the teacher; 'Tommy likes nature study because he likes Mr Smith who teach him'. Later on it is still through the teacher's personality that Tommy is learning the subject–discipline: but he is coming to be skilfully weaned from the teacher to the strong meat of the subject; he has now learned to take the responsibility of its discipline upon himself. He now knows how to use libraries and how to read books or organize his own expeditions.

What we have been saying has emphasized the teacher's influence, even to the point of weaning from that influence. But the natures of the children taught, and the teacher's knowledge of thi, is a potent factor in the growth of their learning. 'Knowledge' of his children is several kinds. He must know something about children in general and about children of that age and intelligence range in particular. He must in other words, have some objective psychological knowledge. He must also have some objective knowledge of them as individuals something a little like what would be called in medicine their 'case histories'. He comes to know their background difficulties, their temperamental 'blocks' and facilities, their dominant interests. All of this knowledge has to be acquired, and it can in a sense, be pigeon -holed. But the effective use of such knowledge would not be adequately described as taking the ideas 'out of the pigeon-holes'. Acquired objective knowledge had not only to be 'pigeon-holed' but assimilated, and the assimilated knowledge can be used relevantly only in the vital act of the teacher. His knowledge will help him to help them in the way they need, to teach them better. It will help him too to temper his ow enthusiasm to their needs. Without this, he can easily become a bore.

But even more is required than this skilled one-way knowledge and intuitive perception. So far, we have been speaking of the children as objects of his knowledge, and of his teaching. This is almost true of the more formal types of teaching. But where there is freedom and activity (using the word activity' in a wide sens). The children's freedom and initiative is continually changing the teaching situation, so that the teacher, although he has a general plan of campaign, must adapt himself continually to a dialogue, actual or implicit. And this is not an continually adaptation only, but a total one; and the relationship to the pupils is when everything is going well, one between person and person. The whole now fairly familiar philosophy of the I -Thou can be applied here. In an atmosphere of freedom the child and the teacher are open to each other. The teacher had authority and greater experienc. He has much to give. But he has much to receive too. Where the relationships are what they should be, he is learning and experiencing on a fresh way through his encounter with the free inquiring minds of his pupils. It is not too much to say that not only is he education his pupils, but 'becoming educated' is taking place here and now in the persons of the children and teacher alike in the small free community of the happy classroom. The children are learning something for the first time, and the teacher is rediscovering, and discovering new significance through the eyes of his pupils. This is one of the delights of 'teaching', through sympathetic understanding dialogue to enjoy the discovery of other younger minds and to recover, perhaps, the springtime of learning.

Because of the subtlety and complexity of this relationship, a teacher never knows the results of his work–for good or ill. The odd word or look or gesture, in or out of the classroom (not only within the four walls of the school), may spark off something significant which remains all the pupil's life. Conversely, what the teacher thought he was doing, and thought good, may have had little influence upon the children's characters, development and real education.

Authority : The Qualities of the Good Teacher

All these things require many qualities, of intellect, sensibility, character and will in the teacher. When things go will, their success is in part the fruit of these qualities—though in success the qualities are simply taken for granted and hardly noticed. But things do not, of course, always go well, and then the need for the qualities becomes more apparent. The tidy-minded teacher who likes a clear plan and likes things to go according to plan, might be a good enough lecturer, but may be an indifferently successful teacher. (I say 'good enough' lecturer, for the good lecturer ought to be aware imaginatively of the general temper of his hearers.) He is very easily tempted to resist and perhaps to resent the untidiness of interruption, the raising of irrelevancies—or what, in the neat plan, seem to him to be irrelevancies–the loose ends which may seem to lead away from the central point. Things become more difficult still for him if question asked, on new lines of investigation suggested, seem to show up his own inadequacies of preparation or understanding. The young teacher especially is apt at such a point to exercise his authority, not liking to acknowledge his own puzzlement or confusion. The experienced good teacher, on the other hand, one who is both master of his subject and at the same time continually learning more of it, may use such occasions as growing points for new discovery and fresh illumination. But this needs confidence; and it is confidence which in part springs from humility, humility in face of the subject and in face of the pupils, the sort of humility which in fact earns the pupil's respect rather than their contempt. In this way, it is character, shown by the way of the teacher's whole approach and attitude, which 'teachers' more effectively than anything else. It is intellectual and moral education at the same time.

The qualities of character needed by the teacher are, of course, seen in a more obvious way when the situation is in a plain sense a 'moral' one. Rebellion, indiscipline, open or covert, is a challenge to the teacher's status. It is very tempting for him to regard it as a personal challenge and to act in an authoritarian way, teacher *versus* pupil. (Sometimes this reaction is necessary.) But, as the good teacher of a 'subject' submits himself to the 'authority' of the subject, and to the 'cause' of teaching, so the teacher in his moral capacity regards himself and his pupils as under the 'authority' of moral principles. It is the teacher's duty as a more experienced and mature person, to lead his pupils to moral as to intellectual responsibility, and he is much, he more likely to be successful if, in his dealings with younger people, he does not yield to the temptation of playing the role of an absolut. If, by understanding the problem of the rebellious at the point where it hurts most (and perhaps hurts both the pupil and his teacher), he can help his pupil to understand himself and to seek after his own solution, the 'cure is likely to be most effective. Learning here, as in intellectual learning, is best when it can be a co-operation between persons. Of course it is often far more difficult than this, But always, it requires as much sympathy, objectivity, humility, firmness, as one can muster.

If the above, very sketchy, account of teaching and the demands upon the teacher is sound as far as it goes, it sets a programme for the professional education and training of teachers.

What, in review, are its main *desiderata*? Any stress on this or that aspect will of course depend upon the kind range of teaching which we have in view. For the *infant* teacher, sympathy with and understanding of children their growth and their needs, are of paramount importance. In the junior school understanding of the basic skills and of the best ways of teaching them, of field's of knowledge gradually emerging out of concrete experience will be essential. The secondary modern school teacher will be concerned with the development of the same thing, but with an eye in the life interests of the pupils as they approach the time when they will leave school take up jobs, organize their own leisure, marry, become citizens. The grammar school teacher is expected to have a greater 'subject', expertise, but in the walled protection of the 'subject', he has somehow to cope with the danger of fragmentation which can arise out of high specialization, and to see his teaching as relevant to the lives of his pupils. The *technical school* teacher has his expertise; but it is particularly important for him to understand the meaning of 'liberal' education; he too is faced with the problem of fragmentation though in a different form. These are some obvious emphases. It should be hardly necessary to say that they are only emphases, are not exclusive of one another, and that many other qualities and attitudes are needed. The grammar school teacher, for example, ought not to assume that life begins at eleven plus or that its function can ever be a solely 'academic' one; the teacher of young children, in her essential concern for the understanding of and attention to children now, has to learn the pattern of later growth, and has to realize that one's idea of children's growth can never be adequate without study of what human nature in its maturity *should* be. 'The end is in the beginning.' It is sometimes too easily assumed that the *whole* programme for teacher education can be summed up in the word 'child-study'.

9

Education of Teachers

This chapter might be called, a little pedantically, 'Some principles of the practice of the professional education of school teachers'. It will deal mainly with the fundamental elements which ought to be included in this professional education, with some of the ways in which these may be developed, and with some of the practical limitations under which teacher-educators must work.

Most of applies to the professional education of all teachers—whether graduates "training" for one year after taking their degrees, or taking a four-year course concurrently with the degree or, non-graduates, participating in the new three–year courses in training colleges. But the limitations of time in the one-year course for graduates obviously create their special problems; from time to time I shall refer to those specifically.

Everything that follows is to be read in intrinsic relation to the philosophy of education. I have stressed, for instance, that the "application of principles to practice' takes place always through the transforming medium of personality and personal action. From this it follows that the quality and vitality of the teachers of teachers will more than anything else determining the quality of the professional education which their students will receive.

But though a truism and even a platitude, it is indispensable to keep it in mind; it is all too easy to think of a topic like the present one merely in terms of syllabus, curriculum, timetable, organization.........

A dominating belief is that educative teaching arises in a situation of interpersonal relations, in which the educated character and personality of the teacher is a major influencing force. Educative teaching takes place within this interpersonal situation; that does not mean that this gives the whole story; of course it does not.

Teaching is a highly differentiated and complex function, requiring special knowledge of different kinds and many 'techniques'. On the other hand, unless all this knowledge and these techniques are assimilated into the creative and individual hour to hour decisions of personal teaching, they have no meaning and may do more harm than good.

We have, then, to take the personal development of the student in certain directions as the centre and core of teacher education. 'Personal development' here does not imply any overwhelming concentration on the internal life of the student with constant emphasis on introspection—though introspection has its place. Personal development, reasonably conceived, takes place through interchange and dialogue with the world of things and people and ideas. This process can be conveniently itemized under a number of headings— so long as it is remembered that the process of growth, though very complex, is single, continuous and organic, so that — when it is healthy — every part of it affects every other part. When things go wrong in teacher education it is usually because some of the parts of it get unduly emphasized, or become separated from the others. At one time, for instance, the aim of teacher education is thought to be chiefly the training in skills and techniques of teaching, or in 'classroom management'; at another it is 'efficient subject teaching'; at another, understanding child psychology .... It would be equally a mistake to think that 'personality development' is the one and only thing that matters, or that this can take place in a vigorous way unless all the other important things are happening too. With these provisos, we may safely proceed to list some of the most important emphases. I shall give the headings first, later dealing with each in turn, some briefly, some more fully.

(i) We have argued throughout that the teacher must experience and come to terms with *values* at a deep level. (ii) He must, to the best of his ability, think philosophically about the nature of education and its setting. (iii) He must pay a new kind of attention to the subjects or areas of his teaching, trying to understand on the one hand 'the philosophy of the subject', and on the other hand to understand, both theoretically and practically, the methods and techniques of teaching it (iv) he has to learn to meet and to understand children; in so doing he may learn a great deal about himself. (v) He must develop and enlarge his mind by beginning to explore new fields of knowledge, some of which contain information which he should have if he is to be properly equipped as a teacher. These include the history, system and organization of education, some understanding of the social background of the children he will teach, some knowledge of the psychology of children, their development, their physical and mental health. (This is, or should be, inseparably related to his contact with children, and his own increasing self-knoweldge.) (vi) Over and above the 'techniques' of teaching— or interspersed with them—he has to learn, by experience, discussion and reflection, what the living personal situation of teaching can and should be. ((vii) A part of this is learned in actual teaching practice—but this practical experience bears its best fruits only when it is integrally related to the whole of the rest of his professional education.

Looked at from one point of view, this is quite an impossible programme to carry out for the graduate who has only one year to spend. (In one respect at least graduates in

England or elsewhere who spread their study of education over a number of years are more fortunate than those who have to get what they can out of a year.) It is 'impossible', that is to say, if one thinks of this year as a year of academic *achievement* in any way comparable to the academic achievement of a degree course, in which intensive study is possible over a number of years. Because it is often—by those of rigid 'academic' habits of mind—misconceived in this way, the 'training' year is frequently unfairly criticized as an academic 'let-down', as a superficial smattering to which it is beneath the dignity of university graduates to give serious attention. No doubt, if so conceived, it can be so. But in my view the assumptions is a seer blunder. What such a year can do, and ought to do, is to introduce and open up new fields of thought and experience and practice; everything should be planned and done with this in view. This is a 're-orientation' year. The graduate student comes to it with his specialized academic knowledge. He is confronted with the new practical challenge of becoming a teacher, for which his orthodox academic education has prepared him little; it may even have bent him in *wrong* directions. He has to make a new adjustment, with the whole of himself—not with his intellect only. He cannot possibly complete this adjustment in the short time of what is in fact much less than one year. In truth it is an adjustment which goes on taking place during a lifetime. Everything he receives and learns during the year, therefore, should as far as possible be a stimulating introduction to new ways of feeling and thinking and acting and to new fields of relevant knowledge, given and taken in such a way that the student will be intrigued and interested. Stirred up to have some idea of the 'size'—the depth and height and extent and implications—of his job, he should be moved to go on from where, in his 'education' years, he makes a mere beginning. The student who is given, and is willing to receive, this kind of an introductory professional education, will say (and does say) that his 'training' year is, in an important sense, a new beginning of his education. (If this does not happen we shal hear the usual conventional—and complacent—clalp-trap about a 'waste of time'). He quickly learns that the aim is not to turn him out as an 'efficient' teacher (fr good teaching is only learned after considerable experiensce), but to prepare him to become and intelligent and perspicacious learner of a job seen in its magnitude and proporitions.

There is an important corollary to all this. If a year's course for the graduate is only the beginning of an introduction to professional education, it ought to be recognized routine that teachers should receive 'in-service' leave from time to time to reflect upon and consider their job in the light of their riper experience. This at present is badly lacking. It is common knowledge that experienced teachers can gain enormously by the proper king of 'refresher' courses.

With these ideas of re-orientation and adjustment in mind, how may the main aims of teacher education be implemented?

Learning Values

(i) The student must realize *values* in his own experience at as deep a level as he can. Values are learnt through experiencing them. It is without doubts helpful to hear about the important values in talks and lectures, before and after experience of them. But as values they can only be realized in personal lived experience. Much of this experience is, or should be, gained through the student's education before he arrives, and part of his new duty is to take stock of what he already has. But at this stage he also needs to experience freshly. He can do so in all sorts of ways—by exploring some new art of craft (alone or along with others in a group), by taking part in drama or music or poetry reading, by critical discussion of these (or of films, broadcasts, television programmes), by excursions or visits (including school visits), by club work...... He may learn much through contact with a tutor whose view of his teaching field is fresh to the student, or perhaps by informal contacts in the tutor's home. He may learn a lot by taking the chance to go off by himself to think

But specially in this year new values can often be discovered through students contacts with one another over their teaching experience in schools. Discussing perhaps a problem of discipline which has arisen during teaching practice (What would you have done in the circumstances?') different, perhaps sharply opposed, opinions will be expressed; individual personalities react in various ways: some are mortified by indiscipline, others are angry, others comparatively unruffled. These reactions, seen in one's contemporaries, bring out, modify and educate one's own; students can learn from each other as they may be unable to learn from someone in 'authority', and they learn quite as much through their own emotional—maybe strongly emotional—reactions as through their intellects. Or perhaps a student who has given an unsuccessful lesson tends to camouflage it before his tutor, or even himself. In a group, however, one of the members happens to be not so inhibited, and acknowledges or even proclaims publicly his failure. This to the others is impressive and important. They may then be embodiment to admit their own mistakes; and nothing is more educative than free honest discussion of the reasons for what went wrong. The weaker are encouraged to think (and feel) again. The sharing of failures, learning to be objective instead of covering up, can be the most rewarding of experiences. Students may learn entirely new and much more genuine values from sharing their experiences, either among themselves privately or under the guidance of a tutor who keeps his own authority in background—and, it should be added, is equally ready to admit and to discuss his own mistakes in his dealings with them.

Philosophical Thinking

(ii) Not a great deal more needs to be said about this. Since most students (graduate or non-graduate) in England very unfortunately know no philosophy, a guiding course of lectures is indispensable, their purpose being to illustrate by example the ways of philosophical thinking, and to bring out the main questions relevant to education. But formal lectures, although necessary, are in themselves only a guide and a stimulus to taught, reading and discussion. Discussion, indeed, is the life-blood of philosophy; it can be stimulated and directed if necessary by pre-planned topics culled from contemporary writings in the press and elsewhere which have a general bearing on questions of education and which are in a broad way related to the lectures. Or it may be helped by the discussion of carefully chosen books. There are many different ways of achieving the same result, the guiding principles being that the students should feel the issues to be alive and relevant, that they should be encouraged to discuss them at a fundamental level, and that they should find their own personal answers (or, if questions cannot be answers easily, that they should be clearly put). The difficult talk of assuring students that it is genuine thinking which is asked for, with questioning as important as answering, can to some extent be helped by ensuring that the examination questions are such as to encourage students to tackle them in their own individual independent ways. If an introduction to philosophy of education does no more than encourage a care for the use of language, and a watchful eye to scrutinize the tags and catchwords which so beset educational journalism and talk, it will at least have done some good- though, as we have seen, there is much more to it than that .

Techniques: General Knowledge: Proper Proportions

(iii) I have already said something on the importance of thinking freshly about 'the philosophy of the subject'. In addition to this there is much to be learnt about the methods and techniques of teaching a subject of area of study. The two things, of course, go together; one cannot, as I have suggested, teach mathematics or history in the right way if one does not understand the nature of what one is teaching; 'techniques' arise out of the structure of the subject; and its place in the curriculum is well judged only if one understands its nature. But techniques also depend on other things too, for example upon psychological understanding. Piaget and others have helped us to understand how important it is to relate, for instance, the teaching of mathematics to the image-and concept-forming stage of the child's development. Psychological knowledge of children's interests, or the ways in which they learn a foreign language, or to read, or to imagine a poem, knowledge which apprises the teacher of individual differences in children, which enlightens him about the ways in which emotional attitudes affect the capacity to learn ... all this and much more is inseparably part of the knowledge of techniques and methods of teaching. As always, teaching experience is a challenge to questioning, questions are tentatively and in a general way answered by 'theory', which in turn modifies the teacher's discriminative apprehension, and in that way his practice. The gradual acquisition of teaching skills is contributed to by all sorts of factors; good tutorial work makes the student-teacher aware of them in a way which makes teaching an intelligent art.

(iv) The need to meet and understand children is implied in most of what has been already said. It will be referred to again under heading (vi) below.

(v) The 'educated teacher' does not deserve the name if he is not sufficiently well informed of the background knowledge of his profession or does not know where to find out more when and where needed. He must have, as has already been said, a foundation of psychological knowledge. This must to some extent, be a systematic knowledge; the particular areas of information required for, say, the techniques of teaching English cannot be intelligently understood except in a context of general relevant psychological knowledge. The children who are being observed of taught are beings with a past and a future. They are now at a certain stage of development, and the teacher who is competent must know as much as is necessary of the stages of child development. They are growing: how for the grow healthily—in body and mind ? What will help their growth without over-stimulating them? What do their capacities and interests generally tend to be at such-and-such age ranges? How does their intelligence and temperament and interest affect their learning? What do the psychologists mean by 'intelligence', 'temperament' and 'interest'? What does 'learning' mean, and what are the conditions of its happening in the best way? Again, children is school are under 'authority' and under discipline'. What are the psychological phenomena of being under authority? What are the psychological phenomena of being under authority? What are psychologically the best forms of authority? What are the psychological phenomena of being in authority? All these things (and many others like them) can be understood in two quit different ways, which are always and necessarily complementary. One way is the way of experiencing events of the classroom as they happen, and then ruminating upon them as experienced. The other way is the conceptual way, study of the books, hearing the scientific experts on child-development, learning, emotional structure, intelligence; ... In both these ways, too, the teacher should have some knowledge of the social context and background of the children he teaches. Much of the particular knowledge can of course only be acquired through considerable experience of the group of children with which he is concerned. But the teacher should receive, during his professional course, some general foundational knowledge on which to build.

Some basic knowledge of the history of education and of educational ideas, and of the contemporary administrative structure of education, is obviously required. All this can be classed as 'information', but if it seems less immediately and obviously relevant to the work of teaching and educating than the other studies mentioned, it is still necessary for the teacher. It is hardly possible to conceive a responsible English teacher, for example completely ignorant of the administrative system in which he works; he would be working blindly; he would not know what he was doing. He undoubtedly requires some general systematic knowlege of the structure of his own educational set-up. The same is true, in a rather less direct way, of the history of education. History is not, directly, of 'use'. But if we try to imagine an extreme case (which had an actual parallel in Nazi Germany) of a teacher who has simply no knowledge at all of the past history of education, who lives only in the present without background we shall be bound to say that he too is equally blind and directioniess.

Having acknowledged all this, however, it is important to remember the central aim and proportions of the course—particularly if we have the graduate one-year period in mind.

There is, in fact, no time, in a one 'year'of some eighteen academic weeks to study everything equally. There has got to be selection and emphasis, and a principle of selection. I have argued that the central and fundamental purpose of professional education is what some would call an 'existential' one—a *personal* re-orientation of the student, a fresh assessment of himself and of his beliefs, of his relation to other people, a rethinking of the meaning of his subject, and the techniques of teaching it, the new beginnings of an approach to the understanding of children and to the immediate and more remote aims of education. It is an 'existential' approach in the sense that the emphasis is upon the student's discoveries through his own personal experiential life, his 'existence', through his thinking, feeling, deciding, acting. His discoveries are achieved in part, no doubt, by his learning about many things; but during this brief formative period it is that information and thinking which can be brought most directly to bear upon his personal orientation to the teaching and educating of children which is of the first importance.

If this principle is accepted (in addition to all the other important things mentioned), it will follow that the informative background knowledge of history and administrative structure shield be regarded as subsidiary to the rest. Students should receive enough of it to realize its importance, to have a general idea of its proportions, and to be able to find their way about so that they can explore it at greater leisure (possibly in a later advanced course).

(*vi*) and (*vii*) I have left to the last—in this 'list'—the learning 'by experience, discussion and reflection, what the living personal situation of teaching can and should be'. It is absurd, of course, to divide things in this way; only the limitations of having to say things *seriatim* makes it necessary. For this personal learning of what teaching and education can be is necessarily integral with everything else that has been said. The remarks which follow are only glosses, or arbitrarily chosen illustrations of ways in which students may gain more intimate insight into what educative teaching and learning really are.

The Problem of Overcoming Stereotypes; Teaching and Art

One of the things which has to be overcome is domination of the 'stereotype' idea of the teacher. It is very difficult for the student beginning to teach not to think of himself as playing a role, or cutting a figure, or otherwise conforming himself to his idea of what a 'teacher' should look like and how a 'teacher' should act. This is not always made better by observing demonstration lessons (though of course a lot can be learned here). The student may watch, with justified admiration, the ways in which a master of the art deals with children and the teaching of a topic. Next time when he is on his own he tries to emulate the admired teacher. If he is a good actor he may be successful up to a point—and again I am not arguing that there is no value in observation and even some imitation. But it does not take him far; he is an insecure immature copyist. The teacher is himself, not another, and if playing the 'sedulous ape' teaches the beginner something, it is something which also has to be unlearned as he discovers his own 'style'. But it is just as likely that his attempts to copy the figure which he admires will break down; 'x can do it so easily; I can't. When the principle of watching a good teacher at work is carried to the extreme of attempting to 'train' a teacher by regarding him as a sort of apprentice exclusively to one master (as is frequently advocated in current journalism and elsewhere), the very worst results can follow.

The domination of the stereotype-image is bad for a number of reasons. The student teacher is focusing his attention on the wrong thing-*himself* as acting a part worked out for him (at least to a considerable extent) by another. He should be thinking of the job, of what he is teaching, of the children as learning, of what is happening to and in them, rather than of his own success. Again, what he needs is *principled* understanding of the task in hand as it now presents itself, not a formula to be applied. If he can cast his mind back to the philosophy of teaching, he will realize that it is not himself-doing (or performing a role) which chiefly matters, but the imaginative understanding of the children's learning. The analogy of art is helpful here. 'Form' in art is not the application of a previously prepared ready-made pattern to something else, the matter or material. True aesthetic form is something which is unique and utterly individual to this work of art (e.g., this poem), watch is discovered in its embodied reality and nowhere else. So a teacher errs if he thinks that a 'lesson' is something the shape of which can be finally fixed beforehand, and which is then 'taught' to the children who 'learn' it. Of course the teacher has to prepare his lessons (as the artist may ruminate long on what he is going to do), and of course he knows generally the sort of children he is going to teach and the conditions under which he will teach them (as the artist knows the material he is going to work with). Nevertheless what the good teacher is really doing by *his* imaginative art is to bring to birth new discovery in the children's minds and imaginations, and this never happens till the actual event in which they with their independence participate. This is what matters—not the teacher's successful carrying out of an act or even 'getting across' what he had his mind before he started—important as that plan may be in its own place and time. Good teaching is the midwife of discovery.

The domination of another stereotype—of teaching as a technique—is also a danger. There are, of course, 'techniques', as we have said. But if techniques are conceived as practical formulae to be put into operation, prescribed modes of procedure providing the answer beforehand as it were, there will be applied science but not genuine teaching. The same analogy can be applied as before. The artist possesses high technical skill, and has to learn it. But the artist best learns his techniques as and when he requires it, on the job, and in the service of his art. In his practice of art, his techniques are being used all the time, but they are servants and not master, subsidiary and not principal. They have to be learned and assimilated till they become second nature, subservient to the central artistic purpose. So with the good teacher.

It is, of course, easy to say all these things, and very difficult to do them. Saying them is of some value; but as always they have to be learnt in experience and action.

Developing Imaginative Sympathy for Children's learning

The experience of the student teacher as a teacher is only beginning, and can ripen only with time. Nevertheless some things can be done during a year of professional education to increase the capacity for intelligent learning from experience and to help the imaginative understanding of the dynamics of teaching-learning: some have been mentioned. One great advantage of practice in art or craft, or example, is that it develops the sense of the importance of discovering the right thing to do as one goes along. This can be 'transferred' to the experience of teaching. Another advantage of beginning to learn a new art or craft during a professional course is that in coping with hitherto unexperienced difficulties one is in much the same position as the children being taught, who are learning new things. Experience and analysis of one's own difficulties, related to theirs, helps through actual experience the understanding of their leaning. If the student's learning takes place within a group, he may learn, in many ways, through sharing and discussing the difficulties of others. If he has a marked preference for working alone, an examination of his own reactions may well help him to understand the child who appears solitary and who prefers to do things alone. (If he prefers to work in a group he may better help the children who have to do things in 'bunches'). Another, more theoretical, way of helping the student to understand what 'being educated' means is to ask him to write a critical essay on his own education—and miss-education.

With much the same ends in view, a number of my colleagues in London have tried in various forms an experiment described by one of them as follows:

> 'To bring home the reality of self observation I find it is useful to ask the students to make some detailed introspection in structured present situations. Throughout, the function of this is continually linked with the understanding of the child's problems,s or predicament, and written descriptions can remain anonymous should the student wish. For example,

when discussing intelligence I set them a problem such as the following to solve, Which is designed to be sufficiently difficult to tax them to their extreme limits. 'There are twelve pennies, one of which is different in weight from the others. You are required to find which is the different penny and whether it is heavier or lighter than the others. You have scales available but you are allowed only three weighings.' I assure them that a solution is possible and that there is no trick in the question. I ask them to write an account of their thought processes, their feelings, tensions, etc. This leads on to the student's own early childhood memories, fears, anxieties, achievement of moral standards, winning and losing, the basis of character development.

It can be seen that experiments of this did although they are concentrated on a moment of educational experience, go forbidden the moment, and raise many important questions of psychology and philosophy.

Teaching Practice

It is for this reason that 'teaching practice' must be seen as an integral part of the whole professional course. This may seem obvious enough in the light of all that has been said; nevertheless it is easily possible to misconceive the function of teaching practice. It is easy to assume that is means nothing more than some practice in teaching, and initiation into the real thing, in which as far as possible the conditions of professional life are reproduced, but for a short period. Of course teaching practice *includes* this, with the reservation that this temporary experience can never exactly reproduce professional life-any more than 'trial marriage' could possibly reproduce the full conditions of married life. But 'teaching practice 'is a great deal more than practice in teaching, much more, for examples, than the practice a student may have before he starts his course. Teaching practice is indeed a practical experiment carried out in the light of a theory—or better, carried out in the light of everything else that goes on during the professional course. Not just practice, but a first attempt at personal embodiment in teaching of all that is being assimilated through the teacher's education.

It is for this reason that the main control and direction of it ought, so far as is practicable, to be in the hands of the tutor (or tutors) in charge of the student throughout the course. To say this is in no way to under-estimate the hospitality of the schools, nor to belittle the important part which the teacher in the school can play in helping the student to teach better. This is indeed an essential contribution—and for more than the reason that the tutor can only be in school for part of the time. But the teacher's part here is one of cooperation rather than of main direction. For this reason it is very important that there should be coming and going between the school and the Department of College as far as time will permit—the tutor being familiar with the school, its staff and its aims, and the teacher having a fair general idea of the dominating ideas of the professional year. But the teacher has, of course, his full job in school; his time and energy are limited; he has to guide the student as best he can, sometimes under difficult circumstances. The tutor, on the other hand, lives and works within the professional department, he has to learn, slowly and perhaps painfully, the complex implications of his own unique function. He learns it mainly by absorption, by daily contact with his colleagues who are making their own, and varying, contributions to the same single end. It is by this kind of living together in a community that "theory" and 'practice' become a part of single organism—and something of this unity can be realized in turn by the students.

(If these things are true, it will follow that the suggestion, sometimes made, that the 'practical training' of the student should be left entirely to the teacher in school, must be rejected outright. If one wanted effectively to divide 'theory' from 'practice', this would be the way to do it.)

'The Materialism of the Curriculum' and Educative Learning: Conclusion

I spoke earlier of what I called 'the materialism of the

curriculum'—the deadening tendency to count up subjects 'done', to measure a teacher's success in terms of the amount of the syllabus covered for the examination. (To give an actual verbatim quotation: 'In this school we didn't teach what's not in the syllabus'). In some schools there is a hard inertia of materialistic counting against which it is difficult for an intelligent young teacher to make headway, and which may dangerously discourage and perhaps disillusion him. It is all made worse by the vicious habit of second-and third-hand learning—memorizing answers ready worked out for the pupil in diagrams and textbooks, with no real mental enjoyment of anything real—whether it be science, or poetry, or history. This is a deep-seated evil; many of the students are victims of it themselves; all of them have been though the examination mill.

The evil is not only deep but widespread; obviously it cannot be cured easily or quickly—even if we optimistically assume that it is not a chronic disease. But some things may be done, even in a short professional year, to provide a little yeast which may in slow time help to leaven the lump.

Something may be gained if students are encouraged to reflect upon their own preparation for examinations and on the reasons for their own comparative success (or comparative failure). Did they succeed by officially approved merit-riciousness, and if so, what do they now think of its effects on their won true education? Or did they fall short of success because this kind of cramming simply did not work for them? What was wrong? Or were they fortunate in receiving a more liberal education, but a bit disillusioned because it did not seem to fit the procrustean examination bed? Or did they find that their more liberal education made it easy to take examinations almost in their stride? Again, has this or that student discovered sadly he was slower than other people, had to work laboriously for perhaps very moderate results? Whatever the case, the analysis of the reasons, particularly if carried out under the guidance of a good tutor, in company and in discussion with others, can prove not only to illuminate the individual experience, but to develop better understanding of bad and good education and the difficulties of children.

In these ways students may be led to think constructively and positively about the educative (as opposed to the 'materialists') teaching of their own field and its relation to examinations. Each discipline has its own order, and it is dangerous to generalize, unless after an extensive survey. But might it not be said that in a course of study leading to the G.C.E. at 'O' level the first two or three years might well be spent in free and enjoyable (though guided) exploration of the basic principles of a subjects, leaving the details to be learned—perhaps with a good deal of hard grinding—which could at that later stage be cheerfully expected? This, I am told, works well in Biology. Might it not be expected to apply, *mutatis mutandis*, in other fields? Is it not educationally self-evident that it is better for children to learn the 'discipline' of a subject through direct and genuine engagement with it rather than, as so often happens, being warned to conform to what they do not yet understand (and taught in this way may never come to understand at all), and to memorize it? To be able to repeat the 'correct'opinions about literature, to be able to reproduce the scientific textbook definitions and diagrams, to remember and to apply the mathematical formulae and procedures-what does it profit a child if he gains all this and loses his soul—his native power of enthralled absorption in drama or poetry, in the ways in which nature, living and animate, 'works', in the fascinating logic of mathematics? The slavish way is not only depressive of natural intellectual and emotional vitality; it is a sin against children's integrity. Most of us would fiercely condemn the introduction of children to noxious drugtaking which in time destroys their human capacities. We do not always see that by certain ways of teaching we are forcing in children the deadly habit of what Plato calls 'the lie in the soul', and so maiming a natural capacity for integrity. Too often from the beginning of their secondary education they are taught to pretend to what they do not possess; if they can produce the right appearance of conformity to what is expected they can romp through.

The complex cause of this evil it would be impossible-and irrelevant—to discuss here. The question which is relevant for the teacher is whether bad methods—which seem to get children through their examinations—are necessary, or even expedient, to attain this result? Among other reasons, it is fear and insecurity which drives teachers to cling to the abstractions of syllabus—headings and textbooks. These have 'authority', and conform to authority—and to the powerful authority of the examiners—seems to be the way of earning the title of 'efficient'. But is the way of fear the only way? There are good teachers, large numbers of them, who teach educatively, and whose 'results' are excellent. Since even keen young teachers after first appointment easily fall prey to the cynicism of their elders, it is of great importance for students during their professionally education to have a chance of looking into the relation between educative teaching and examination success.

I have tried in this concluding chapter to view the several parts of teacher education—theory of various kinds, practical teaching, knowledge of children, the development of the students' own experiences individual and social, the learning of techniques...in relation to one another and to the one central aim of that vital educative experience which is the other side of educative teaching. Once again (and for the last time) the imaginative and co-operative understanding of this complex aim—and not merely its intellectual formulation—is that which gives life to every part of the professional training period.

10

Development of Comparative Education

The purpose of (reviewing) the development of comparative education is not simply to trace through materials that have been examined many times before, but rather to search out in the predecessors of modern comparative education those elements of their thought pertinent to understanding their motives for undertaking comparative work, the types of data they used, the ways they handled the data, and their interpretations of them. The analysis reveals the gradual, unsteady emergence of an empirically based, social scientific approach in comparative education, the history of which begins with simple narrative sometimes naive, but often astute, and ends, for the present, with the application of the sophisticated methods now being employed in the social sciences.

The development of comparative education has been marked by five identifiable stages, each characterized by a different motive for comparative study and each producing a different genre of work.

The earliest stage, the period of (*travelers' tales*,) was prompted by simple curiosity.

Second came a period of *educational borrowing*, when the desire to learn useful lessons from foreign practices was the major motivation.

In the third stage, *international educational cooperation* was stressed in the interests of world harmony and mutual improvement among nations.

Since the beginning of the twentieth century, *two more states* have appeared, both concerned with seeking explanations for the wide variety of educational and social phenomena observed around the globe.

The first of these attempted to *identify the forces and (factors shaping national educational systems)*.

The second, and the latest, may be termed (*the stage of social science explanation*). Which uses the empirical, quantitative methods of economics, political science, and sociology to clarify relationships between education and society.

These stages are far from being discrete in time: each of these types of work in comparative education has persisted down to the present and may be observed in the contemporary literature, and rarely can any contributor to the field be confined within a single category. But the categorization suggested, loose though it is, provides a convenient, unforced framework within which to review the development of the field.

The first and most primitive comparative education observations were the tales brought home by travelers to foreign parts. Such reports were essentially the work of amateurs who included in more general descriptions of institutions and practices abroad details of foreign ways of raising children. These rapporteurs tended to emphasize exotic information simply because it threw into sharp contrast the familiar practices and institutions of their homelands. Curiosity was the mainspring of their voyages, and local color the attraction of their descriptions. Only the rare observer could extract systematic conclusions with explanatory value from a mass of indiscriminately reported impressions. In the form of superior journalism, this style of work remains a prominent feature of writing on foreign countries today.

From the beginning of the nineteenth century, coincident with the rise of national systems of education in Europe, journeys abroad were made by travelers with a specialized interest in educational matters. No longer motivated by general curiosity, they went the rounds of foreign countries to discover information useful for charting the course of education in their own countries.

This group of precursors of modern comparative education were predominantly educational politicians, experts, and activists. Often they traveled not at their own expense, or following their private interest, but as emissaries, sometimes self-appointed, of their national governments. They concerned themselves with educational theory, methodology, finance, and organization. Teacher training, instructional methods, and alternatives to traditionally accepted curricula were matters of major importance for them.

Though their reports now focused sharply upon the schools, characteristics associated with travelers' tales persisted: many of the reports took the form of encyclopedic descriptions of foreign school systems, perhaps enlivened here and there with anecdotes, but rarely explanatory. Of necessity, objectivity and detachment were lacking, for these educational emissaries, committed as they were to the cause of education in their own countries, mostly saw and reported from abroad merely what they judged would advance their domestic enterprises.

This was a period, too, when exchange of information about foreign countries and particularly about foreign education was considered desirable *simply to break down the barriers of ignorance that divided nation from nation*. Encyclopedic work was still the fashion, but it was argued that the very process of systematically amassing and publishing information on foreign countries would require extensive exchanges of scholars, students, and publications. The resulting network of international contacts would of itself help promote international understanding, as well as the improvement of social and, in particular, educational institutions around the world.

Coincident with the rise of the social sciences towards the end of the nineteenth century there came a recognition of the importance of the dynamic relationships knitting education and society. *Education was seen as the mirror of society*; but society, in turn, was molded partly by the schools. Changes in one were revealed in the other. The concern now was to understand the interaction of education and society by analyzing the historical forces and contemporary factors that had shaped both.

Moreover, exponents of this approach were interested in more than laying bare the nature of these relationships. They began to consider the possibility of using their conclusions to steer educational reform and so engineer the future shape of society.

In this phase of comparative education, studies of foreign schooling became to a considerable extent studies of national character and the institutions that help form it. They relied heavily on history and tended to strike a deterministic note. Problems of cause and effect preoccupied comparative educators, but inevitably their discussion quickly descended into a familiar circularity: national character determines education, and education determines national character. Where to break in to this perplexing circle was a question not easily answered.

A significant strengthening of the explanatory powers of the social sciences took place after World War I. Many governments improved the quantity and quality of their statistical series, and statistical techniques became much more sophisticated. Partly in response to these new possibilities, the social sciences came to rely more and more upon quantitative methods; and the demands of researchers stimulated the production of yet more statistical material.

This was particularly true in economics and sociology, and in later years this trend extended to political science and even to anthropology.

Quantitative methods were adopted not only in the social sciences, perse, but also in some branches of education, particularly in psychology and psychometrics.

In this manner, the humanistic origins of the social sciences, which accounted for their early philosophical and historical emphases, were gradually overlaid by new concerns and methods of an empirical and quantitative nature. Comparative education slowly followed the same path.

Since World War II these trends have accelerated and the empirical orientation of the social sciences has begun to reshape comparative education. Contemporary cross-national study in education is thus founded upon the twin bases of vastly increased bodies of data and improved techniques in social science research. Empirical, quantitative methods in comparative education are still beset with serious difficulties, but there can be little doubt that their potential contribution to the field is so great that they will have to be reckoned with.

It is now possible to review a century and a half of development and progress since the proposals of Marc-Antoine Jullien de Paris in 1817. This was the period when "pantometry" held sway, indiscriminate measuring was a fad, and hopes were strong that a science of education could emerge from massive collections of data, expressed wherever possible in numerical form.

The early quantitative approaches in comparative education failed (as did pantometry in general) partly because they were inappropriately applied, partly because the sources of data and the means of their collection were even more limited than they are today, and finally because the dangers arising from personal and cultural bias were barely recognized.

At that time the failure of primitive quantitative approaches was not crucial since comparative education was directed mainly toward selective cultural borrowing and was little concerned with the problems of explanation. However, suspicion of statistics persisted even as comparative education moved toward the search for explanation.

The qualitative interpretations of Sadler, Kandel, and Hans were magnificent attempts to explain the dynamics of education and society, largely without reference to statistical and quantitative data. From Sadler on, the common approach relied on the identification of forces and factors (Triebkrafte) in the search for explanation.

Initially, the emphasis was historical; later, sociological, political, and even anthropological factors were introduced. However, the most recent stage in comparative education and cognate fields reverses the classic post-Sadlerian approach : the forces and factors that previously had been the bases for explanation have now themselves become objects of inquiry.

At the same time as the social sciences were developing increasing sophistication in quantification, nonquantitative explanations tended to be ignored. If comparative education was to fulfill its potential as a tool for educational planning, it had to offer a means of reliable prediction. Without a quantitative base, it appeared, this could not be adequately achieved.

During a century and a half comparative education has moved from the stage of curiosity to the stage of analysis.

This movement may be discerned along three dimensions.

From indiscriminate data gathering to vastly greater precision:From philanthropy in international educational cooperation to professionalism and from analysis based on intuition toward scientific explanation.

First, comparative education has advanced from the stage of curiosity exemplified by Bache's enormous and indiscriminate collections of pedagogical material to the equally vast but now highly structured collections of data of the IEA project.

Second, the early workers in the last century were imbued with humanitarian and philanthropic intentions. They saw the international exchange of educational information as good in itself, but with the exception of Jullien they could not conceive of it as a possible object of conscious, planned, international cooperation. Since the foundation of the International Bureau of Education after World War I, and of Unesco, OECD, and the World Bank after World War II, Jullien's dream has been partially realized. The work of these organizations is in the hands of specialists. Thus, what began with philanthropy has ended with professionalism.

The third and perhaps the most significant dimension along which comparative education has advanced concerns the search for explanation.

Early workers were motivated by a vague sense of the differences among nations, an interest in what was going on abroad, and the intention of learning useful lessons. Even when the search for explanations superseded these earlier motivations and when the theories of comparative educators developed comprehensiveness and a sense of the dynamic interrelation of education and society, their approach was largely intuitive.

In the most recent phase, a new order of work has appeared in which no explanation can be deemed satisfactory unless validated by rigorous scientific testing.

Comparative Education as a Field of Inquiry

> *"It seems very pretty," she said when she had finished it, "but it's rather hard to understand." (You see she didn't like to confess, even to herself, that she couldn't make it out at all.) "Somehow it seems to fill my head with ideas – only I don't exactly know what they are!"*

So far, this section has been concerned with the value of the method of science as a way of knowing and its major features as a way of investigating social reality. It is now necessary to consider the special characteristics of comparative education and the case for applying empirical methods to its study.

Comparative education began with observations about

foreign peoples and their education and developed into descriptions of foreign school systems. Inherent in this work was the practical aim of borrowing from abroad useful educational devices for the improvement of education at home.

The descriptive phase gradually expanded to include examination of the social, political, and historical context in which school systems developed. A further dimension was added to the description of these relationships as comparative educators proceeded to consider the dynamic interaction between education and its societal setting.

Most recently, comparative education has entered yet a new phase in which cross-national data are used to test propositions about the relationship of education to society.

Comparative education is thus part of the wider attempt to explain phenomena, first, within educational systems and institutions, and second, surrounding education and linking it with its social environment. Attempts to do the first lead to a concern with the technology of education: the methods, practices, and outcomes of different modes of instruction, organization, supervision, administration, and finance. Where attention is paid to the teaching-learning process in a number of countries, educational psychology and particularly psychometrics are especially relevant.

Insofar as comparative education is concerned with pedagogy, the work has largely been done by teachers, administrators, and educational psychologists seeking to comprehend and possibly to improve the instructional work of the schools, and it is useful to term this branch of the subject comparative pedagogy.

But to the extent that comparative education has looked outside the confines of the classroom and the school system, its concerns and its data have overlapped with the interests of social scientists, some of whom have recently undertaken systematic comparative study of education as a social phenomenon.

Comparative education has one foot firmly planted in pedagogy and the other in the wider area of the social science. Concern with the form and function of the school has, however, united these two aspects of the field by concentrating attention on similar kinds of data and complementary topics.

A second unifying element, and possibly a more important one, has recently become apparent in a common movement toward empirical and quantitative methods of inquiry.

Notably, the IEA study has welded together the two aspects of comparative education: concern with technology of education (comparative pedagogy) and with the interaction of schooling and its social context.

Comparative education in its most recent phase emerges as the attempt to use cross-national data to test propositions about the relationship between education and society and between teaching practices and learning outcomes.

Characteristic Problems of Comparative Education

> *"Well in our country." said Alice, still panting a little. "you'd generally get to somewhere else- if you ran very fast for a long time as we've been doing." "A slow sort of country!" saïd the Queen. "Now, here, you see, it takes all the running you can do, to keep in the same place.*

The serious problems of the field are not hard to perceive. For the comparative educator the nagging questions persist: why do we know so little for certain in comparative education, and why does comparative education hardly figure at all in the list of recognized fields of comparative study (history, sociology, religion, literature, economics, political science)?

A recent compendium of scientific findings about human behavior includes a great deal of material on education, but can report nothing that relies on cross-national research in this area. Similarly, a review article by an outstandingly well-informed scholar on the status of comparative studies in the United States makes not a single mention of comparative education.

A number of problems appear fundamental to comparative education and presumably must be met head on and overcome if the field is ever to realize its potential. They are the problems of bias, utility of results, and eclecticism in both methodology and data.

Bias may arise at every stage of the comparative educator's work, from the identification of problems to the collection of data, their interpretation, and the conclusions drawn from them. Ethnocentrism is an obvious source of bias in comparative education: inevitably investigators view foreign societies through a selective and distorting screen interposed by their cultural experience. But there is a vastly more important source of bias embedded in the whole field of comparative education and, indeed, in the social sciences in general.

This entire edifice of knowledge is part of the intellectual achievement of the Western world during the past two centuries and reflects the secularism, liberalism, and humanism of the modern Western tradition. Just as the development of the physical sciences in the West has been the story of man's attempt to extend his control over his physical environment, so the development of the social sciences similarly has sought to extend man's control over his social environment.

Difficult though it may be for the observer brought up in this tradition to recognize, the instrumental view itself provides a value system that must bias perceptions. For example, movement toward a secular, humanistic, liberal, and industrialized society is equated with progress and is endowed with positive value. Comparative educators have fully shared this bias, as their writings reveal. Until very recently their attention was concentrated almost exclusively on Western-type societies and their consideration of other societies is still too frequently cast in terms of movement toward Western structures and processes.

"The tendency has been to regard non-Western nations as in some way primitive forms and to assume that their natural development will follow Western precedents." Moreover, these attitudes have not been a monopoly of comparative educators and social scientists in the West; they have been shared in good measure by their colleagues in Japan, India, and a host of contemporary developing countries.

As a result, comparative education has devoted primary attention to problems of change and progress; relating education to economic growth, social amelioration, and political development. Compared to the volumes produced on these topics, the amount of attention paid to conservation of existing institutions has been insignificant.

Moreover, those who have concerned themselves with the maintenance and continuity of present social and cultural modes have been labelled traditionalist and reactionary. Yet there are clearly some very important and legitimate problems to be examined in this area.

The culturally imposed filter affects not only the topics selected for study, but also the data. It is merely trite to observe that the selection of some topics and the ignoring of others will inevitably condition the type of data collected. But the problem is compounded in comparative education, where an investigator from an alien culture often is unable to recognize the relevance of certain types of data for the solution of the problem he has chosen.

When the comparative educator examines the relationship between education and economic development in, say, India, he is naturally attracted to an examination of those formal educational institutions for which statistics and data have been collected. Among these data he tends to search out just those elements he has learned are important in the models with which he is familiar.

What has not already been identified for him and what has not in his past experience seemed to have much importance may not be taken into account.

Thus, modernization and education in India may be examined on the basis of the number of technical school places opened and filled. This procedure simply reflects the role of formal technical education in Western societies. Yet the most important means of modernization in Indian society may be increasing availability of automobiles, bicycles, water pumps, and so forth-all the Western–type machines that impose on their operators disciplines of use, maintenance, and repair.

Insofar as the comparative educator is interested in examining the relationship between education and development, he would be utterly misled by giving attention just to the formal system of education and neglecting the informal educational effects of introducing Western machinery.

One stimulus to improved work in a field is the ease of movement between the research findings in the field and their practical applications. Although comparative interest sprang from a desire to improve education by studying foreign models, the difficulties involved in extensive foreign borrowing eventually became apparent.

The later comparative studies of the role of education in society provided a mass of descriptive and sometimes interpretive writing that provided little practical guidance to educational policy makers, whatever may have been its value for scholarship. One of the major incentives for a reawakened interest in comparative education in recent years had been the expectation that lessons drawn from comparative study could be use to aid in the development of the new nations.

However, comparative education still remains far from realizing these hopes and the findings of comparative educators as yet rarely enter into the considerations of planners of national education systems, for their predictive value has yet to be demonstrated.

Another important problem of comparative education warrants discussion. Is it possible to distinguish clearly a problem in comparative education from problems in the economics of education, sociology of education, and so on? In other words, is there a clear definition of comparative education as a field of inquiry?

If at present comparative education is suffering from an identity crisis, one reason may be its eclecticism. When anthropologists, sociologists, economists, political scientists, historians, and philosophers can all make some claim to expertise in the field, it becomes extremely difficult to identify its limits with respect to both method and data. There is no consensus about the area of discourse over which comparative educators properly may range.

The ranking of a new field of inquiry in the "pecking order" of academic respectability depends on the "hardness" of its data or the rigor of its methods. As an eminent economist expressed the idea, ...economics is by its nature a softer and less exact science than, say, conventional physics. Now in a hard, exact science a practitioner does not really have to know much about methodology. Indeed, even if he is definitely a misguided methodologist, the subject itself has a selfcleansing property which renders harmless his aberrations. By contrast, a scholar in economics who is fundamentally confused concerning the relationship of definition, tautology, logical implication, empirical hypothesis, and factual refutation may spend a lifetime shadow–boxing with reality.

In a sense, therefore, in order to earn his daily bread as a fruitful contributor to knowledge, the practitioner of an intermediately hard science like economics must come to terms with methodological problems. I stress the importance of intermediate hardness because when one descends lower still, say to certain areas of sociology that are almost completely without substantive content, it may not matter much one way or the other what truths or errors about scientific method are involved-for the reason that nothing matters.

The data used in comparative education are notoriously "soft," and consequently there is a high premium on methodological rigor. Yet comparative education cannot be regarded as an enterprise with its own raison d'etre so long as it has neither a well substantiated theoretical framework nor distinctive concepts of its own. Comparative education can expect no assured place in the hierarchy of academic studies until its data and methods are clarified and their relation to one another recognized.

The Potential of Comparative Education

"If there's no meaning in it," said the King, "that saves a world of trouble, you know, as we needn't try to find any."

These multifarious difficulties nothwithstanding, the field undoubtedly contains considerable potential, arising from two sources: the special value of the cross-national dimension for studying educational issues and the arena for interdisciplinary collaboration that the field provides.

Not all propositions in education and society require crossnational treatment, but with respect to two types of validation, cross-national work is mandatory.

First, quite obviously, some generalizations simply cannot be tested by using data from one country alone since there is not sufficient variation in the single case. For example, a test of the hypothesis that there is a relation between centralization of national educational administration and students' achievement levels inevitably requires cross-national inquiry.

Second, the single case permits no more than a particular statement to be made, and it is only on the basis of cross-national research that propositions established by study of a single case can be generalized and further refined. This point merits further discussion.

Even in single-country studies, the cross-national dimension can enrich explanation. Confined to domestic data, a historical study of the expansion of higher education in the United States may be able to provide genetic explanations for its present state, but there is no doubt that such a particular study will gain by being set in the context of higher educational developments in other countries.

Of course the expansion of higher education in the United States cannot be properly understood apart from such foreign developments as the flight of German intellectuals after the failure of the 1848 Revolution in Prussia, the foreign experiences of American students and professors, and the emphasis on graduate research imported from Germany. Here is the classic justification for the comparative dimension: including foreign data in a single-country study enhances explanation of domestic phenomena. But, more important, if a hypothesis is tested within the confines of only one society there can be no certainty that the conclusions do not have merely parochial validity.

Suppose that a study of the social outcomes of the expansion of higher education in the United States shows that expansion has promoted intergenerational social mobility from lower to middle socioeconomic levels, but not from middle to upper levels. Even if this result is regarded as having a high level of accuracy for the United States, it is only by investigating the same topic in other countries that the full value of the United States finding can be exploited.

Suppose that in extending this study to England, similar conclusions are reached. A double bonus is derived from the broadened scope of the study: the United States findings are further validated, and the statement about the relationship between the expansion of higher education and social mobility in the United States now becomes more general.

Alternatively, it may be revealed that what was found to be true of the relationship between higher education and social mobility in the United States is not true in England. This should lead immediately to the suspicion that the relationship is much more complex than first thought.

When confronted with evidence to two different sets of social outcomes as a result of similar educational expansion in the two countries, the investigator is forced to abandon any simplistic explanation of the phenomena. He must reconsider the entire problem and undertake an investigation embracing more factors and more cases in order to develop a more comprehensive theory.

One of the great advantages of comparative investigation is precisely this heuristic potential.

Comparative education can provide an arena where representatives of different disciplines come together to their mutual benefit, forcing investigators out of their narrow specializations. The field has often been considered a natural candidate for interdisciplinary work by reason of the particular problems and data it treats.

Indeed, many of the important topics that fall to comparative education can be handled satisfactorily only in an interdisciplinary manner. For example, no study of education and national development is conceivable solely within the confines of a single discipline; it must draw from a wide range of behavioral and social sciences.

However, comparative education is multi-rather than interdisciplinary in both its origins and current state. Every branch of social science has made use of educational data from various countries; in return, comparative education has drawn data and concepts from the social sciences. As previously stressed, this has been a cause of much confusion concerning the scope and limits of the field. But its multidisciplinary character could be transformed into an interdisciplinary effort if the data, concepts, and methods of the several social sciences were systematically focused on the testing of specific socioeducational propositions. Then, what has been a constant source of difficulty might become instead an asset.

There are many topics of common interest to educational investigators and social scientists. All may share an interest in the social dimensions of education. For example, its political ramifications will interest political scientists, as much as educators. Because all aspects of the society cannot be treated together at one time, problems in comparative education cannot profitably be expressed holistically in terms of relationships between education as a whole and society as a whole. Rather, they must be expressed in terms of some specific aspect of education and some limited sector of the total societal context.

Therefore it is necessary to consider the total social context as made up of several overlapping sectors: for example, the economy, the ideology (religious, political, and social), the social structure, and the political structure.

Consequently,among the common problems comparative education is concerned with are the schools and economic development, the impact of different ideologies on education, education and class structure, and education and the formation of social and political elites.

These categories are not entirely arbitrary, but coincide with some major approaches to the study of society, as represented by the several social sciences. At the same time it should be emphasized that they are by no means the only ways of categorizing the total area of interest in comparative education.

Because so many propositions can profitably be tested crossnationally, it should not be surprising that the area of comparative education is occupied by educators and social scientists equally. Yet comparative education is potentially more than a congeries of data and perspectives from the social sciences applied to education in different countries. Neither the topic of education nor the cross-national dimension is central to any of the social sciences; nor are social science concerns and the cross-national dimension central to the work of educators.

The field of comparative education is best defined as an intersection of the social sciences, education, and cross-national study. Consequently, a problem in comparative education is the common concern of both social scientists and educators, but the exclusive concern of neither.

There are, of course, severe problems involved in interdisciplinary studies. Commonly they have been accused of sacrificing depth and rigorousness to breadth and modishness. In addition, specialists in one discipline have difficulty in understanding the concepts, assumptions, and modes of proof of other disciplines. They often find it very difficult to appreciate the strategies, let alone the tactics, employed by other specialists to tackle a problem.

But apart from the common focus of study (explanation of specific educational phenomena in their social context), there is one fundamental factor that promises to promote depth and rigor while uniting the disciplines engaged in comparative eduction. This is the scientific method, a mode of inquiry that is not merely a set of procedures or techniques, but an approach toward establishing belief. Everything that has been presented in this section has pointed to the indispensable role of comparative work in social science explanation of educational phenomena. The implication that must be drawn from this is that comparative education is not just an exotic excursion from the main track of education studies, but that *the comparative method provides one of the major routes for validating the most important propositions about education and society*. Where controlled experimentation is impossible, controlled investigation, which inevitably calls for comparative study, is essential.

It is certainly important to identify more precisely than ever the substantive problems of education and society that demand attention and that can provide the arena for fruitful contributions from the social sciences. Moreover, not only is comparative study required for satisfactory explanation in problems of education and society but the empirical methods of the social sciences must be embraced if the full potential of the comparative approach is to be realized. Of central importance then, will be the effort to develop in comparative education a systematic, controlled, empirical, and critical methodology.

Toward a Science of Comparative Education

The exotic lure of foreign places, manners, and customs is overwhelming. The simple acts of going and seeing for oneself and the unpredictable joys of serendipity become their own rewards; and surely if we visit abroad enough, read diligently, and cooperate with others of like interest, comparative study must get somewhere. Yet the painful truth is that it may not get anywhere at all. It may simply go around in a circle, repeating over and over again the same stale "facts," refurbished from time to time. Or comparative study may stumble over important findings, but have no notion how they fit in to the surrounding territory, how exactly they were arrived at, or how to make the best use of them now that they have been discovered. It has been the single argument of this book that, armed with the question. "Where do I wish to go?" and intent on using and improving a map to reach his destination, the wandering scholar in cross-national data greatly betters his chances of undertaking a journey that will be valuable both to himself and to his colleagues in the field.

At some stage of development, most disciplines have had to give thought to several related questions. What material and which problems lie squarly within the purview of the discipline, and which lie outside? What, if any, are the characteristic methods of the field? And what are the criteria for determining whether a piece of work in the field is good, bad, or indifferent? Comparative education today is forced hard against these question, and twist and turn as they may, comparative educators have to try to provide answers that are satisfactory to themselves, to their colleagues in adjacent areas of education studies, and to colleagues working in the social sciences.

Much of this book has been devoted to an attempt to give some answer to the first two questions. The territory of comparative education has been defined as the intersection of the social sciences, education studies, and the cross-national dimension, so that the hallmark of work properly claiming to be comparative education is that it lies neatly within that intersection. In addition, it has been argued, the characteristic methods of the field presently can be specified no more rigorously than that they are (or should be) derived from the social sciences. But the third question, which demands the establishment of criteria for the evaluation of work in comparative education, has remained largely unanswered, both in the larger world of work in comparative education and so far in this volume.

Such criteria are most urgently needed everywhere in the field: by those who do research and write in comparative education, by journal editors who must judge whether or not to publish work submitted, by those who teach the subject and by students seeking to learn, and not least by planners wishing to base decisions for the reform and development of educational systems at least partly on the findings of comparative education. Yet it is no secret that the minimum criteria simply do not exist.

Writing in the field tends to be largely descriptive, anecdotal, or hortatory. Publishing is indiscriminate, and though every genre of work is represented the factual and narrative items vastly outnumber the carefully explanatory.

Courses in comparative education are characteristically haphazard and eclectic; beginning courses in comparative education offered in colleges and universities provide students with widely dissimilar treatments of the field, in both subject matter and method of approach. And woe to the planner, either national or international, who relies on the findings of comparative education to sustain his search for some guiding principles of educational development, for he will come away from a survey of the literature with very little of value.

This absence of generally accepted criteria against which to evaluate work in comparative education can best be explained by reference to the antecedents of the field. Until quite recently it has been dominated by simple curiosity about foreign lands and customs, or by a desire to borrow foreign practices or by the hope of promoting international brotherhood and cooperation.

These motives, while highly laudable, are inadequate bases to sustain a field of study. Only since the beginning of the century has the task of explanation moved to the center of the stage, and historical and philosophical methods been used to interpret educational and social phenomena with great perceptivity, scholarliness, and intuitive insight. But even here a consistent and defensible methodology has been largely lacking.

Comparative education for the most part has not had as its goal the provision of validated explanations, nor have its results been assessed, as a matter of routine, for their predictive value. In short, the real potential of comparative study has gone largely unexploited. Instead of using cross-national data to test the validity of statements about relationships between education and society, comparative education has for too long remained simply a pleasantly exotic field in which those who happened to have some experience of foreign education can busy themselves.

The development of the social sciences along empirical lines has, however, opened up a new arena for comparative work. Many propositions already validated in individual (case-study) situations are prime candidates for cross-national testing of their wider applicability, while many other propositions simply cannot be tested at all without recourse to comparative models and data.

Most important of all, perhaps, the method of work enjoined by an empirical social science approach provides the criteria needed for evaluating work in comparative education. Systematic, controlled, empirical, and (wherever possible) quantitative investigation of explicitly stated hypotheses is the hallmark of the contemporary social sciences; it needs to become a modus operandi of those who would call themselves comparative educators, too.

To the extent that the investigator in cross-national research is crystal-clear in his own mind and makes quite clear to his readers precisely which hypothetical proposition he is testing, he furnishes himself with a focus for research and his readers with a clear guide to understanding the implications of the results achieved. By contrast, to the extent that work using cross-national educational data is unsystematic, lacks explicit controls, appeals for proof to authority or intuition rather than to the facts, and ignores possibilities of quantification of variables it is poor social science and therefore poor comparative education . Unfortunately, to date, far too much of what passes for comparative education would fail on these essential tests.

Even in a single-country case study, it must be emphasized, only the most preliminary work can afford to proceed innocent of an explicitly stated hypothesis, clearly defined concepts and variables, and announcement of the minimum standards of proof to be accepted as validation of the hypothesis. Case studies that neglect these basic features of scientific work risk remaining isolated fragments of knowledge, unconnected to a wider understanding of the phenomena with which they deal. A series of separate country-bycountry studies is no substitute for work that is overtly comparative from the beginning and is designed specifically to test hypotheses cross–nationally.

Although explanation is the ultimate aim of all scientific (and hence of all comparative) work in education, the process of explanation often yields some significant by-products. Important new information may be garnered about the educational and social systems of the world; concepts that previously appeared to have universal validity may be tested against the variety of global experience and shown to have validity only under certain specified conditions; and help may be provided to planners trying to improve the effectiveness of educational systems.

None of these by-products of the scientific, comparative enterprise is to be despised. Indeed, frustrated by the complexities of the problems we choose to examine and the inadequacy of the tools at our command, they may turn out to be the only secure fruits of our labors, and we may need to console ourselves with the thought that half a loaf is better than none. But insofar as investigators actually prefer the byproducts of quanta of information or concept-validation to the main goal of explanation, they are settling for second-best.

Without doubt, there is a place for work that sets out simply to collect cross-national material, describe phenomena, and classify data. For example, in the literature of comparative education there are many studies of curricular developments, examination requirements, enrollment patterns, administrative structures, modes of financial provision, and so forth. Furthermore, the continual updating and extension of such compendia and catalogs is a necessary and valuable contribution. But devising and developing a taxonomy of comparative education items is only a preliminary of, and perhaps a concomitant to fruitful comparative work. In no sense does it penetrate to the core of the undertaking.

The scholar who collects data on, say, teacher training practices for European secondary education, arranges them in convenient categories, discusses the validity of the categories and the reliability of the information, and goes no further, is stopping short just at the point where a comparative investigation begins.

He can, and often does, suggest tentative explanations for some of the phenomena he has uncovered, but it is the precise formulation of hypotheses, discussion of the theoretical justifications for advancing them, and the statement and operationalizing of concepts and indicators that represents the essence of comparative work in education. It goes far beyond the business of assembling data simply for informational purposes, important and difficult though even that task may be.

A special question arises concerning the role of history in comparative education. The historian aims at providing what is called genetic explanation of events in time; that is, he endeavors to demonstrate how particular events were caused by a convergence of prior happenings, forces, and factors. Thus, the historian attempts to explain the Education Act of 1944 in Britain by referring to the variety of social, political, and education phenomena preceding the passage of the bill into law.

Comparative educators, using historical approaches, have attempted to make genetic explanations of educational phenomena on a cross-national basis, and in the process have written some extraordinarily insightful and readable books. But these studies share the weakness of most traditional historical studies: their conclusions rely largely on the private insights of their authors, not only regarding which categories are valid and which data are relevant, but also on the matter of what quantity and quality of evidence constitute proof of a particular assertion.

The new history recognizes these difficulties in the older style of historical work and is moving towards a more empirical and, where possible, quantified approach. As this movement succeeds in establishing in historical studies what is essentially the approach advocated throughout this volume, empirically-oriented comparative educators will acquire an additional instrument for their work. To the scholarly insights of the old historians will be added a measure of the empirical rigor of the new, to the benefit of both.

The criteria of the empirically based social sciences are not offered as a simple nostrum for all the unsolved problems of comparative education. Indeed, advocacy of the scientific approach adds a host of new difficulties to the many already evident. The problems involved in proceeding toward rigorous, scientific explanation in comparative education are not to be dismissed lightly.

In education, as in the wider social context, both data and concepts are far from satisfactory. Data abound in some areas while remaining quite scanty elsewhere. Not only is the accuracy of much of the available statistical information highly questionable, but the reliability of nonquantified, descriptive material is very limited.

More confusing still, the margin of error or the extent of unreliability is unpredictable, varying according to the country observed, the date of collection, and the kinds of data reported. Concepts tend to be at least as elusive. For example, the common use of such terms as democracy, socialization, or even secondary education as categories for observing, grouping and interpreting data cannot be satisfactory in the absence of agreement on operational definitions. Yet even generally acceptable, functional definitions are difficult to achieve.

Perhaps comparative education is suffering more from the imprecisions inherent in the term education than from vagueness in the term comparative, but whatever the source of the difficulty, typologies and explanatory concepts in comparative education remain crude, questionable, and largely unvalidated. Data and concepts tend to be narrowly ad hoc, and notions of causality are at best primitive. These are the hallmarks of any field of study in the first stages of its search for a distinguishing methodology and universe of discourse.

Concern with data and definition of concepts must not be allowed to obscure a more important goal, that of exploiting the full explanatory and instrumental values of comparative studies in education. Though the explanatory value of work motivated by the desire to import foreign educational practices or to develop a spirit of international harmony has not been high, there is a sense in which useful lessons can be learned.

Sir Michael Sadler was right when he saw the practical value of studying foreign education and society in the chance to improve understanding of one's own country. Isaac Kandel, too, was right when he viewed each nation's educational system as a species of laboratory where a particular attempt was being made to solve a more general set of social, political and historical problems. But realization of the instrumental and learning potential of comparative education depends upon using a method that will avoid the a prior judgments and biases that have characterized so much of the earlier work.

As one observer has put it, the instrumental value of comparative study is great, provided one can avoid the three main traps of foreign observation: the Pago-Pago fallacy, which tends to say of everything, "How quaint!" the Victorian lady-in-waiting fallacy, which leads us to wrinkle our noses in disgust and exclaim, "How wrong!" and the Judy O'Grady fallacy, which dismisses the wild variety of human experience with the easy plea, "It's the same the whole world over!"

Especially in studying foreign nations and cultures, bias is a major problem, whether it stems from a conscious attempt of the investigator to prove a case for the superiority or inferiority of his own country's education, or from an unconscious imposition on data and conclusions of merely personal or parochial values implicitly assumed to be universal.

Although there are grave problems inherent in every effort to study education and society comparatively, and severe additional problems raised by attempts to apply social science techniques to comparative work, the promise both of the general field of comparative education and of the specific methods advocated here remains great. The potential of the field, as we have argued, lies first in the promise of extending the generality of propositions beyond the confines of a single society; second, in the provision of an arena where propositions, testable only in a cross-national context, can be investigated; third, as a field for interdisciplinary work; and finally, as an instrument for planners and policy makers.

These potentialities will be realized only if satisfactory criteria for assessing contributions to comparative education can be developed. This in turn is contingent upon securing convincing methods of validating research findings. Intuitive studies, even when bent on explanation and concerned with causation, provide inadequate proof; empirical investigation offers the hope of a more satisfactory system of validation. It provides an instrument for cutting through the circularities of reasoning inherent in even the best of the traditional studies.

On the other hand, a purely inductive approach cannot be advocated. Simply to roam over the facts and to draw generalizations from them invites repetition of the errors of the past: encyclopedism (only now perhaps rendered more economical by the efficiency of electronic computers), observer bias and arbitrariness, and absence of criteria to guide the observer on the questions of which data are important and how much is enough.

A method that incorporates the intuitive insights and speculative reflections of the observer, but submits them to systematic, empirical testing appears to offer the best hope for the progress of comparative education. It provides teachers with something teachable and students with something eminently learnable and useful. Furthermore, it provides a criterion for evaluating research in comparative education, since each step in the process of investigation is always open to scrutiny, and conclusions and inferences are publicly arrived at.

Researchers find built in to the hypothetico-inductive approach the expectation that their inquiries will be replicated and the validity of their data, methods, and conclusions subjected to the critical inspection of peers.

Finally, because it is heuristic and open-ended, the social scientific method offers the researchers of one generation the hope of building securely on the work of their predecessors.

Clearer aims when doing research and more precise criteria after research has been completed are the essential requirements at the present stage of comparative study. The comparative educator needs to start with the questions: "Where do I want to go?" and "How will I know when I have arrived?" for the answers point the way toward an influential, intellectually cogent, and elegant science of comparative education.

11

National Education

Thought and word, it has been well said, are inchoate action; and every institution that considers its moral or legal right as an insufficient guarantee for its continued existence tries to control not only men's actions but their thoughts and words.

Every government that is interested in maintaining the *status quo* thus finds itself invariably trying to mould the thoughts and opinions of men, not merely in those spheres that directly affect the governmental institutions but in all the varied phases of human activity.

The best method of such a control has been at all times recognised to lie in the effective manipulation of the educational machinery of the community. The extreme republicanism of the government of France is being imposed upon the community by its educational policy, just in the same way as the autocratic monarchy of Prussia tried to perpetuate itself by a State control of the universities.

This principle, which has been from time immemorial the mainstay of every party in power, is best illustrated by the educational policy of the British government in India. Indeed, education seems to have been at no time free and unhindered in our country. Brahminical India used all the power which it possessed in trying to impose a status education which would perpetuate its own supremacy. It is easy for a critic to find exact parallels for our present educational disabilities in the general policy of Brahminical India. If we now object that education is given to us through the medium of a foreign language, it could effectively be pointed out that Brahminical India did the same thing, insisted on education through Sanskrit, which being the language of the conquering Aryans, was a foreign language to the vast majority of the inhabitants of that time as English is to-day. If we now object that naval and military education is prohibited and opportunities for higher engineering and constructive skill are denied to us under the British government, it could be pointed out that the punishment for a Sudra *hearing* the sacred words of the Vedas was mutilation. And that at no time of Indian history were educational disabilities so wide, and so rigorously enforced as in Brahminical India.

Such an argument does our cause no harm. It only establishes beyond doubt our principle that the powers that be have always tried 'to continue to be' by an effective control of opinion through the educational machinery. In India under Britain, as in India under the Brahmins, the preservation of racial supremacy is the fundamental and apparently unalterable maxim of policy. This distrust of freedom is the basic fact that we have to face, and any reconstruction of Indian educational values must be preceded by a change in this essentially wrong attitude to wards social growth.

Indian education is now wholly under the control of the State. The state manages and moulds educational policy and ideal as thoroughly and as effectively as ever the Church or the Jesuits did. The universities are founded on government charter and exist on its sufferance. Their governing bodies are government controlled. Their examinations are the only gateway to government appointment, thus discouraging all independent educational attempts. It inspects the curriculum, discourage the extensive diffusion of certain others, and tries to circumscribe the intellect in narrow grooves. It limits the activity of the teacher, prohibits him from having opinion on vital question, imposes upon him obligations which no honourable and patriotic citizen could accept. The history of the progressive systematisation of this distruct of freedom, of the progressive adoption of the principle of status education, of the progressive elaboration of the methodology to realise that principle.

The universal control of our educational institutions by the state is the most demoralising fact in the complicated problem of our national existence. Even such institutions as the Benares Hindu University, which comes in to existence with the blessing of the Government, do not by any means escape this vigorous and all-embracing control of the Indian bureaucracy. It is suspected and watched. The Government reserves the right of disapproving the nomination of any professor. It refuses to sanction Hindi as the medium of education. When even such a conservative institution is under suspicion, it is impossible that independent experiments such as the Gurukula and the Santiniketan should be left alone. The Government is keeping a watchful eye on them and we may be certain that it would never allow those institutions in any way to interfere with its general policy of educational control.

This however is not the only defect of our educational policy. An education for the express purpose of maintaining status relations necessarily tends of maintaining status relations necessarily tends to become formal. Its methodology becomes rigid and loses its meaning. As it is animated rigid and loses its progression but only by a desire to better the machinery, its formalism comes to be of the most deadening type ensuring a 'Chinese' type of stationary society. Such a process is inevitable and the educational policy of the British Government since 1835 has shown this more conclusively than ever.

Macaulay wrote his omniscient minute in that year. It laid once and for ever the basis of the Anglo-Indian system of education. We are not concerned here with a criticism of that system; our business in this essay is to analyse and interpret a National educational ideal. What we have to recognise with regard to the Anglo Indian system is that from 1834 its tendency has been to become progressively unreal, so that to-day it is a machinery which stunts our growth, a mass of unreality expressing no meaning and capable of expressing none, a system which tortures us by its elaboration, and kills our mind and soul by its barrenness.

Lord Curzon was the only Viceroy who came to India with any ideas on education. He recognised the mischief that had been done in the preceding 65 years and valiantly tried to reform it. In an address to the Educational Conference at Simla he expressed in his own magniloquent style all the glaring defects of the Anglo Indian system. He declaimedwith vehemence against the 'attempt to transplant the smaller educational flora from the hot houses of Europe' into an entirely different atmosphere. The never-ending revolution of the examination wheel by which the educational fate of a man was settled met with the violent disapprobation of Lord Curzon, Indian education, he admitted, is restricted in its aims and destructive in its methods. 'It is of no use.' says he, 'to turn out respectable clerks, munsiffs or vakils if this is done at the expense of the intellect of the nation. '

Lord Curzon's criticism of the educational policy of the British Government was crushing and conclusive. But his reformative attempt, it must be admitted, ended in a total failure. His ideal was not free education, but an education, controlled by the State. The Apostle of Efficiency cannot tolerate a variety of institutions with different ideals and methods. They must needs be regulated by the State. The Universities already under Government influence must become directly Government controlled; otherwise they won't be efficient—as though efficiency were the end of educational institutions. The Raleigh Commission reported very much as Lord Curzon desired. In spite of the vigorous protest of Sir Gurudas Banerjee, the Commission came to the conclusion that the cost of higher education should be raised and that a greater control of the university by the Government will tend to educational efficiency.

The Indian national movement had watched with great anxiety the restless activity of Lord Curzon in this field. The Congress awoke at last to the extreme importance of the problem when Lord Curzon showed them that the future of their country was being moulded by an Anglo—Indian Committee. Till now the Congress had shown a fatuous indifference to this necessity of a national programme in education and the fatal danger of allowing an alien Government full control of the training of the youth of the nation, patent enough to ordinary observers of political life, were completely ignored by the Congress until this time. It is true that a few devoted spirits of the Congress movement had for a long time seen the imperative character of this problem. Surendra Nath Banerjee. Gopal Krishna Gokhale, and a few others had very early in their career recognised the necessity of national control in education and had realised that the problem of national education touched very vitally the life and death of nations. They had in their different spheres tried to solve that problem independently of the Government. But the Congress itself confined its activities to the strictly political problems as if the source from which all political action derived its motive force was not a question of politics at all.

But the threatening activity of the Viceroy awoke the Congress from its characteristic slumber. The changed character of the Congress, its new and unbending nationalism, its gradual emancipation from the Bombay clique, all contributed to the general activity and life which that movement showed during the latter part of the Curzonian regime. Lord Curzon's attempt to raise the cost of higher education was therefore met with a direct challenge. The Congress at Benares enunciated the formula of 'National Education under National Control.' Later events showed that this formula was interpreted in two entirely different ways by the two different parties. The vital difference between the two parties showed itself even in the interpretation of this non-political programme. To the Moderates of the Gokhale type national education and national control meant only an extension of the field for Indians in the Service and a greater study of Indians subjects in the universities. To the Nationalists this formula meant something very different. They interpreted it to mean the complete nationalisation of educational machinery and absolute boycott of all the institutions where the hand of the Government was suspected. Thus the Congress committed itself to an undeined formula which only covered, as all formula are perhaps meant to cover, fundamental differences of opinion. Behind the united demand for national education under national control which the Congress put forward in 1905, it was easy for the acute observer to see the uncompromising hostility between the Moderates and the Nationalists.

The cleavage of opinion on the matter became vital when from the domain of congressional discussion an attempt was made to translate it into the field of action. Bengal instituted a Council of National Education and it seemed for a time that the educational monopoly of the Government was passing out of its hands. But the Bengal attempt failed as it was bound to fail. A division between the purse and the brain of a concern cannot indeed conduce to its success. The Hindu revival which was at the basis of the new nationalist movement had scarcely affected the moderates. They were still the 'crowning product of the British rule,' as one of them expressed it. They still looked to England for inspiration. They were unwilling to nationalise education completely lest 'the crowning product of the British rule' might become extinct. The Nationalist party had no such fears. They looked not to Europe but to India itself for inspiration. To them, all the faith of the moderates in the wonderful effects of the western education was but one of the many vile superstitions which the Anglo Indian system had sedulously cultivated. As the experiment of national education progressed, this divergence of opinion came more and more to the front. In a few years' time the whole system had completely broken down. Few tears need be wasted on the failure of this scheme. It only emphasised once more the fundamental political truth that all great institutions that shape and mould the destiny of nations begin in individuals, and not in collective organised groups. The great pre-revolutionary educational force in Europe was the Society of Jesus and it had its origin in the brain of Ignatius Loyola. Comenius, Pestallozi and Froebel and all the rest of the great teachers that have revolutionised the educational systems of the world and thus directed the thought and evolution of mankind into widely different moulds were individuals and the institutions that they set up did not owe their origin to the collective initiation of a group but to individual attempts to realise what society had generally laughed at as impracticable dreams. In this matter as in others real progress can come only by the action of individuals and the Bengal National Council of Education had this 'basic fault.' It was left for an individual, the most eminent that Bengal has produced after Chaitanya, to realise the ideal of National Education and Rabindranath Tagore's school at Bolpur can in this way be said to be the contribution of Bengal to the solution of this problem. We shall examine it later.

The Bengal Council was perhaps the most typical attempt of modern Anglicised and 'progressive' India in the educational field. But the most remarkable experiment both in educational ideal and pedagogic methodology came not from Bengal but from the Punjab. The Arya Samaj and the Hindu revival brought with them not only a new interpretation of the doctrines of the Aryan religion but also a new outlook on life, and a new conception of mental training. The Aryas recognised more fully than the Congressionists that the development of an independent system of education must precede all attempts at reconstruction and readjustment of the bases of Indian society. This new attitude and outlook materialised in the Gurukula at Hardwar.

The Gurukula ideal of education is essentially different, not only from the Anglo-Indian system but from the educational ideals of any of the modern countries. It is an attempt to revitalise the ascetic spirit of the ancient Hindu culture. It is an experiment in assimilating as much of modern science as is essential with the spirit of our ancient civilisation. The Gurukula tries to found an Indian University, Indian in every sense, out of which would arise a new Indian nation breathing the old and sacred atmosphere of the Vedas but tasting and relishing all that is useful and fine in the thought, literature and science of the modern nations.

This is, we might say at once, the right ideal. But in the systematic elaboration of its methodology the Gurukula system tends both to an ascetic severity, and a cast-iron formalism. In taking the children away from the realities of domestic life and interning them for very nearly 18 years in the unreal surrounding of a Himalayan monastery, the Arya Samaj theorists show an absolute ignorance of the fundamental ideas of education. They forget the essential truth that an education which does not keep the child in touch with the realities of domestic life is no education at all; that to be left after 20 years of restless mental activity in an unexplained and to him inexplicable environment is not only harmful but positively destructive; that such a divorce of life in knowledge and life in reality can only lead to intellectual insincerity absolutely incompatible with true education.

The answer which the Aryasamajists make to this argument is that family influence in India is on the whole detrimental to the full development of the child and that the less he sees of his family in his formative years the better. This line of argument takes for granted that it is for his elders to settle what is good for the child, and in effect that the mind of the child is soft clay to be moulded and shaped as his elders desire. This is the doctrine against which the great Comenius and the no less great Rousseau preached with such unanswerable logic. The child's mind is not a virgin soil to use the famous metaphor of Comenius, to be sown by the teacher in a formal pattern. This is the basic flaw of the Gurukula system. It treats the children as so much raw material to be manufactured by a longtime process into pious, patriotic, philosophical and literary citizens capable of carrying the Message of the Great Arya Civilisation to all the known parts of the world.

Another and perhaps more effective criticism on the Hardwar ideal is that it is essentially revivalistic and therefore lacking in the element of progression. The ideals of yesterday are useless if they are not interpreted from the point of view of the life of to-day . The *Gurukulas* were prevalent full 2000 years ago and it is a vain attempt even if it were possible to revitalise an institution which flourished under widely different conditions and in a very different time. No nation can go back and least of all could we who boast of having had a continuous civilised existence of 4000 years, afford to go back to a particular phase of our national evolution. Societal traditions have their place in educational systems and in India, or at least in the India of the Indians, such traditions are stronger than even a traditionalist could wish. Every system of education should have both the binding conservatism of the social tradition and the fluidal mobility of a progressional element. The former is the hold of the past. The latter is the problem of the present and the call of the future. In Indian institutions the former is predominant; the latter is deplorably lacking. The Gurukula of Hardwar shows this defect of our institutions more conspicuously than anything in modern India.

The principle of individual freedom so crushed out in Hardwar for uniformity of pattern is found to be the fundamental principle of the *Santiniketan* of Rabindranath Tagore. The Bengal Council was not an educational experiment; it was a solemn futility meant to be an educational demonstration. But that unrest which drove the fatuous Congress to do something in its own extremely futile manner led the most fertile mind of modern Bengal to embark on an educational experiment the most unique of its kind in India. The School at Bolpur showed once more that experiment must begin, especially when the raw material on which it is begun is the most precious element in the nation, with the tested instincts of creative genius, and not by the commercial application of a uniform principle. The Santiniketan grew out of Tagore's brains as the Academy grew out of Plato's and the Bonnal School out of Pestalozzi's dreams.

Educational practice has from time immemorial been divided, as one writer well put it, into that which works through rules more than through sympathy and that which puts sympathy before rule. The Hardwar system exemplifies the first: the Bolpur system exemplifies the second. The Hardwar system works through the class, assumes a uniformity of intelligence and interest. Santiniketan works through the individual, treats 'each case on its own merit' with no uniformity of pattern and preconceived notions as to what the child ought to be when grown up. It assumes that every child is born good but with different degrees of instinct, feeling and intelligence. The aim of all is the same but the capability of realising it differs in degree. Thus each individual should be ministered to in the fashion that fits him and brings out and developes his qualities and not in the measure of another's wants and desires.

The teaching of tradition tends to societal control: individual liberty tends to social freedom; but societal control and individual freedom; are not incompatible when we recognise that, individual liberty finds its highest and truest expression only under societal control. But though they are not necessarily incompatible popular instinct is right when it draws a dividing line between the rigid formalism of the traditionalist and the sympathetic guidance of the individualist. The Gurukula stands for the control and therefore for the limitation of the future by the experience or the realised ideal of the past. Bolpur stands for the ideal of free development deriving inspiration from tradition, but hindered as little as possible by the deadweight of a desire to bring back into existence an institution out of which life had flown centuries ago.

Both the Gurukula and the Santiniketan are only individual attempts at the solution of a national problem. Realisation of great principles can only come through the spontaneous energy of individuals: but institutions meant for remedying crying evils have to originate, not in the creative genius of a single man, but in the general consciousness of a nation and its collective initiative. The Benares Hindu University is essentially a work of this kind. It is not the realisation of a great principle or ideal but simply an attempt to remedy the most conspicuous of all the evils of the Anglo-Indian system of education. Macaulay had written with the sublime impudence that characterised his peculiar talents that the Indian *risorgimento* can come only through the wide diffusion of European culture and that Indian civilisation, whatever it may have been worth, was as dead as the Assyrian. The falsity of this view was manifest from its beginning. Its importance lies in its results rather than on its merits. From that day dates the deplorable divorce of Indian education from Indian thought and Indian feeling. The universities of India were but factories where a few were manufactured into Graduates and a good many more wrecked in the voyage of their intellectual life.

What the Hindu University has attempted to do is to bring Indian education into conformity with Indian culture. With its many and patent faults we need not concern ourselves. What we should recognise clearly is that the Hindu University differs essentially from the Anglo-Indian Universities in that the former exists for the express purpose of interpreting Hindu culture, and as the material and tangible expression of the cultural unity of India. Thus the Benaras University is a far-reaching experiment remedial in its primary character but creating a new atmosphere, vitalising old traditions, interpreting racial ideals and spreading the thought and feeling of ancient and modern India.

Here we have the right ideal. But in the execution of that ideal lies unsolved the problem of national education. The Benares University is as effectively controlled by the Government as its own institutions. The experiment is so important, the probable effects from it so far-reaching, the success or failure of it so vital, that the Government acting on this irrational distrust of free and unshackled education considered itself justified in imposing its own authority on it. But when all is said of the influence of Government, of the reactionary character of any institution that exists to interpret ancient ideals and not primarily to search for truth, of the mischief that it may originate due to its sectarian character of the great and crying evils such as the caste system which it may perpetuate, when all is said, the Benares Hindu University remains a capital fact which is bound to influence our national evolution certainly in a much better way than the Anglo-Indian institutions.

Its chief defect we have noticed before. It is remedial and therefore supplementary. It does not solve the educational problem of nationalist India. It does not even face the issue boldly. But this must be admitted that it is a great step forward. It is the natural nucleus of any national experiment in education. Around it would gather institutions united in their diversity, inspired by the majestic flow of the sacred Ganges which now as before is held sacred by the great majority of Indian Population.

Up to now our work has been entirely critical and estimative. The greater task of stating and analysing the problem and interpreting the tendency of the new nationalists towards it remains.

What most strikes anyone who approaches the problem of Indian education from any point of view, is its appalling magnitude. Here is a country with a population of 315 millions whose future salvation depends greatly upon the careful study and the right solution of this problem. Here is a not inconsiderable portion of the human kind whose destiny depends a great deal upon those who have the foresight to see and the energy and the enthusiasm to realise a right educational ideal. The problem is indeed bewildering in its variety. It is an if one entered a primeval forest, thick and crowded with trees, with no gleam of light to guide one's steps, with soft grass and wild creepers covering many a pitfall. But if it is difficult, nay almost impossible to traverse, we must also admit the temptation to persevere in the attempt is as great, seeing that beyond this dark and untraversed forest lies the promised land, the land of a free and educated population.

Out of the wild variety of this problem three factors stand out towering above the rest. They are the questions of a common language, of the education of women, and of the general policy and the institutions by which to realise it. The first question is whether India should be treated as a cultural unity whether a new All-Indian language, a modified *Arya Bhasha* embodying not only the culture of Ancient India, but assimilating the contribution of the Mussalman inhabitants should be consciously evolved. The second question is whether we should perpetuate the status relation between men and women in education, whether an absolute equality of sexes in educational practice is not bound to affect adversely the free progress of family and social development. Whether a different educational ideal for women is not desirable, possible and practicable. The third question is the question of the educational principles and institutions; whether a uniform general policy is desirable, if desirable how far it should be carried, whether the realisations of great principles does not come from the co-ordination of tested units, whether it would be more desirable to nationalise interest than to universalise it. Such are the main outlines of the problem which the nationalist has to face not only when India governs herself but even to-day, because without at least a partial solution of the educational problem Swaraj would remain an unrealised ideal.

The first question—that of a common language, is one of the most pressing of our problems not only from an educational, but from a general nationalist point of view. Without it all our efforts at united action must for ever remain virtually ineffective. It is true that before the British dominion India was one in feeling, thought and culture. But to-day by the influence of a foreign language her different provinces are tending to a difference even in these vital points. This process of disintegration can be arrested only by a common language. Is such a thing possible; if possible, can Indian Nationalists unaided by the all-pervading machinery of government realise it? This is the first question we have to answer.

That English can never serve the purpose of a common language is a manifest fact that requires no argument to prove. It is so utterly foreign to us that education in it involves an enormous waste of mental power. This waste is suffered not only by those whose natural gifts are so overflowing as to be indifferent to its effects but by everyone who desires to be educated in India. This is the explanation of the enormous number of failures in our universities, and of that unique and therefore all the more heartrending phenomenon of the Indian educational world the "failed B.A." English can never become anything but the language for a microscopic minority of our inhabitants—the *cidevant* Eurasian. For us Indians it is and it will ever be a language in which to commit literary suicide, a tongue which stifles our expressive faculties, a medium, of expression which kills all the thinking power of our mind. The use of a foreign language as the medium of our higher education leaves us without a national genius in literature, in sciences and in thought. Lord Curzon was essentially right, though in a negative sense, when he said that the raising of the cost of higher education would tend to the betterment of India. Such an administrative act would limit the classes who would be affected by this intellectual ravage. It would confine the intellectual exploitation to the very few who are rich. The ordinary man, though he does not gain, surely does not lose by this arrangement.

Setting aside therefore the impossible sup-position that English can at any time be the common language of India we are left with two alternatives, to wit:—that we should choose as our common language either an unused language—a dead language as it is erroneously called—Sanskrit, Prakrit, or Classical Persian, or, one of the chief Indian vernaculars, such as Hindi, Bengali or Tamil. Of these two possible alternatives we can dismiss the first with a few words. True that Sanskrit has the merit of being known and studied all over India. It has also the merit of being the common basis of all the Indian languages. But at *no time* does it seem to have been extensively spoken in India and it is hardly possible that such a perfect language with all its different verbal forms could ever be spoken by the ordinary man. Persian, of course, has little claim to be the common language, and Prakrit, less.

Thus we are left with indubitable fact that the common language of India can only be one of the three or four chief vernaculars of India. The problem more plainly stated becomes this: which language are we to choose, from among the great vernaculars of India as the medium of higher education and the basis of higher communal life? The apparent contest is between Hindustani, Bengali and Tamil. But the contest seems to me to be only an apparent one. Neither Tamil nor Bengali, however cultivated their literatures be, can claim to be anything but the language of a particular province, a language spoken by a sub-nationality. But the case of Hindustani is different. The Hindustani-speaking people do not inhabit a particular marked out portion of India. It is in fact understood all over North India. It is understood in a slightly different form by all the Mussalman inhabitants of India and this fact alone makes its claim a matter of incontestable weight. Also it has a double alphabet which, peculiarly enough, is in this case not a hindrance but an additional claim. Its Nagari character makes it acceptable to all Hindus; its Urdu character makes it acceptable to all Mussalmans. Thus an acceptance of Hindustani would preserve the continuity of our civilisation both for our Muslim brethren and for ourselves.

The word Hindustani in the sense which Giersonhas given to it i.e. the language which the ordinary man speaks in Northern India, of which both Urdu and Hindi are mere literary offshoots. I am convineced that the bad feeling that existed between the two communies with regard to Urdu and Hindi does not effect oure argument in favuur of Hindustani.

It is an interesting and supremely important subject which we would have liked to discuss with greater elaboration had the limits of this essay permitted it. However before entering into the consideration of the next question we would attempt to answer one important objection that is commonly raised against the evolution of an Indian common language. Will not the adoption of any one Indian language, say Hindustani for example, as our *lingua franca* adversely affect the growth of our vernaculars? Will not the language in which Chandidas and Rabindranath Tagore wrote, say these, become in course of time, like Gaelic in Ireland, merely a dead tradition. Will not the sublime Tirukural, and the no less sublime songs of Ramdas, become like the wonderful poems of the Welsh bards, or the reputed epics of the Aztecs, mere object of curiosity for the antiquarians? The fear is legitimate, though groundless. The unique greatness of India lies in its wonderful diversity, and the ideal of a great India must always remain a diversity-ideal. Is the attempt to create a common language an attempt to create a uniformity of thought and expression? If it is, it is the word Hindustani in the sense which Gierson has given to it i.e. the language which the ordinary man speakes in Northern India, of which both Urdu and Hindi are mere literary offshoots. I am convinced that the bad feeling that existed between the two communies with regard to Urdu and Hindi does not effect our argument in favour of *Hindustani treason* to India. But under no conceivable circumstances can it be so. A second language taught and spoken as such can never replace a well cultivated mother tongue. The Bengali would be proud of his tongue as the Tamilian, the Gujarati, the Punjabi and the Malayali would be. They would be cultivated with greater zest and interest as the knowledge of the other Indian languages grew among the people. The objection therefore is groundless.

The proper education of women is the next problem. We have noticed that this problem has to be treated in three main lines, which are—first, whether we should perpetuate the status relation between men and women in education, secondly, whether the Indian family life does not demand a peculiar consideration in our educational problem, thirdly, whether a different educational ideal for our women cannot without breaking the continuity of our culture be evolved from our past.

The Indian nation can never be free till the Indian woman has ceased to be a slave. The Indian nation can never be educated till the Indian woman has ceased to be ignorant. I am not saying that the Indian womanhood is bound in slavery, or that it is blinded by ignorance. But the fact is that both in the relative status of sexes and in the idea of their education our present system affords room for very considerable modification. Is that modification to come through the activities of the social reformers or by the extensive diffusion of education. The difference between the two processes is great indeed. The social reformers try to impose their ideas on the generality, believing implicity in the infallibility of the reforms they advocate. The social reform temperament is the temperament of the missionary. On the other hand the process of social evolution through the wider diffusion of education is essentially a process of raising the general standard of opinion and thus making social reform the real expression of the conscious will of the community.

The question however arises whether we are to perpetuate the status relation of sexes in our educational system. The process of human evolution has surely been in the progressive differentiation of sexes which has now become a dominant and capital fact in all organised societies. The question of sexual status and education affects us in an entirely different way. At present the education of our females, such as it is, is entirely in relation to the family and not to the community. It is designed so as to make the child as it grows up a sweet and docile wife, an ideal mother, and when she reaches that age a self-sacrificing widow and able head of the family. This ideal is absolutely right as far as it goes. But it does not go far. It gives no place for the relation of women to the community. That relation is only implied in a very limited sense in the ideal mother. The business of the mother, as far as the community is concerned, according to this ideal, is to rear up ideal citizens. Naturally the question arises; does the social relationship of women end with rearing up excellent soldiers and sagacious politicians? Is she merely a means and not an end in herself? Can her faculties be fully and freely developed except in relation to the organised community, and, by limiting her to the smallest possible community, the family.

This brings us to the second question whether such an extension of feminine activity through a different ideal of education which, while perpetuating the healthy status relation of sexes, does not limit the female to the family, would affect adversely that vital point of our civilisation—the joint family system. It is by no means clear whether a higher individuation of the units that compose the family would tend to its breakup and it does not seem to be true that a freer interpretation of the position of women in society must lead to a disintegration of the family. What seems quite clear is that the joint family system as it is, with all its merits, tends very considerably to be a deadweight in the matter of freer, fuller and healthier family life, and a purification of it in its essentials can come only through the increased intelligence of women. Female education as long as it is imparted with the view of perpetuating the status relation of the sexes or on the other hand is based on the idea that such differences ought not to exist, would remain wholly unreal, disturbing the whole fabric of social organisation and sapping the very vital roots of all social existence. The education of women, such as is given in India to-day, inclines to the second alternative of ignoring the existence of sexual differences. That is why female education in India has been a totally disturbing instead of a consolidating, factor in social life. The Indian joint family life being indeed the realised truth of a thousand generations requires a peculiar consideration in our educational problem. Our ideal should not be to destroy but to purify it.

Does this ideal mean a break in the continuity of our civilisation? In spite of the opinion of Sir. C. Sankaran Nair, no sensible man has ever believed that according to Hindu ideals woman is created to minister to man's wants. The Hindu ideal of womanhood has been the ideal—not the European conception of a helpmate for man soothing his distracted hours—of a necessary counterpart without whom man by himself cannot attain salvation. What Sri Krishna asks his old playmate Kuchela when that pious devotee visited the Lord, is whether the female rishi suited him in every way. Indeed, according to the Hindu ideal man and woman are like the twin blade of a pair of scissors each impotent and insufficient in itself and capable of action only in combination. There is no superiority or inferiority in their relations. The right ideal is to make both the blades as keen as possible. This not only does not mean a break in the continuity of the Hindu tradition but is in entire conformity with its spirit. Such is the opinion of those who have devoted their life work to the cause of female education. Prof. Karve in founding the women's university has the same ideal. The Gurukula authorities in establishing an institution for girls gives the authority of orthodox Hinduism to this ideal.

Now it remains to discuss whether a general educational programme under these conditions is possible, and whether such a policy would be desirable as laying down the main lines of our educational development. A general policy means at least an attempt on the part of the powers that be to lay down certain things as the essential minimum of education. This power in the hands of a government generally tends to a control of the educational system. That is eminently undesirable, even if it comes from a strictly nationalist Indian Government. Education, unless we want to travesty it as a governmental instrument, must necessarily be free and unhampered. Thus a general policy can be laid down only to this extent, that is, the Government while encouraging, by every means in its power, should leave education outside the scope of its general activities except in so far as to remedy such manifest evils as a monopoly by any particular community, or a general in activity in any particular field. The Government should make primary education free and compulsory, but in no case should it insist on a general curriculum for the whole of India. It should be left to the discrimination of the local authorities prescribing however that in such subjects, as elementary Arithmetic of which the realised experiments of the past centuries have convincingly proved the utility, a minimum standard should be set. Only up to this has the Government any right of interference. In its educational policy the Government's activity should be one of co-ordination of educational institutions.

How then are we to realise this ideal of free and compulsory primary education, absolutely under local control, with the least possible interference from the governmental authorities? Is it by a system of free universities as in America or by a system of local effort supplemented by board schools as in England? The answer is difficult. But this much we can say without any fear of contradiction: A national programme of education in a country like India whose greatness lies in the rich diversity of her people, her ideas and her life, must essentially be a programme of local effort, of individual experiment and of provincial and national co-ordination. The Government can therefore never lay down an educational policy. If it did, such a policy would only create a mechanical process of instruction without any local colour, without any conformity with the realities of life, without any attempt to create intellectual sincerity. The realisation of any ideal, however good, can come only through the general prevalence of individual experiments in that direction. A state can never successfully impose it on the community, without transforming the character of that ideal.

To summarise what we have said till now. The nationalist movement in India is threatened to-day by a grave danger, that of an inquisitorial control by the state of the educational machinery. On the face of it, therefore, a nationalist programme in education becomes an imperative necessity. From the earliest days of the national movement the more farsighted among them had seen this. But their efforts remained mainly local until the hand to Lord Curzon imposed on an unwilling Congress the necessity of enunciating a general policy in education. The translation of that policy from the realm of speech to that of action ended in complete failure. But other experiments, such as the Gurukula which attempts to revive the ascetic spirit of the ancient Hindus and the Santiniketan which tries to realise the principle of individual freedom, arose out of that educational unrest. The Banaras University expressed in a tangible form the dissatisfaction of the best moderate mind with the Anglo-Indian system of education.

But a really nationalist ideal in education has not yet been authoritatively elaborated. Such an ideal must take into consideration the problem of a common language which in the opinion of the present writer can only be Hindustani. It must also give particular attention to the education of our women without attempting to disintegrate the joint family system. Finally a national educational programme must be a programme of local effort and national co-ordination. It is unnecessary to forecast whether such an ideal is immediately practicable. Any diversity-ideal can only be a matter of growth though not necessarily slow. The nationalist effort in education, therefore, should be directed not chiefly towards any attempt to mould the governmental policy but in building up local institutions of a great variety of character and embodying different national ideals and culture. Therein alone lies the hope of nationalism, for nationalism ignorant is nationalism ineffective.

Let us remember this and then we shall have no more fear of the future. In the past India was great: the present is not without hope: but with out united effort her future shall indeed be greater than either her present or even past. It depends upon us and let it not be said of us that the Spirit of Time in determining the fate of our Motherland tried us in the ordeal of fire and found us wanting.

K.M. Pannikar

12

Education For Nationalism And Internationalism

Radhakrishan wrote that :

> "We must refine the spirit of patriotism so as to make it a pathway from man to mankind."

No nation can survive if the people belonging to it are not prepared to sacrifice their all for its welfare. No nation can flourish if its citizens do not have a deep love and affection towards it and no nation can blossom if the people are not prepared to lay down their liv1es gladly in its service. It is, therefore, no wonder if in all ages in almost all the countries of the world and at all times nationalism had been regarded as the most pious, most desirable trait to be inculcated among the citizens.

Nationalism has been eulogised by the poets and idealized by the philosophers. It has been theorized by the politicians and actually practised by the men of arms. On the one hand, it has brought to the surface those urges, motives for actions and the feeling of patriotism which have all through been the distinctive characteristics of a human from his nonhuman ancestors and on the other those lesser feelings, low impulses and narrow attitudes which have brought miseries to the world in the form of wars, strifes and riots, The nationalism has been preached for the love of one's own countrymen and it has also preached for the hatred, aggressiveness an hostility against the people who belong to the other nations. We like the first and consider it as vital to human existence but we cannot neglect the second which is for the wiping out of the human existence itself. If we love the first can we hate the second is a broad question which is being discussed today in all the human communities. Some feel that nationalism in both of its aspects is worthy of practice. Others consider the second which they call as narrow nationalism as unworthy of practice and preach for only the first as fit to be inculcated among the citizens of the nations. A third group is of the opinion that nationalism has outlived its utility and now there should be developed the ideas on international understanding. They can be considered as the supporters of internationalism. However, the world today is neither prepared to accept nationalism in both its aspects, nor internationalism in the form of one world government or in some other similar form It is thinking in terms of some mid-course. It believes in the development of the feelings of nationalism in the context of internationalism. For achieving this end educations considered to be the most influential and efficacious agency. Let us explore this further and concentrate towards the role of education in spreading the feelings of nationalism and the plans for its reorganization so that the people of the world may develop an international outlook while all the time they remain devoted nationalists. By devoted nationalists we mean that they will have profound respect towards their nation and an unflinching faithfulness to it. By international outlook we mean that they will have feeling of universal brotherhood and a good–will towards the problems of all the citizens of the world.

Difference Between Patriotism and Nationalism

According to Brubacher. "Nationalism ordinarily indicates a wider scope of loyalty than patriotism". Ordinarily the meaning of nationalism is taken to be in broader sense than the patriotism. The patriotism is limited to the love of that country where one has been born. But in nationalism the love of one's race, language, tradition and culture all are involved.

History of Patriotic Education

The ancient Roman and Greeks believed in the inculcation of the virtues of patriotism among their people. The Jews during the Biblical, period also believed in imparting education for patriotism. During Renaissance in Europe the patriotic education was being given a high place. In 18th century in Europe a feeling began to develop that patriotic education should be given less importance and education for the welfare of all the countries and nations should be organized. But the French Revolution in 1779 had put a stumbling–block in the spread and growth of such an idea. After this revolution education became more patriotic throughout Europe, La Chalotais, Roland, Diderot and Condorcet in France; Francke, Hecher Fichte in Germany became the chief exponents of nationalism in education.

In United States of America, the feeling of nationalism developed in the 19th century. To Jefferson, Mann and Bernard goes the credit of promoting the nationalistic conceptions of education. In ancient India education was nationalist only to a limited extent. In this country, more stress was laid on moral values. The slogan "my country right or wrong" was seldom raised in India. In the British period, the education was far removed from patriotic feelings. The Britishers never wanted the Indian people to develop any sort of nationalistic outlook. The strength of their government lay in their keeping the masses ignorant and unpatriotic. But there was all time an under–current of patriotism which was flowing among the Indian people. The Indian National Congress under the leadership of Mahatma Gandhi had created a stir among the Indian masses and awakened in them a feeling of strong nationalism. After independence, education for nationalism attained different significance. It is now attuned to the development of such a citizenry which believes in the oneness of the country and the sacredness of its boundaries, which considers the constitution to be supreme and democratic way of living as the cherished goal, which strives for the socialistic pattern of the society and which is prepared to fight vigorously with the internal and the external enemies of the country.

Meaning of Nationalism

The nationalism is the cementing force that binds the citizens of a country in an unity. It motivates the man to sacrifice his individual good to the good of the nation. The patriotic citizens of a country sacrifice their own interests for the well-being of the nation. The spirit of nationalism makes the individual will subject to the national will and the nation takes the position of a metaphysical entity where nothing is considered above it. the individual citizens resolve their differences, close their ranks and bind themselves in strong bonds to achieve one goal and that is to serve the nation safeguarding it from external dangers. The force of nationalism is considered superior to all other earthly forces. It is through it alone that individuals are led to believe that they may attain their goals of life. An unpatriotic or anti-national person is considered as worst type of the sinner and a morally deprived person.

Education for Nationalism

An important aim of education is to socialize individuals and to bind them in the bonds of unity. Nationalism is the greatest force which makes unity possible in whole of the country. For the inculcation of the spirit of nationalism among the people education can play the greatest role. It is on account of this that almost all countries consider it their prime duty to provide facilities for such education to the children that they become better citizens and develop feelings of patriotism towards their country. There are also certain nations which believe that complete control over education should be exercised so that through it the children are moulded in such a manner that they always consider their nation or country as supreme which require an unflinching loyalty on their part. The organization of education in such countries is such that every educational aspect is controlled by the state and directed towards this goal that the children from the very beginning of their lives begin to consider *"country above everything else"*

Education for nationalism in reality refers to such education which is imparted for national unity and for the inculcation of the spirit of social service. This type of education is oriented towards national reconstruction and national progress. The national unity is possible only when the citizens belonging to different races, classes, social groups, states, province or cultural groups develop a feeling of love toward their nation and strive together for the national progress and for the furtherance of the national interests.

No nation can progress and prosper if its citizens are not adequately educated. Through education, the social and economic life of the country is made better and better progress is brought about in the nation. The nation always degenerates if there are superstitions, bad tradition and evil customs. For example, in India, the caste differences, low position of women in society and dowry system etc., have taken the nation to the downward roads of degradation. To eradicate the social evils and to encourage the feeling of nationalism education can play the most important role. The education directs the attention of the citizens towards social evils and creates such emotional and intellectual environment which takes the society towards purity and goodness. They almost all the educationalists are agreed on this point that Indian education be directed towards the inculcation of national feeling and the spread of social reforms.

The education helps in national progress when it leads to the economics betterment of the country. Through the vocational education the citizens of the State are prepared for earning their living and in this way there are brought reforms in their economic conditions. In our country, the poverty of the people is greatly responsible for the lack of the spirit of nationalism among them. But government of independent India is taking adequate steps towards the economic betterment of the people. Through the Five-Year-Plans, efforts are being made to bring about economic prosperity in the country.

Side by side with the economic and social progress the national feeling also develops through medium of a national language. The country can be bound in an unity through the national language. The citizens are made aware of the greatness of the country through it. It creates in them a love for the country, a pride in its greatness and a sentiment of patriotism. Therefore, it is extremely necessary that all the citizens are given training in their national language. In India, the constitution recognizes fourteen languages. Besides these there are many more languages which are mostly the different dialects of the same language. In this way there are a multiplicity of languages Constitutionally Hindi is recognized as the national language. But even after more than fifteen years of the promulgation of the constitution Hindi has not replaced English as the official language. More than this there is growing a bitter opposition towards its adoption. Some of the southern and eastern Indians are making a case for the continuation of English. They do not agree that Hindi should be given the place of the national language of the country. This is a bad situation. The language problem is assuming big proportions and is ready to strike at the very roots of national solidarity.

There is a great controversy about the part the religious education play in developing the national feelings. However, it seems that in those countries where the nation belongs to only one religious group there is more unity. But it must be remembered that same religion is not a precondition for national unity. In the present times, the religious education is not being much encouraged. The reason for this is obvious. In a modern country there are usually found citizens belonging to number of religious or denominational groups add it had become very difficult to decide the type of the religious education which ought to be given to all the citizens. Many countries therefore, feel that religious education should not be given any place in the school curriculum. But this seems to be not a very healthy point of view. For the moral development of the citizens of a country, the religious education is very necessary. However, in a multireligious country the religious education should not to be limited to the education of any particular religion but should be based on the great principles of all the religions.

In giving education for nationalism it is also essential that the individuals should be taught to sacrifice their interests for the interests of the nation. Since the individuals have a tendency to look to only their personal benefit, it is essential that among the citizens a respect towards the laws of the country be developed. The laws which are framed by the government are for the good of the citizens and they put a check on such of their behavior patterns and actions which have an anti-national or anti–social tinge.

Defects in the Education for Nationalism

That education which develops narrow and blind patriotism should be discouraged because such education develops narrow outlook the citizens. The citizens find everything good in their nation and everything bad in the other nations. Narrow type of education for nationalism develops such a feeling among the citizens that they lose all sense of proportion and justice, fair play and human consideration in their dealings with the citizens of nations. They follow the dictums of their own government in a mechanized way. Their individual ideas never find an opportunity to blossom. They are made weak, timid and inferior so far as their own nation and their government is concerned but are taught to hate, destroy and demolish everything belonging to the people of the other nation. Their personality is developed only partially and they lose all equanimity in those situations where the other people than their own are involved. For developing nationalism or patriotism to this extent education based on falsehood is encourged. The citizens are taught that history which is only a bundle of lies and those books whose every page is full of falsehood so that the glory of their nation is dramatised and the meanness of other nations is magnified. The government and organisation of their own country are idealized and everything associated with other nations is contemptuously described. The citizens are taught that their nation never commits errors, is never tyrannical and never takes wrong steps. The result of all to this is that the citizens forget that there are other nations in the world and there are other people who are in no way inferior to them. They many a time intoxicated with their own greatness attack the other nations and set a flame whole of the world. The main reason for the last two Great Wars was narrow nationalism. The Nazi Germany and fascist Italy have brought untold miseries to the people of the world through their preachings of narrow nationalistic philosophy.

In the end we say that education for nationalism should be given but it should not be for the inculcation of narrow nationalism. It is good to love one's motherland but this love should not create hatred towards the other lands. The education should endeavour to promote international view-point.

INTERNATIONALISM IN EDUCATION

Today the world has become more compact. The people living in distant regions and lands have been brought closer. The scientific inventions have reduced the distance by means of rapid modes of communications. Now any happening in any part of the world casts its influence over the people throughout the world. The people living in lands which were considered quite distant are now taken to be neighbours. If the war breaks our in Cypres of Vietnam, Whole of the world becomes alive to the dangers of war immediately. The social or economic condition of the one nation creates problems for a large number of other nation. Any internal happening in one country influences the conditions in the other countries. Thus all the nations take an interest in the happenings of the other nations. Any internal or external problem of a nation cannot be solved by itself unless and until it gets some sympathetic understanding of the other nations. In case such an understanding is not forthcoming then there develop tensions. The nations begin to prepare for war and the distrust of each other rapidly develops. Under such situation, any spark anywhere is considered sufficient to flame up whole of the world. It is, therefore,of utmost importance that education for international understanding should be given.

Growth of the Idea of International in Education

Pierre Dubius may be considered to be one of the early exponents of the international education. More than six centuries ago he advocated the establishment of international schools. He hoped that these schools would get finances from the expenditure saved through the elimination of war. In 17 th century, Comenius urged that there should be created Pansophic colleges. He thought that in these college scholars from all over the world would work together and bring about universal peace. In the 19th century we find a Frenchman, Jullien by name, who suggested the forming of a commission which was to gather and disseminate information among different European nations. His idea in the formation such a commission was to improve education everywhere in Europe and also to promote international peace. In 1912, President Taft of U.S.A was interested in the promotion of the idea of international education. In this connection, name of Fannie F. Andrews may be mentioned. President Taft made efforts to call an International Conference at Hague. But his efforts failed as a number of nations put impediments in its formation. Still in 1914 when war broke out such a conference met. After war, Mrs Andrews advocated the incorporation of an international office of education in the League of Nations. But the nations after the devastation of war were in no mood to think about such a proposition. The economic and political needs of the time were more urgent and so the efforts of Mrs. Andrews again failed.

There was no further development till 1921 when this idea reappeared at the suggestion of Leon Bourgesis. The League of Nations at his suggestion recommended that a commission of eminent educators and scientists be formed. This commission was to *"study the questions of international co-*

operation and education." Besides this, the commission was also thought to be a sort of advisory body to the League to advise it about the course of action which might *"facilitate intellectual exchange among the nations, especially as concerns the communication of scientific data and methods of education."* This proposal was, however, opposed and the word education was deleted. In 1926 a commission of intellectual co-operation was created. This may be considered to be the first international body to promote a better understanding among different nations through co-operation in intellectual spheres. But unfortunately this commission failed to achieve anything. The main reasons for its failure were: lack of real power attached to it, lack of official status,insufficient personnel and inadequacy of funds. A group of educators in 1925 independently founded an "International Bureau of Education." It was patronized by small nations but bigger nations kept themselves aloof from it.

At diplomatic level however, U.S.A. U. K. France and Germany organized 'cultural relations programmes." These programmes were organised to have better contacts with the people of the other countries and to make them better understand their own plans, policies and cultures. These cultural mission cannot be taken to be the promoters of international education as their functions were more in line with nationalistic outlook rather than with the promotion internationalism.

The rise of Fascism in Italy and Nazism in Germany encouraged narrow nationalism among the citizens of different countries. All the ideas of internationalism were thrown out and World War broke out in 1939. The Second World War, however, was responsible for focussing the attention towards internationalism. After the war nations began to make efforts that more international amity might develop and education began to be considered as the most important means to achieve this goal. During the Second World War itself the education ministers of those countries which were conquered by the Nazis met and deliberated upon the plans of educational re-construction after the war. After the war, the representatives of Russia and U.S.A. also participated in these conferences and in United Nations Charter provisions were made for the promotion of intellectual understanding and co-operation through education.

It was decided that 'in order to promote international stability the United Nation shall promote international cultural and educational co-operation." To put this in operation, a conference was called in London which created 'United Nations Educational, Scientific and Cultural Organization (UNESCO).

UNITED NATIONS ORGANIZATION

United Nations Organization was established as an agency responsible for the maintenance of world peace. Its membership was made open to all the countries of the world. The foundation of this organization was laid on the principle that the differences and the quarrels among various nations can be resolved through discussions and other peaceful methods. In the United Nations Charter, the clause containing the Human Rights was incorporated. These Rights provided complete freedom to all the nations to set up their own internal policies. In fact the main purpose of this organization was to encourage mutual friendship and universal peace. There were established many other subsidiary organizations attached to this big organization. They were UNESCO, World Health Organization and International Labour Organization. In the education sphere, UNESCO is performing the most important function for the promotion of world peace.

UNITED NATIONS EDUCATIONAL, SCIENTFIC AND CULTURAL ORGANIZATION (UNESCO)

In the preamble to the UNESCO constitution, the following words are of special significance and warrant careful attention:

> The Government of the States Parties to this Constitution, on behalf of their People, Declare that since wars begin in the minds of men, it is in the minds of men that defences of peace must be constructed.

> That a peace based exclusively upon the political and economic arrangement of government would not be a peace which could secure the unanimous, lasting and sincere support, be founded, if it is not to fail, upon the intellectual and moral solidarity of mankind.

For these reasons,

> The States Parties to this Constitution, believing in full and equal opportunities for education for all in the unrestricted pursuit of objective truth, and in the free exchange of ideas and knowledge, are agreed and determined to develop and increase the means of communication between their peoples and to employ these means for the purposes of mutual understanding and truer and more perfect knowledge of each other's lives.

In consequence whereof,

> they do hereby create the United Nations Educational Scientific and Cultural Organization for the purpose of advancing through the educational and scientific and cultural relations of the peoples of the world, the objectives of international peace and of the common welfare of mankind for which the United Nation Organization was established and which its charter proclaims. From the above it will be clear that UNESCO is a body mainly concerned with the common welfare of mankind and promoting peace and international understanding.

Education for Internationalism. It is only through education that internationalism can be developed. According to Bertrand Russell education may not bring internationalism from political point of view but education is the only agency through which it is possible to develop the feeling of internationalism. It is through education that the attention of the public can be drawn towards internationalism. Today, in the world, public opinion is the most potent factor in deciding about the peace or war. If public opinion is for peace then would peace becomes easier. Therefore, education should be so organized that it may promote the feelings of internationalism.

Aims of Education for International Understanding

In the present times the development of international understanding is considered **an important aim of education.** For the achievement of this aim it is necessary that obstacles in the path of international understanding are removed through education. In this connection the following are to be noted:

1. The primary aim of education is to develop a power of independent thinking. Through independent thinking the people will develop the capability of discerning good from bad, truth from falsehood. They will not be led away by false propaganda and will try to solve each and every national or international problem with insight, intellect and in an atmosphere free from anger and emotionalism.

2. Through education, the attention of the humanity will be directed towards the evil effects of war and the suffering and miseries caused to the people as a result thereof. Thus education will create a hatred towards war and a love towards peaceful living.

3. The education will focus the attention towards the evil effects of narrow nationalism.

4. The education will discourage the feelings of supremacy of certain races, colour or creed among the citizens of different nations.

5. The education will focus the attention towards the dependence of one nation on the other in the present-day world. It will inculcate a feeling among all the people that now no nation can live in aloofness. Each nation needs certain, material raw or finished which can only be supplied by the other nations. Thus, the needs of all the nations can be better satisfied if there is international amity and understanding.

6. The education will make special efforts to reduce the fear complex among different nations. The reason

for cold war is always a fear complex. This leads to a race for armament and the nations live in perpetual dread of the other nations. Russia is afraid that U.S.A. might not attack it and U.S.A. fears that if Russia is quite strong then it will attack U.S.A. and destroy it. Thus both the countries put all their energies in preparing for war and the world is brought on the brink of a major catastrophe. The aim of education for internationalism will therefore, be the eradication from the minds of different nations, of those complexes which lead to mutual hatred,fear and enmity.

In the end, we may say that the major aim of education is to prepare citizens for world citizenship. The meaning of world citizenship is that the individual pays attention towards the good of all the human beings. The individual understands that the citizens of whole of the world are his friends and he has to live with in close amity.

Curriculum for Education for Internationalism

For internationalism the curriculum for education should be properly organized. The following things are to be kept in mind in the framing of the curriculum:

(A) Curricular Programme. In the curriculum there should be included the cultural and artistic, 'endowments of different' nations and societies. There should be developed such a curriculum which is representative of the cultural heritage of all the nations.

1. Whatever literature is to be included in the curriculum that must be a part of international literature. In the curriculum of each nation, the best literature of the other nations must be included.

2. The scientific and technical education should be given from an international point of view. In the process of the development of sciences, various nations have participated and they have all given their best

contributions. The scientific inventions and discoveries have benefited most of the nation and they have been responsible in raising the standards of living of the human population throughout the world. It is, therefore, necessary that contents of the educational curriculum should consist of the study of the application of scientific knowledge to the eradication of hunger, want and poverty and the enrichment of the human life.

3. The curriculum in history should also promote the feelings of internationalism. The main aim of the curriculum in history should be to acquaint the pupils with the life and work great leaders of the world. In the teaching of history not only the culture of one's own country be given a place of importance but the culture and civilization of the other nations should also be taught. But it should be remembered that in teaching history the biography of such leaders of different nations be taught who are famous as the angels of peace.

4. In the geography curriculum, there should be the description of different nations of the world. The children should be made conversant with the customs, modes of living food, clothes, etc., of various countries. Besides this the curriculum in geography should include the descriptions of the agricultural products, the main industries, manufactured goods etc., of different countries. Special efforts should be made to create an understanding among the students that each and every country is dependent upon others for various types of industrial and agricultural goods.

5. The curriculum in a number of other subjects such as arts, psychology and philosophy etc., should be so organized that the feelings of internationalism are encouraged. Through psychology, the citizens of one country should be made to understand the

attitudes of the citizens of the other countries. They should also be made to realize that among all the people of the world there are similar impulses and tendencies. From psychological view-point this fact had to be made explicit that basically there are no differences between peoples of different castes, colours or nationalities. Similarly, philosophy by putting emphasis on the same fundamental aims of human life should encourage the feelings of internationalism.

(B) Co-curricular Activities. Through the co-curricular activities also internationalism can be promoted.

1. Through group games the children learn quickly that the individuals are dependent upon one another and they cannot live alone in the world. The international games and competitions between athletes of different nations also help very greatly in mutual understanding.

2. Through cultural conferences the feeling of internationalism can be developed. By celebrating the birthdays of all great leaders of different countries and by focussing attention towards their work and achievement better understanding among the people of one's country towards nationals of other countries can be inculcated. Besides this, in these conferences, the problems of the different nations of the world can be studied and their desirable solutions chalked out. In the schools and colleges, the magazines and other publications can be printed and exchanged with the schools and colleges of the other countries.

3. In the schools and colleges lectures and talks can be arranged of those great people of the other nations who might be visiting the country at that particular time.

4. The students should be made acquainted with the

miseries and the calamities which have fallen over the people of the other nations and they should be encouraged to collect subscriptions, etc.

5. Besides the above the children should be encouraged to have pen-friendship and they should be encouraged to develop such interests which may promote international good–will.

Methods of Teaching for Internationalism

For the promotion of internationalism such teaching methods should be adopted which discourage the feeling of narrow citizenship and develop the feeling of world cirtizenship. The teaching of different subjects should be done in such a way that international view-point is promoted. The teacher will be capable of inculcating the feelings of international brotherhood and international understanding when they themselves will have profound faith in internationalism.

Teacher and Internationalism

As described above, the personality of the teacher himself has an important place in the promotion of the feeling of internationalism among the students. If during teaching the teacher emphasizes international outlook on controversial questions then among the children the feeling of internationalism are easily inculcated. But if the teacher teaches from the narrow nationalistic point of view, then the children's ideas are not focussed towards internationalism. The teachers are always greatly responsible for the education of the feelings of jealousy, hatred etc., and for the promotion of the ideals of world peace. Their teaching may raise the belief of the children in the equality of human beings. They may teach that the differences of caste, religion, colour, etc, are only external covers and the human race is one. Thus they can inculcate the ideals of one world family.

13

Planning and Education

"Planning in general may be sufficiently defined as any attempt to organise resources for the attainment of a chosen end or ends; it is in other words, purposeful action." In this sense everyone can be considered planner. But its use is particularly made in connection with a 'Nation'. The nation plans for the good of the country as a whole. The planning in India is thus a purposeful action. It has certain objectives and ends to achieve. All of these are, however, directed towards the provision of the opportunities to the Indian masses to lead a good life. The welfare of all the citizens through planned approach toward s the harnessing of all the resources of the country is the basic idea in planning in this country.

The planning in India is essentially "Democratic planning". It is democratic because the ends or purposes of planning are not imposed from without. They are chosen by the representatives of the people in the Parliament. A government formed by a political party which has sought election on an election manifesto which had sponsored certain ends or objectives of national welfare when it tries to embody them in the administrative framework can not be accused of authoritarianism. The elected government in this country when puts its faith in planned development of the country to achieve 'a good life' for its citizens is planning democratically.

The present concept in democracy is based on economics of welfare. Ordway Tead has described it in these words: "The purpose of economic effort is the well-being of all the people. We do not live to work. Economically, consumption is the aim, and until the interests of all the people as consumers are taken adequate account of, the economic system is at *odds* with democratic profession." The interests of all the people either as producers or consumers have to be given attention to. Gone are the days when the problems of economics referred to the problems of production only and it was thought that production could only be stimulated if there is protection to the industry and huge profits for the owners are assured. Now the consumer is more in the central periphery of any economic system. Production is supposed to increase if there are more consumers and more consumers will be there if there is a wide distribution of income. This idea is basic economic idea in a democratic system today. Also democracy believes in equality principle. In economics it is expressed in terms of welfare principle which implies that there should be a more equal distribution of wealth It is assumed that the national wealth is produced by the collective effort of the whole people. Thus, for the general national welfare a greater degree of equality is necessary. It would be a logical consequence of "the democratic conception of justice". Economically, a more equal distribution is necessary because it will produce more consumers or we may repeat a phrase "distribution of purchasing power", as a stimulus for more production. More production leads to more national wealth.

To achieve the more rational distribution of wealth as well as to have integration and co-ordination in national economy a 'planed economy' is needed. The co-ordination as described by Berkson is the inter-relating of the productive forces of the nation as a whole: agriculture to industry; supplies of labour to available plants; imports to exports. Integration of the national economy, according to him "involves currency control, management of credits, guiding the investment of capital; co-ordination refers to the development of locality and regions but, above all, it means national planning under agencies of the federal government". The planned economy refers to the "looking towards the future, adjusting the economy to developing needs, to new discoveries and to changing facts". This means that planning will lead to the "progressive improvement of human life". It is a principle of liberalism which was and is still highly valued in democracy. Planning is scientific approach to settle the economic issues, to consciously regulate the forces of supply and demand, to achieve the individual good through the satisfaction of his social needs. It strives to achieve a higher standard of living through proper utilization of material and social resources of the nation. Thus we may again repeat that there is no conflict between the planned economy and the principles of democracy. What we wish to achieve through democracy for an individual and society we practically proceed to achieve it through a planned approach. This approach ensures the conservation of natural resources, conservation of human resources through adequate health and recreational programmes and social security. It provides equality of educational opportunities and assures an adequate standard of living.

There are some who object to planning since they feel that it is a totalitarian concept. They point towards USSR and say that the planning there has been done in a totalitarian set-up. They accuse the planning in India on two counts :

(i) Planning and democracy are two alien concepts. When there is planning there are restrictions on individual freedom. This comes in violent conflict with the principle of liberty in democracy. The government controls all the resources and the government becomes the sole determiner of the direction of individuals; efforts, may they be in the sphere of their personal, social or economic life. The government stamps its authority on all the means of production and distribution. The free trade and commerce are put under restraint and private enterprise is replaced by public enterprise. These things are acceptable in a communist regime or a regime where the totalitarianism prevails but not in a democratic country.

(ii) The planning in a democratic country cannot be successful. It is considered that the planning in a country like U.S.S.R. where there is a very high degree of concentration, economic and political power has been successful because of these elements. Since in democracy they will be lacking, the planning is bound to fail.

As may be seen, both these objections are to some extent contradictory to each other and if we successfuly answer the first one second one might still be there without any refutation. Anyway we may emphasize that the planning in a democratic country like India is essential. A free market and a free economy there has resulted in the concentration of wealth in a few hands while the millions have starved. Thus a restriction on the enterprise of unscrupulous and greedy people is necessarily required. Secondly, the national resources of the country require proper tapping. This can only be achieved where there is some planned effort. In an unplanned economy, some resources may undergo undue strains and stresses while others may go neglected. Thirdly, the internal resources alone cannot raise the standard of living or can uplift the masses. For this foreign aid is required. If this aid is taken on a national footing in accordance with the necessities for the planned development of the country it will rapidly be able to stand on its own legs. On the other hand, there are chances of either too little foreign aid or an aid given in such a manner that the country might be put under economic slavery.

These and many other reasons make planning a necessity in this country. Since we have already said that planning in this country has not been imposed from without but has been chosen and hence it is democratic in nature. In fact, it has followed an evolutionary process. It has evolved out with the 'socialistic pattern' concept of the society. It is not limited to the economic sphere but has extended to the total life of the citizens. It is centralized no doubt but its emphasis is on decentralized units at village level. It restricts the private enterprise but also promotes its activities so far as they are in national interests. It has been successful in democracy as the achievements of India's three plans indicate.

Social Objectives in Planning

The economic aspects of planning are quite obvious. They are nicely described by P. S. Lokanathan in a seminar on Planning held on November 26, 1959. He said, "The only reason we are driven to plan is the necessity to achieve economic goals bigger than are likely to be realised with planning. We are not content with the results that might be achieved with the resources that are now in sight....the whole point of planning is to increase productivity and savings and mobilise them for economic growth. This we can do by adopting policies aimed at national objectives".

To increase productivity and to achieve economic growth are laudable objectives but one has to realise that these objectives are meaningless unless the social existing atmosphere is fully taken into account and efforts are made to reform and re-orient it towards the objectives or ends desired to be achieved through planning.

A Government of India's publication clearly keeps social aspect tied together with the economic progress in planning. It says, "From the beginning, it has been stressed that the objective of planned development is not only to increase production and attain higher levels of living, but also to secure a social and economic order based on the values of freedom and democracy in which "justice, social, economic and political, shall inform all the institutions of national life." It is the primary aim of the plans to provide the basic necessities to all persons within the community and at the same time, to emphasise the place of human values in economic and social development.

"In December 1954, Parliament declared that the broad objective of economic policy should be to achieve the socialist pattern of society." In the previous chapter, we have described our concept of socialist pattern of society. To achieve such a society, the planning is of utmost necessity. The existing economic and social institutions of the country need to be replaced or transformed so that the society of our aspirations may be created. Thus an analysis of the present institutions with respect to their role in the evolvement of a socialist society and to make them vital instruments for the desirable changes in the social order is the task which has to be performed with care and on the basis of a planned programme. A socialistic pattern of society has the basis requirement of equitable distribution of wealth which should be produced more and more through better techniques of production in which science and technology play their role. Both the production and distribution are economic factors which have deeper social significance also. The means of production employed, the people involved in better production are as much important as the increased production. If the capitalist increases his wealth and keeps it to himself the community will not benefit by him, so also the community's interests suffer at the hands of a person who uses dishonest means to increase productivity. Such people keep money with themselves or the wealth is distributed among only a few while the majority goes on living in poor conditions. This is the negation of socialist ideals and cannot be tolerated. Thus planning for social and community development can never be ignored if the society on socialist pattern has to develop. The planning will not only be limited to the achievement of ends but also to the means adopted. Mahatma Gandhi has said, "For me the identity of means is as important as the identity of ends." This ideal has to be kept in view in planning. Pandit Nehru has also said, "so long as we do not adhere to right means, the end will not be right and fresh evil will flow from it. This was the essence of Gandhiji's message and mankind will have to appreciate it in order to see and act clearly."

The determination of social objectives, the means to attain them and the evaluation of the extent to which they have been achieved in order to re-define the objectives and replan the means are all linked with education. Even though the politician, the economist or the social worker may claim to take the initiative in all these fields the confusion regarding them can only be removed through a proper approach of educational leaders towards them. Thus, the effective role of education in planning cannot be over-emphasized.

Education and Planning

The education and planning are linked in essentially two ways. One is that planning itself is an educational process and second is that the fruits of planning can yield results only when the people are educated to make full use of the increased means of production and understand the objectives of planning and try consciously to achieve them.

The goals of planning and education in a democratic country are similar. Both aim at good life of all the citizens. While one equips the individual for living a good life the other supplies the means to achieve this ideal. The education trains the mind and shapes the heart. It inculcates the right ideals for social living. It creates faith in human dignity and human labour. It equips the individuals to earn their own living, to stand on their own legs and to achieve their welfare through their own efforts. The planning through the proper harnessing of the resources of the nation helps the individuals to bring a change for the better in their individual, social and economic make-up. It strives to achieve the objectives which education sets before the nation as worthy of achievement. In this process it also helps to develop the education system itself so that the educated men of the nation help in the building of a better social order and move forward to set higher targets of social and economic significance for achievement before the nation. Education is thus the means as well as the consequence of planning. Planning is the determinant and the determiner of education. Better education leads to better planning and better planning leads to the tremendous development in education both in its content and quantity.

Today planning has become the fact of our national life. We plan for progress and prosperity. India needs planning because it has to go a long way to achieve socialistic pattern.

She is backward and poor. Through proper control of her resources and their utilization, the nation has to be made rich and set on an onward march towards progress. India's five-year plans have these objectives in view. The Planning Commission has been set up in the country in 1950 to plan for the country's development . It is making five-year plans for the country for progress and for the attainment of goals and objectives for providing good life to the citizens. At the time of setting up the Planning Commission, the Government of India issued the following resolution:[6]

The Planning Commission will :

1. make an assessment oi the material, capital and human resources of the country including technical personnel and investigate the possibilities of augmenting such of these resources as are found deficient in relation to the nation's requirements ;
2. formulate a plan for the most effective and planned utilization of the country's resources;
3. on a determination of priorities, define the stages in which the plan should be carried out and propose the allocation of resources for the due completion of each stage;
4. indicate the factors which are tending to retard economic development and determine the conditions which, in view of the current social and political situation, should be established for the successful execution of the plan;
5. determine the nature of the machinery which may be necessary for securing the successful implementation of each stage of the plan in all its aspects;
6. appraise from time to time the progress achieved in the execution of each stage of the plan and recommend the adjustment of policy and measures that such appraisal may show to be necessary ; and

7. make such interim or ancillary recommendations as appear to be appropriate for facilitating the discharge of the duties assigned to it or on a consideration of the prevailing economic conditions, current policies, measures and development programmes or on an examination such specific problems as may be referred to it for advice by the Central or State Government.

In keeping with the above the Planning Commission has drawn a number of five-year plans. The first covered the period 1951-56, the second 1956-61, and the third 1961-66. The fourth plan was introduced only in 1969, after three annual plans. All these plans have the basic objective of "providing sound foundations for sustained economic growth, for increasing opportunities for gainful employment and improving living standards and working conditions for the masses". But as we have emphasized in the previous chapters in this book, the sound foundations for sustained economic growth, as well as for providing gainful employment opportunities and for raising standards for living, education is the most potent and vital factor. Thus, the five-year plans of this country have a great meaningful significance to educator. He has objectives before him and he has to plan his own work so that these objectives may be attained. The plans at the national level provide direction and resources to the educationist. It is for him to make full use of both in planning for the educational development.

We have here made an effort to draw three phases of relationship between planning and education. To enumerate them again, we may say,

(i) education leads to planning,

(ii) planning helps to bring qualitative and quantitative improvement in education,

(iii) planning at national level provides directions and resources to the educational worker to draw plans for education.

There may seem to be some overlapping between the second and the third phase. Let discuss these phases in some more detail.

Education Leads to Planning

An individual satisfied with his lot seldom resorts to planning. A nation well-contented will pay little head to planning. A nation, however, will resort to planning when it is conscious of its poor conditions and has high aspirations to improve its lot. Russia first of all resorted to planning because the Bolshevik revolution had acquainted the nation with its backwardness and had created a desire to raise the level and status of the nation. It was the academic mind in Russia which led to this realisation and the creation of such a desire. It was also the academic mind which realized that the progress and development of a nation requires phased programmes of nearer targets to achieve the distant goals.

The nation's progress is possible when its resources are harnessed, its means of production and distribution are re-oriented towards the desirable goals. The educated mind realized that no nation has magic lamp of Aladdin to bring prosperity and progress at one stroke. For this, a planned approach to the problem is essential.

The education helped in developing the concept of planning and in making the nation realize the importance of it. This task it did in three ways: (i) by making the nation conscious of its social and economic condition; (ii) by inculcating high aspirations, among the people of the nation to improve their lot; and (iii) by making them realize that their aspirations can only be realized if the nation proceeds towards the task of reconstructing itself in a planned manner. It has to take stock of the present situation and then to plan how it can achieve the goals which it aspires for.

In India, the consciousness of backwardness came with the political movement. The politicians helped imbibe the aspirations for a good life and emphasized the need for planning. But this does not mean that education has played no role in this country in motivating planning. It was through education that a window on the Western world was opened and the Indian mind was made conscious of the country's backwardness. The education broadened Indian's vision and out of his lethargy and fatalistic attitude of false contentment he was lifted to aspire for a better life. It was also education which made the Indian mind conversant with the success of planning in the progress of other nations and a realisation that the resources of the nation shall yield no fruits if their utilization is not done in a planned manner.

It may also be emphasized here that the success of plans depends upon how the people take to planning. If the people are ignorant and indifferent towards plans they will not prove to be beneficial. The reason is obvious. The people will not work for the achievement of targets set in the plan and will adopt critical attitude towards the plan itself. This will greatly obstruct the planners in their task. An example, may be given here. The production of fertilizers has been given a high priority in the five - year plans. Now these fertilizers are meant for the use of the farmer. The farmer is ignorant of their use and is full of superstitions. He looks with great suspicion at any attempt made to popularize them. Now non-use of the fertilizers means the failure of planning because as they are not used by the farmers they do not lead to high production. The money spent on them is purely wasted and the economy of the country is further shattered. The ignorant farmer plays in the hands of the opposition parties and becomes critical of the planners. He accuses them for plan failures while all the time he is really the culprit. Thus, education can in no case be divorced from planning. Education for 'successful planning' and 'plan for education' should be the all important slogans.

Planning leads to quantitative and qualitative improvement in education

The education leads to planning and the planning is successful through proper education. It is thus considered of utmost importance that planning should lead to higher quantitative and qualitative achievements in education. In fact, all the plans in all the countries keep education at the priority list in fixing the long-term or short-term targets. In India also education is being given an adequate importance in the five - year plans. It is expected that more education with better content will lead to higher social and economic development. Thus, the planning here has led to tremendous development of education both in content and numbers during the last three plan periods.

We may give some figures to emphasize how the educational development has taken place in this country during the three plan periods.

Table - Pupils in Age-Group 6-11

Year	Enrolment in classes I-V (in lakhs)			Percentage of population in age-group 6-11		
	Boys	Girls	Total	Boys	Girls	Total
1950-51	137.7	53.8	191.5	59.8	24.6	42.6
1955-56 (end of first plan period)	175.3	76.4	251.7	70.3	32.4	52.9
1960-61 (end of second plan period)	233.8	109.6	343.4	80.5	40.4	61.1
1965-66 (end of third plan period)	301.2	195.2	496.4	90.4	61.6	76.4

Source : Third Five-Year Plan, op. cit., p. 580

The above figures show that in each plan period a tremendous increase in enrolment in 6-11 age-group has taken place. The enrolment in 1965-66 increased nearly 2.5 times from that in 1950-51. This achievement is possible only because there is planned effort to increase enrolment.

The enrolment not only in the age-group 6-11 has

increased but in age-group 11-14 and 14-17 also there is tremendous rise. In the age-group 11-14 there were 31.2 lakh students in schools in 1950-51. In 1965-66 their number was nearly 97.5 lakhs. Similarly, in the age-group 14-17 there were 12.2 lakh students in 1950-51 in secondary schools. In 1965-66 their number was approximately 45.6 lakhs.

The number of Universities increased from 24 in 1950-51 to 32 in 1955-56, to 46 in 1960-61, to 55 in 1963-64, to 62 in 64-65, apart from 9 institutions recognized as of university status. This number is constantly rising.

These are all quantitative improvements. They definitely establish that planning leads to quantitative improvement. But they also enable us to evaluate the successes achieved in planned targets . For example, according to Directive Principles of the Constitution, universal compulsory primary education should have come to the country by now but the planning has failed to achieve it and the target is still distant.

The three plans have not only led to quantitative development but also to the qualitative. There have been concentrated programmes for the training of teachers and at present a large number of teachers in the schools are trained. These trained teachers are greatly helpful in raising the quality. The following table gives the number of the trained teachers and the training institutions in three plan periods.

Table - Trained Teachers and Training Institutions

Item	1950-51	1955-56 (likely achievement)	1960-61	1965-66
		Targets		
Training Institutions				
training schools	782	930	1307	424
training colleges	53	107	236	312
teachers	5379186	91249	91000	1266000
trained teachers	316124	423192	591500	949500

percentage of trained teachers	58.8	61.2	65.0	75.0
Middle School				
teachers	85496	148394	230000	360000
trained teachers	45569	86810	149500	270000
percentage of trained teachers	53.3	58.5	65.0	75.0
High/Secondary				
Higher teachers	126504	189794	229000	290000
trained teachers	68059	113307	155720	217500
percentage of trained teachers	53.8	59.7	68.0	75.0

Source: Third Five-Year Plan, op. cit., p. 575.

Thus by the end of third plan in primary, middle and high schools there were nearly 75% trained teachers.

There are also many schemes to improve the school equipment and to establish better community school relationships. The community's aid is sought in many school programmes such as organisation of enrolment drives, persuading parents to send girls to schools, construction of school buildings, and provision of additional equipment and furniture to schools and of mid-day meals and free clothing for the poorer children. The states, Madras, Kerala, Andhra Pradesh, Mysore and Orissa are making efforts to provide mid-day meals to the children. In Madras alone nearly one million more children have been benefited by the end of third plan over and above one million who were already getting this benefit at the beginning of the plan.

In the second and third plans of India, many steps have been taken to enlarge the content of secondary educational process. There have been established a number of multi-purpose schools with provision of a number of elective subjects alone with and in addition to the academic course. The improved facilities for teaching of science, provision of educational and vocational guidance, improvement of the examination and evaluation system have all been achieved to quite an appreciable extent during the plan periods.

Many important steps have been taken to provide science education in the secondary schools and to improve its teaching. By the end of the second plan, a programme of general or elementary science of an elective standard had been provided in about 4625 schools. To encourage the creative and original activity science clubs in selected secondary schools and training colleges have been established. Their number was 450 by the end of the second plan. In third plan 9500 out of 21,800 secondary schools were to have science as an elective subject also. The steps have also been taken to review and modify science syllabi in various states. To remove the shortage of science teachers and to improve the quality of science education, increasing facilities of science education are provided at the University stage and also arrangements are made for various types of in-service training in content and methodology for the existing science teachers. A scheme of science talent search has also been introduced with a view to identifying promising talent at the secondary stage and providing opportunities for its development.

During the first Two Plans, 2115 multi-purpose schools were established. These schools offered one or more practical courses in Technology, Agriculture, Commerce, Home Science and Fine Arts in addition to humanities and science. In the third plan only 331 new schools were added but the programmes have also been undertaken to consolidate the work done in this field and to strengthen the institutions already established. An integrated teacher training programme was undertaken and for this purpose four Regional colleges were established.

During the Second Plan, in addition to setting up of a Central Bureau of Educational and Vocational Guidance, State Bureaux of Educational and Vocational Guidance were established in 12 states. These Bureaux are providing training to the career masters and counsellors. They are also organising guidance services for schools and constructing tests. In the third plan, these Bureaux were further strengthened and helped to carry their guidance programmes farther into the field.

Besides the above steps for the qualitative improvements in the secondary education, a number of steps to strengthen the library services in the schools and to provide in-service training to the secondary school teachers through the extension service programmes were also undertaken.

In the University education there is much qualitative and quantitative improvement. To check the deterioration of standards by a great increase in enrolment in Universities and colleges, the third plan provided more facilities for diverting students to vocational and technological education.

The University Grants Commission is assisting the Universities and post-graduate departments of colleges in the development of post-graduate studies and research. Assistance during the plan periods is given to the Universities and colleges for additional accommodation, laboratory equipment and library facilities. To strengthen the science syllabi in the Universities and to provide better teaching to the increasing numbers adequate steps are being taken by providing more funds to the Universities to purchase better equipment and to appoint qualified staff.

In the second plan, eleven Rural Institutes were established with the object of providing higher education after the secondary stage to the rural students in their own setting for developing rural leadership, and for stimulating active participation of the rural population in welfare and community development programmes. By the end of Second Plan, the enrolment in Rural Institutes was over 2300. But the scheme of Rural Institutes is still not in full swing. The reasons are the difficulty in their working and in their not meeting adequately the man-power requirements for rural development. In the third plan, the problem of rural institutes was fully examined and the steps taken to make them really the institutes of great value for the rural development programmes.

The qualitative improvement in higher education was also sought through three year-degree course in arts, science and commerce following the higher secondary school examination. In the plans, the funds and facilities were provided to the Universities to adopt this type of course. The plans also made provision for other reforms along with three-year degree course which included improvement in the teacher-pupil ratio, introduction of tutorial system, general education, improvement of libraries, laboratories and instructional buildings.

To provide facilities for education to the deserving but poor students provision for a great number of scholarships was made in five-year plans. Expenditure on scholarship programmes rose from about Rs. 3.5 crores in 1950-51, to over Rs. 8 crores in 1955-56, to about Rs. 11 crores in 1957-58 and to about Rs. 18 crores in 1960-61. In the third plan this was raised to 37 crores. During the second and third plan periods, the Ministry of Education had undertaken a number of schemes for the provision of scholarship to the deserving students. There is now a national scholarship scheme for outstanding students at the post-matriculation stage. Scholarships are being provided for overseas studies and a number of scholarship schemes are there to help the backward classes.

Besides the above schemes for qualitative improvement, a number of other steps have been taken to improve education at all levels. The teachers' salary scales were revised. Steps were taken to organise vigorous programmes of research in educational objectives, method and techniques through the all-India Research Institutes like "The National Institute of Basic Education" etc. During the third plan, the National Institute of Educational Research and Training had been established which had merged in itself the existing Central Institutes. This institute is undertaking various programmes of qualitative improvements in education.

The emphasis on scientific and technological research in the plans had also helped much in qualitative improvements in these fields. The plans for research in Agriculture had proved to be not only beneficial for agricultural education but to the nation as a whole. A provision of Rs. 130 crores was made in the third plan for research in various technological and scientific fields as against Rs. 72 crores in the second plan.

Drawing of Plans for Education

The planning in all the spheres of national life is of great importance. But of an equal importance is the planned development in the various fields within their own scope of work. The planning at national level fixes priorities and allots funds for various aspects of national development. The planning in specific fields envisages a programme of development in their own spheres. This programme is also based on priorities to various aspects of improvements within the fields and to the funds allotted to it or it expects to be allotted to it by the National Planning Commission. Thus, the over-all national plan envisages planning within the fields and without the fields. Both types of planning are essential for the national development of the country.

The various aspects of education require a planned approach towards their development . The educational planner has to fix the priorities and the targets to be achieved within a given period of time so that the national objectives set forward can be achieved through phased programmes. If there is no adequate planning, the growth throughout the field will be haphazard. The planning brings to the conscious level the objectives to be achieved, helps in fixing targets and enables the better organization of work by distributing it among well-defined units. After independence, India's tremendous progress in the field of education is due to the planned approach towards it. The expenditure on education in the pre-independence period shows a haphazard progress so far as its impact on national income is considered. But after independence, the expenditure on education shows an impact which is much more orderly in nature. In one of the papers it has been shown that the correlation of educational expenditure and national income is much higher in the post-independence era than in the pre-independence period.

How the plans in education should be drawn? The very first thing will be to define the objectives. It may be said that the broader objectives will be the same as the objectives of national planning. It will be the secondary objectives which will be needed to be identified. For example, the objective of the socialist pattern of society will be the broader objective for education as well. Some of the secondary objectives derived from this may be described as follows:

(i) To provide equality of opportunities to all the people to get education;

(ii) To make education available to even the humblest and poorest of the citizen;

(iii) To make education productive so that with education may come economic riches;

(iv) To organize education so that the desirable social changes are brought in the community;

(v) To make provisions for higher education, scientific education, technical education, medical education and agricultural education so that adequate man power is available for the various projects of national development in the country.

After the identification of the objectives the next step is to fix priorities within the resources available. What our late Prime Minister Nehru said about the priorities in national planning also holds good here. He said : "A country which wants to progress, wants to progress in a hundred ways. We have, therefore, to take into consideration the order of preference– what is first, what is second, and what is third ? There are so many things we want to do in India, and we want to do them quickly and passionately". In planning in education, we will also like to do many things but we cannot do everything and so it is necessary to fix preferences.

In the last few chapters we have described how these priorities should be determined. We have described that India needs literacy, universal compulsory elementary education, a well planned secondary education, an education in sciences, agriculture and technology and an education for the upliftment of rural population. All these are 'musts' for establishing a 'socialistic pattern of society'. All these, therefore, need to be given priority. In any scheme of educational development all these should find a place. But if the funds are limited, the priorities are to be further narrowed down so as to curtail the developmental programme to only the basic requirements in the beginning. The plans should be drawn in such a manner that within the resources available the development is maximum and the chances of returns to the investment made are the greatest.

For drawing a five-year plan for educational development, the answers to the following questions must necessarily be sought :

(i) What are the primary and secondary objectives?

(ii) What is the existing situation with regard to these objectives? This implies that an assessment of the progress of education in the past should be made and its contribution towards the attainment of the objectives at the time of planning should be evaluated.

(iii) Which aspects of education need priorities? And to what extent? This means that every aspect of education as a contributory factor to the attainment of the objectives should be examined. It should also be seen as to how much development in a particular aspect which is given priority can be sought in the first phase and how much in the next.

(iv) Are enough funds available to proceed with the implementation of the plan? The question of priorities and the funds is greatly linked up. It will be within the funds available that the priorities have to be fixed.

(v) Are there enough other resources to implement the planned programme? Many a time a plan is made for rapid expansion of say primary education but it is not assessed simultaneously if the teachers, buildings, equipment etc. would be available.

(vi) Are there adequate personnel to administer and organise the execution of the planned programmes? For this the trained personnel will be required. No plan can be successful if in its implementation there are not enough qualified people. For example, we say that high priority should be given to universal compulsory elementary education but when it comes to the administrators to put the scheme in operation they falter and the programmes go a begging. Many nice schemes are lost to red-tapism, many to official lethargy, priggishness and aristocratic or autocratic approach.

(vii) How far the plan will lead to over-all increase in productivity in the economic sense ? The education as an investment should always be kept in sight. In the plan efforts should be made to purge out the factors which lead to wastage of effort and money. For example, if we plan for higher education we must see that the persons who are highly educated can add to the national prosperity. A graduate or post-graduate unemployed adds to the wastage, so also a failure means wastage. Thus the planning for higher education should be in keeping with the man-power needs of the country and only those who have talent and calibre, should be allowed to proceed to get higher education.

(viii) Are there adequate provisions for evaluating the plan progress from time to time ? The degree to which the targets set are being achieved at different stages of the plan must be assessed from time to time. Wherever there are weaknesses they should be removed and steps should be taken to strengthen the efforts towards the achievement of the targets.

(ix) Does this plan take into account the future development in the years which follow after the plans or in the next plans? It means that it has to be seen if the plan is limited to only one five year period or may be extended to the other periods which follow. The perspective planning in planning for five year periods should not be lost sight of. Pandit Nehru had emphasized this by saying, "planning, therefore, consists in having an objective–not only an immediate objective, but a more distant objective. You cannot plan only for tomorrow, you have to plan for years, and in the case of a nation, you have to plan for generations. Therefore, planning means perspective planning. After such long term planning, you come to planning for tomorrow and today."

The above nine-point analytical inventory may form the fundamentals of planning in all the fields but specifically it is good for planning in education.

In the end, we again repeat the words of our late Prime Minister Nehru who during his address to the Parliament said:

> "planning is the exercise of intelligence to deal with facts and situations as they are and find a way to solve problems. Everybody plans, and ought to plan, whether he runs a shop or an industry or a plant or a State. In this world today, where everything is more and more governed by developments of science and technology, the idea of things happening by themselves, that is, the laissez-faire theory, is almost considered the verge of absurdity except by a few who profit greatly under it at the cost of the many. Nobody in this House, I trust, stands for the profit of the few at the cost of the many."

Thus planning means an organized way of doing things. It leads to the attainment of objectives through intelligent approach to the utilization of the resources of the nation.

At present, the criticisms directed against our plans and planning body are gaining momentum. The Planning Commission is referred to as "White Elephant". A study by the Indian Institute of Public Administration some time back has revealed that the Planning Commission's sanctioned staff has increased about five times in 11 years–from 224 in 1951-52 to

1,131 in 1963-64. In its editorial of 11th Sept. 64, 'The Tribune' criticizes this state of affairs. It writes: "The 100 per cent increase in its own strength makes the 4 percent, or even less, annual increase in the national income pale into insignificance. In recent years, the rate of the country's growth has slackened but the Commission's has gone up." The editorial further mentions, "Little wonder that, despite colossal expenditure, the Commission has failed to build up an institutional framework adequate in the needs and aspirations of the semi-starved, ill-clad ill-housed masses. The basic problems of poverty and unemployment remain unsolved when the Planning Commission itself has a cumbersome and top heavy establishment which lives in an ivory tower and has ceased to be effective."

Many of these criticism may be justified. But they should not deter us from planning. Let us plan and when we frame our plans and are in difficulty let us remember the *Talisman* given by Gandhiji and apply it to find whether our efforts are in the right direction. Gandhiji said:

> I will give you a talisman. Whenever you are in doubt or when the self becomes too much with you, apply the following test. Recall the face of the poorest and the weakest man whom you may have seen, and ask yourself if the step you contemplate is going to be of any use to him. Will he gain anything by it? Will it restore him to a control over his own life and destiny? In other words, will it lead to swaraj for the hungry and spiritually starving millions? Then you will find your doubt and yourself melting away."

14

The Administration of Education

That the impact of the political theory of the State is most noticeable in the public supervision and administration of education will be readily understood when it is remembered that political theory must at some point define clearly the purposes of education and then go on to determine the type of administration which seems best suited to the attainment of the citizen type the State wishes to produce.

It should, however, also be remembered that it was not until the eighteenth and nineteenth centuries that statesmen decided that universal and compulsory education was a desirable aim, and that even then they were more often than not inclined to leave the actual provision of the schools to someone else, usually the parishes and the local communities.

When it became imperative that there should be some centralized control—if only for the reason that to make universal compulsory education a reality and not merely a law on the statute book the State must provide the necessary funds—then the kind of centralized control that was imposed had to take account of the prevailing culture pattern and of the aims and aspirations of the people as a whole as reflected so far in the organization of the school systems in vogue.

Only in countries like Russia, or Germany and Italy under the Nazi and Fascist regimes, where a totalitarian system could be imposed, did it prove in any measure possible to impose a rigidly centralized administration to the exclusion of the participation of the public or any of its associated group. And in the purely totalitarian state, of course, there can be no conflicting opinions and no criticism of theory and practice. Democracy for the Russians, considered from the educational point of view, means training in dialectical materialism and in socialism. Conformity to the Marxist ideal is the aim, and care is taken at all stage and at all levels to control all sources of information which may lead to "the harbouring of dangerous thoughts."

In consequence, the administration of education in Russia, though it is shared by several organization is in effect (as far as policies and details are concerned) controlled entirely by the Council of People's Commissars, by the Central Committee of the Communist Party, and by the Central Planning Commission of which each Minister for Education for each of the sixteen republics in the U.S.S.R. is a member. The Minister for Education thus takes part in deliberations and discussions on all national problems, thereby assuring a close and permanent link at the highest administrative level between education and the life of the Communist State. It is the responsibility of the Ministry of Education for each of the sixteen republics to see to the efficient organization of work in the primary and secondary schools, in the teacher training colleges, in education bureaux, in education laboratories, in educational research institutes, and in the general sphere of adult education. True, there is some decentralization of administration in the sense that local bodies are required to maintain school buildings and approve the appointment of teachers, which is made by the head of the school, who is himself (or herself) a Ministry nominee. They are also expected to take "an active interest" in the provision of facilities for the improvement of the efficiency of "in service" teachers and to provide adequate facilities for out of school activities. They can have no say, however, in the planning of the school syllabus, in the amount of time that shall be allotted to various subjects at various levels, nor in the approach to the teaching of the subjects on the curriculum, nor in the choice of textbooks.

Indeed, there are common or "stable" textbooks prescribed throughout the whole of the U.S.S.R. to ensure that the basic knowledge acquired is the same throughout the whole union, and that it is consistently up to date in accordance with the latest high level pronouncements. There is also a common syllabus for the whole union, and a fixed timetable, to ensure that the main facts are taught to all children in the correct dosage. Apologists will often argue that much initiative is left to the local teacher to supplement all this as he will in accordance with local conditions and requirements, and that he is encouraged to draw on a wide variety of other material to supplement the textbook knowledge, the choice being entirely his. This is true ... but the would be a brave and rash man who attempted anything not in strict accordance with the party line and that was not going to win the immediate approval of the inspectorate!

Inspectors to the schools are appointed by each, Ministry of Education, after some years of teaching experience during which they have proved themselves to be "sound." Their duties are many and their responsibilities considerable, their main task being that of constantly raising the standard of education and discipline in the schools and of co-operating closely with the head of the school to maintain to school's efficiency and reputation at the highest possible level. This means that they are constantly in and out of the school listening to lessons and examining the work of the pupils. If an inspector considers that a lesson has been badly given, he will probably go over it in detail with the teacher in private, analysing it to show what was wrong, and then take the next lesson himself to show how it should be done. It is equally the inspector's duty, together with the head of the school, to recommend a teacher for an award or promotion. Finally, in order to ensure that the inspectors themselves do not in any sense deviate from the party line, and are kept constantly informed of the various shifts and emphasis that are from tine to time required, there is an institute for the training of inspectors, this training being followed up by regular refresher courses held every three months As one Russian university professor once put it: "Our education sets itself the task of creating all-round active, determined possessors of knowledge and of the proletarian world outlook, devoted to communism and communistic morality, builders and defenders of a socialist society." There could be no more direct and simple statement of a completely totalitarian aim.

Of course, several of the Western European democracies-notable amongst which are France, Belgium, Sweden and Holland—enjoy or have enjoyed in varying degrees the mixed blessings of a highly centralized system in many respects not dissimilar from that holding in the U.S.S.R. But there comparison stops short, for the ends to be served in these countries by a policy of centralized control of education are neither political nor ideological, but rather based on a definite theory of education that seems best to suit the peculiar require-ments of the country in the light of its past endeavours and achievements. Again, whilst the character of the administrative machine may be authoritarian, authority and controls are limited to the actual work done in the schools and to providing a uniform school system, and are in no sense extended to cover the private lives of teachers, parents pupils and citizens generally outside the school. A parent or teacher may hold whatever political or religious views he pleases, may freely criticize both the theory and practice of education, and—if he does like what is provided for him by the State—may send his children to a private "free" school or start such a school himself, subject only to general governmental regulations covering adequacy of building and equipment and the employment of suitably qualified teachers, the qualifications exacted from teachers in the "free" schools being by no means necessarily as high as those required for employment under State control. Broadly speaking, such countries among the democracies as to-day have some form of centralization use their powers to make certain that the pupils in the schools have acquired both a certain body of knowledge (for one reason or another considered indispensable) and a mind trained to think for itself. Again, we must remember that without direct intervention on the part of the State the organization and provision of adequate educational facilities for all children would have been impossible in Holland, Belgium and Scandinavia, just as it was proving impossible in England until the passing of the 1944 Education Act which itself proved a step towards a more authoritarian and centralized control.

The advantages that are usually claimed for the centralized system are that opportunities are equalized, and that the rural and more remote areas have as good educational facilities as the more advanced and progressive urban areas; that the quality of education provided is uniform because all schools are provided with teachers possessing the same qualifications; and that the system is efficient because the same standards are set for all schools. This, of course, is only true a point. All teachers are not of equal calibre even if they have all followed identical courses and passed the same examination. Nor, in actual practice, do we find the more able and, more ambitious teacher willing to bury themselves in remote country areas. Nor, Finally, do examination successes show that the same standards of achievement have been achieved in different schools of the same system. A more serious criticism of the tightly centralized system, however, is that local initiative and enterprise is stifled and there is no real incentive to the subgroups seriously to challenge because practised doctrines.

The real vigour of the English educational system has lain in the wide diversity and variety of aims and purposes that have only been made possible through a policy of complete decentralization. The stagnation that has repeatedly been complained of in experimentation in aims and methods in French schools was the inevitable outcome of a strongly centralized system, dating from the 1880's, that whittled away the power and influence of local authorities to virtually nil. It is interesting to note that post-war reforms in English education to be effective have had to initiate a closer control of local responsibility and private enterprise, whereas in France there has had to be a relaxation of control in order to allow what was considered desirable experimentation to take place.

What is obviously wanted in those countries which (unlike America) still believe in the importance to the country as a whole of the formation of an intellectual elite is a careful distribution of functions between the central and the local authorities that achieves real liberty with a high degree of conformity, and it is the proud and justifiable boast of the Dutch that they have managed to do this. The inevitable struggle between Church and State for the control of education led to a series of uneasy compromise in the predominantly Catholic countries, but generally speaking these countries—in particular France and Belgium—achieved a working solution to the problems facing them on a basis of what we might call "liberty without the State system." That is to say, the State has undertaken the maintenance and development of a neutral system of education open to all who care to profit by it. Those sections of the community who are for one reason or another dissatisfied with what the State offers may, if they so wish, establish side by side with the State schools "free" schools which become their entire responsibility. In principle the State adopts a passive attitude towards such schools. There is, however, another solution which might be termed "liberty within the State system," and it is this solution the Dutch have sought. Passivity is replaced by avctive State intervention. Thus the State actively assists the development of such schools as are not neutral, provided certain guarantees are given that the instruction in those schools will be equivalent to, though not necessarily identical with, that given in the neutral schools. Since 1945 both France and Belgium have felt compelled to treat the Catholic "free" schools in their respective countries on not dessimilar lines by granting State subsidies proportionate to those voted for the State schools towards their upkeep and general maintenance.

Alongside all this, however, Holland has devised her own peculiar form of decentralization. Though the Ministry of Education supervises the whole system it most definitely does not act (as in France) as "schoolmaster-in-chief." Its function is to achieve uniformity of standards and of educational opportunity throughout the country; to pay the salaries of all approved teacher in whatever school they serve, to regulate the execution of the programme of studies and the timetable of lessons, to see that regulation effecting efficiency in schools are complied with (e.g. that the number to teachers employed in a given school is not allowed to fall below the basic minimum prescribed by law), to see to it that any group of persons legally in a position to demand the establishment of a "free" school are not denied their rights, and to make a large contribution towards the upkeep of the secondary schools proper (80 percent of the expenses of the commercial secondary schools is met by the Ministry, which also maintains at its own expense forty-nine secondary schools in areas where the proper provision of secondary education by local authorities is difficult). To enable it efficiently to carry out these various duties, the Ministry has an inspectorate consisting of three chief inspectors and fifty-six others assigned to different to districts. There are two architect-inspectors in addition whose sole concern is school buildings, and two inspectors of teacher-training.

The immediate responsibility for the provision of adequate primary, secondary and technical education falls on the local authorities, the public schools being managed by the municipal council and a board consisting of the burgomaster and aldermen, the "free" schools being privately managed but the local authority being held responsible for supplying the necessary school buildings. The local authorities appoint local inspection committees on which parents, teachers and other local citizens are represented. To sum up, the local authorities pay all current expenses and provide the buildings for all types of schools, the Ministry pays all salaries and in addition makes adequate grants towards the efficient maintenance of good secondary education. About 27 percent of the children attend neutral State primary schools, about 28 percent attend "free" Protestant schools, about 43 percent attend "free" Roman Catholic schools, and 2 percent only are in neutral "free" schools—that is to say, schools which belong to no religious body and which equally wish to remain "free" from municipal control. The Dutch love of freedom and independence which probably found its greatest expression for all time in the eighty year's struggle ceaselessly waged to secure freedom from the Spanish yoke finds in modern times its fullest expression in this present system which harmoniously combines the benefits of both a centralized and a decentralized system of educational administration.

As we have already hinted, the situation holding in France is radically different from that In Holland, the local authorities having in effect no say in the policy to be adopted, their functions being restricted in the main to the supply of furnishings, heating, lighting, and so on, and even then being very carefully guided by some specific regulation as to exactly how and when and why and in what measure they shall act. All authority is exercised by the Minister for Education, under the control of Parliament, and by his delegates in each of the seventeen *academies* in to which the country is administratively divided. At the head of each *academie* is the *Recteur*, appointed by the President of the Republic and directly responsible to the Minister. Usually he is chosen from among the university professors, but the only qualification he actually needs is the possession of a doctorate degree. The *Recteur* has almost absolute powers within his *academie*, and he directs the whole system of education from the nursery school upwards to the university, and including the general supervision of all private schools. His administrative assistants include, since the last war, an inspector general for primary education, one for youth and sports, and one or more for technical education. Under his control, and representing both the *Recteur* and the Minister, is an academy inspector for each of the *departements* contained within the *Academie*. The academy inspector controls his team of inspectors who are specialists chosen to cover all types of education offered within any given *departement*. It should be noted that there is in addition a *departmental* council that fulfils in each *departement* the important role of administering the whole of primary education, and in particular holds itself responsible for the recruitment, training and promotion of primary school teachers. This is a traditional arrangement, extending back to the first attempt at organizing primary education in France (that had been entirely neglected by Napoleon) and when the Minister of the Interore, through his prefets, sought an orderly solution.

At the highest level the Minister and his numerous advisers are assisted by a body of special inspectors of national education whose function it is to visit all educational establishments, to report on the teachers therein (in conjunction with the local inspectorate), to keep the Minister constantly informed of the over-all picture of education throughout France, and—most important of all in many ways—to plan the programme of studies for the schools, to think out new lines of approach in view of constantly changing conditions, and to indicate quite clearly and dogmatically what are, in the Ministry's view, the best method of instruction to be adopted. All these inspectors are of, course, specialists in one given branch, though they may from time to time be charged with a job of work that extends beyond the confines of their specially. Since 1946 this rigid top-level structure has been to some extent modified by the formation of various new consultative committees on which the actual teaching personnel are represented, and by widening the representation in the teacher's favour on the important *Conseils d'Enseignement* and *Conseil Superieur* which are concerned with all projects of reform of education. Further, there has been a marked tendency over the last twenty years or so to permit local divergences from the fixed programme of studies, particularly in the last year of the primary school, in technical education, and in advanced and specialized work at the university level or its equivalent.

A further peculiarity of the French system, and one still further accentuating the strongly centralized approach is that all examination without exception are State examinations, and not merely school leaving examination conducted in part or as a whole by the school authorities concerned with the pupil. Any child, provided he fulfils the necessary age qualifications may present himself anywhere for examination in the appropriate subjects, it making no difference whether he has been privately educated at home, or in a State or "free" (usually

Catholic) school. Private "free" establishments can, of course, issue, their own diplomas, but they have no value whatever in securing one of the innumerable appointments which always specify success in one or a number of State examinations. Naturally, the obligation on everybody to present themselves for the State examinations ensures that the programme of work in all "free" establishments will be the same as in the State schools and that the approach to the teaching of the various subjects will not greatly differ. Finally, there is the *concours* or competitive examination where the number accepted does not only depend on the high quality of work achieved but also on the number of places available—for example, the *consours d'agregation* for teachers at a secondary and university level.

This principle of the centralization of education was first enunciated by La Chalotais in 1763, upheld by the writers of the French Revolution, and cast in its final practical, mould by Napoleon in 1808. And Napoleon quite consciously imitated many of the features of the organization of the Society of Jesus that over the preceding centuries had done so much to create an intellectual elite as a basis for a strongly centralized monarchial regime. As he himself put it, he was anxious to secure for the State all the advantage that were obviously secured for the Church of Rome by the Jesuit organization, and to secure a class of civil servant who would have no other ambition except to be useful, and no other interest except public welfare. "My aim in establishing an educational corporation is to be able to direct political and moral opinions." Not unnaturally we find that since France was by this time the spiritual leader of the Latin world, most of these Latin countries followed the model set them by Napoleon for the organization of their educational systems.

In Italy, for example, the centralization of administration was introduced as far as the kingdom of Sardinia was concerned well before the Napoleonic reforme. Napoleon's conquest of the Northern Provinces led to their incorporation in the French empire, and in the south of Italy Joseph Bonaparte and Murat were naturally bound to pursue a policy of close centralization on the approved French model, particularly so when it is remembered that Napoleon owed the germ of his idea for centralization from what he had seen operative in the kingdom of Sardinia. With the founding of the Ministry of Public Instruction in Italy and the passing of the Casati Law of 1859, centralization had been extended to all the provinces, and the Casati Law itself, again following French practice, left primary education to the initiative of the local authorities and maintained only the secondary and higher schools. Under the Fascist regime Gentile was instrumental in reducing the sixty-nine province into nineteen regions that each had their own historical frontiers (an important difference) and in furthering "regional" activities and so allowing each historical region to vary its curricula to suit local bias, local traditions and peculiar outlook. Further, the neutral State schools have never been neutral in the French sense that no religious teaching of any kind shall be done there. It is also to be noted that various attempts made to encourage local self-government in education have proved abortive, and that, mainly for financial reasons, the country as a whole would now seem to prefer centralized system.

Supreme over all education in Italy is the Minister, assisted by an under-secretary with an educational cabinet of his own. Eight director-generals of education are in charge of general affairs and of personnel, and amongst them cover the whole field of education including university and higher education, antiquity and fine arts, academies and libraries and cultural relations. The highest authority in a province is the Chief Inspector of Studies, who is directly responsible for all matters concerning primary education (including teaching appointments) and who also supervises the secondary schools. The actual task of school visitation, inspection and supervision is carried out by a team of school inspectors. The Chief Inspector of Studies also appoints a provincial school council consisting of an expert in primary education (nominated directly by the Minister), professors teacher, a physician and the chief engineer for public works. This council provides the Chief Inspector with all the technical advice he needs and under his chairmanship deals with questions of school organization, including finance and staffing. The Chief Inspector of Studies is a Ministry nominee and representative.

The slight but important divergences from the French system that have appeared indicate the Italian's historical consciousness of regional differences, reflect the constant striving to make him aware of his national entity, and betray a marked Germanic influence (particularly in the conception of the *ginnasi*) and strong Catholic outlook. In the case of Belgium, with its own peculiar stormy history, its strong Catholic and non-Catholic parties, and the linguistic problems presented by the Flemings and the Walloons, there are many differences to be noted. By population and tradition, Belgium of course is not a typical Latin country, and the old system of local and provincial self-government is very much in evidence despite the centralized system that is imposed for the sake of uniformity. According to the usual pattern, there is a Minister with his boards of advisers and a ministerial inspectorate with very wide power of supervision in that they control material organization, curricula, pedagogical, methods, and enforce a strict execution of the law as centrally interpreted. When by the law of 1932 Belgium was officialy divided into Flemish and Wallon areas, so was the inspectorate divided, though each separate body was subordinated to the central control of the Ministry. Whilst it is generally true to say that secondary and higher education is administered directly by the Ministry, and that primary education is left as a responsibility of the local authorities and the provinces (under close supervision of the Ministry inspectorate), it must be remembered that several large towns and provinces still cling jealously to their independence, insist on controlling their own secondary schools, and strive often to keep ahead of rival institution in other towns and provinces in their ability to recruit the best possible teaching staff and to make use of the best and most modern school equipment available. There are in all ten provinces, each with a governor chosen by the king, each with a provincial council elected by popular vote. Similarly, there is in each commune a communal council the executive head of which is the burgomaster assisted by any number of from two to six *echevins* selected by ballot from the rest of the members of the council. Amongst these *e'chevins* one is responsible for educational matters within the commune.

It is, of course, the boast of the Belgians that in accordance with their constitution all education is free in the sense that anybody can open a school. Education generally, however, is of two types: either "free" or Roman Catholic, or State and therefore secular. School figures to-day indicate that the children are roughly divided between the two types of school, there being quite a number of Catholics attending the State schools. The Belgian insistence on the liberty of the subject is further exemplified by the fact that in the State secular schools two hours per week are left open for religious or moral instruction. According to the wishes of the parents, a priest of the appropriate denomination will attend to give this instruction. Where parents do not wish for wish for this, then the children follow a course of moral instruction given by an appropriate teacher. Again, at the level of higher education, the State provides two State universities, one at Ghent for the Flemish-speaking population, one at Liege for the Walloons whose language is French. The Catholics, however, have their own "free" university at Louvain, and a secular "free" university is established in Brussels. Finally, the Catholic schools have established their right to their own body of inspectors, who naturally follow the main directives laid down by the Ministry.

Further flexibility in the system is to be found in that each secondary school has its own leaving examination, the only State interference being through a *Jury d'Homologation* whose job it is, acting in a general supervisory capacity, to ensure that a certain level of attainment is reached—in other words that the national standards are maintained in all schools. Thus there is nothing as impersonal as the *baccalaureat* in France, and no State system of examinations as such—though the system of *concours* is in existence in certain specialized fields though not in effect in teaching.

It is significant to note that a decentralized system of administration developed almost entirely amongst peoples of Germanic origin or tradition where for one reason or another the Roman legal system did not take deep roots and therefore could not supersede the old customs of self-government. The efforts of the monarchy to achieve a strongly centralized State could not wear down the sturdy opposition of the aristocracy (often of bourgeois and of merchant-trader origin) and of the people. And the Reformation further rendered abortive such efforts at centralization as persisted by the organization of the Protestant churches on the basis of a self-governing parish. Whatever centralization was later achieved was willingly conceded by the people as a whole in the interests of national uniformity, though care was none the less taken to preserve the administrative independence of the local authorities. We have already seen how this has worked out in practice in both Holland and Belgium. We must now examine in same detail the systems of more typically decentralized countries such as Germany, the Scandinavian countries, Switzerland, and of course England.

Germany is in many ways untypical in that the decentralization takes the form of allegiance to the *Land* rather than to a local authority, and the *Land* can often be extremely authoritarian in the control it exercises. The Thirty Years War left the various *Lander* divided amongst themselves and Germany as a whole in a state of Political disintegration. As a result the individual *Land*, and not the *Reich*, assumed control of the schools and determined their form and organization, and each *Land* continued to hold and exercise this function until the Weimar Constitution was adopted after the First World War. Articles in this constitution determined a basis for a common school legislation, but nothing was done to implement this, and the *Lander* continued, in the field of education at any rate, to retain complete autonomy. A slight step towards uniformity was taken by agreements negotiated between several *Lander*, when conformity over general standards of education was established. The National Socialists introduced further measures to bring about unification, and created in 1934 the

Reich Ministry of Education. The overwhelming difficulties that faced the Germans on the collapse of the Nazi regime, and the complications involved in having to contend with four separate occupying Power, led once more to the various *Lander* retaining control of school legislation and administration. This time, however, the various Ministers of Education, sensing the need for co-operation between the various *Lander* if the new democratic principles involving a unified Germany were to be realized, formed themselves into a permanent conference which, working quietly and efficiently over the last several years, has done much towards achieving a uniform purpose in education for the whole country. Thus, general agreement has been achieved on: the adoption of grades of equal value and formulation to be used on school reports and certificates; the introduction of optional foreign language instruction in the primary school; principles of political education in school; adoption of uniform principles of spelling; mutual recognition of certificates of maturity (the *Abitur*) entitling admission to the universities; the methods of professional preparation of secondary school teachers; the standardization of school holidays. None the less, much must still be done before the ideal of real harmony in German education is achieved.

Within each *Land* there are three levels of administration: the State Ministry of Education; the Government-District (*Regierungsbezirk*); and the country level, which is either rural or urban. General school policy, curriculum planning, the setting up of examination requirements, the final certification and appointment of teachers, are all handled at the ministerial level. The Government-District and the county levels of administration have functions of local administration and supervision, the supervision of the secondary schools being separate from that of the primary schools and attaching to the Ministry. Both these school authorities, however, receive their directions from the Ministry, and any innovations they may wish to introduce must first of all have ministerial sanction. They are, on the other hand, held responsible for seeing that school regulations in the primary schools and in the intermediate schools are scrupulously observed, for guiding and advising teachers, for the in-service training of young teachers, and for the licensing of private teachers, including those who wish to "tutor" pupils who need or seek special assistance. As in Belgium, the *Abitur* examination is a more informal and "homely" affair than in France, the teachers in the schools setting the examinations the senior inspector for the *Land* (or his deputy) vetting the questions before they are actually put and having the right of choosing among a number or changing them, and always taking part in the important viva voce section of the examination as chairman of the examining panel.

Thus in this modern attempt to proceed along real democratic lines the German people have recognized the right of the memberstates of the Federal Republic to preserve their own particular features of education, and the individual states, in their turn, have devised a working machinery in the Permanent Conference of Ministers of Education for reaching compromises between the administrations of the individual states for the benefit of the cultural way of life all of them. Diversity, which in the past has so largely contributed to the richness of German cultural life, is maintained; bit harmony is encouraged on order to facilitate transfers from the schools of one *Land* to those of another. The goal is not complete uniformity of education throughout the federal Republic, but equivalence base on a centralized *Land* system.

In many ways Switzerland might be considered purely from the point of view of educational administration, as "Germany writ small." The country is divided into twenty-five independent *cantons*, and within these *cantons* there are about three thousand more or less autonomous political communities (*Gemeinden*), each having considerable jurisdictional authority, Education is consequently the joint affair of the *Bund*, of the *canton*, and of the local community; there is no Ministry of Education, but complete delegation of responsibility to local authorities who have, incidentally, always to consider that there are four official national languages for the whole of Switzerland. As in Germany, the *Bund* places the responsibility on the *cantons* for seeing to it that education is "free, adequate, compulsory and without religious discrimination." No attempt is made in the Constitution to define what is meant by "adequate education." The *canton* must decide that, and should a Swiss in any *canton* feel that education is not adequate he is free to appeal to the *Bund* to seek redress. "Compulsory education" means that the *canton* is responsible for seeing that sufficient instruction is received according to local *cantonal* regulations. but not that children shall attend a State school. All schools, however, whether private or public, must achieve a minimum standard of instruction, and *cantonal* inspectors have supervisory control over the curriculum of both private and public schools. All State primary schools and many of the secondary schools are administered directly by the local communities, and the teachers are appointed locally. The local community also maintains the schools and pays teacher's salaries, though the *cantons* lay down compulsory scales of pay and grant subsidies to their local communities. The Federal Government subsidises teacher's salaries, buildings, welfare work and the preparation of teacher for the primary schools. It also pays about half the cost of vocational training and supervises this.

Obviously the Swiss Republic is the only country in Europe where the old system of extreme decentralization has remained practically unchanged. And equally obviously the Swiss have proved that a really high standard of educational endeavour and achievement can be obtained with such a system, rivalling in all spheres the best on all other countries. Differences of language, religion and cultural traditions, dependent in turn on the geograhical configuration of the country, account for the perpetuation of an extreme form of decentralization. Economic circumstances have forced the Swiss to demand to a high standard of education from all and for all. Historical events have led to a real spirit of democracy among the people, and this in turn has led to a stressing of the importance of education as a means of producing the good citizen type who will be a well-informed and progressive member of the community.

The Scandinavian countries are constitutional monarchies in which the function of the Crown are analogous to those of the Crown in Great Britain. The controlling power of government is vested in the people who elect their permanently bodies on a principal of universal suffrage. The dissemination of cultures is wide, and all classes of people play an active part in community and national life. Characteristic also of these countries is that private capitalism and social collectivism are co-extensively. In Sweden, for example, all public utility services are the concern of either the State or the local government—yet almost all industrial workers are privately employed. Throughout Scandinavia generally the whole of the arable land is privately owned and tilled—and yet the farmers form themselves into co-operative societies to market their produce. Finally, it should be noted that the "welfare state" has been long the concern of these countries as a means of achieving real economic and social stability. Education has been deliberately used throughout the centuries to bring about this high degree of voluntary collectivism, and public education as part of the urge towards popular enlightenment that came with the Reformation has been a national concern since the sixteenth century.

The administrations of education, originally in the hands of the Lutheran Church and of local boards, has now become a joint concern of both the State and the local communities. In Norway there is still a "Ministry of Church and Education" which is responsible for all supervision of education, and which for this purpose has a staff of consultants and travelling inspectors for special subjects. The Norwegian "People's School" (primary school) is run by the local authority, its governorship being the direct responsibility of the people. In every municipality there is a school board appointed by the elected municipal council, but which must contain a clergyman of the State Church nominated by the bishop, and a teacher (or teacher) nominated by his own colleagues. This school board is held responsible for the local school administration in compliance with the existing laws of the country. The school board appoints its own teachers, subject to ratification of the appointment by the Ministry. Usually it secures the services of a local school inspector to supervise the administrative as well as the pedagogic side of the school work. An over-all control of primary education is maintained by the Ministry which divides the country into seven administrative districts at the head of each of which is a school director. Any differences of opinion within the school boards, or between the school boards and the directors, may be referred to the Ministry for a final decision. The secondary schools originated from schools opened at the bishop's sees from 1150 onwards, and even to-day still bear in most cases the stamp of their ecclesiastical origins. These schools can be either State or municipally controlled. A State secondary school has a board of governors consisting of the headmaster, a representative of the Ministry, one representatives of the teaching staff, and from one to four member's of the local authorities in whose district the school is situated. The school boards act as governors for the municipally controlled schools. The final school-leaving examination is the same throughout the country and is organized by a special council of secondary education, the members of which are nominated by the King for a period of five years, and who inspect the schools and act as advisers to the Ministry. The total expenditure on education is roughly divided equally between the local authority and the State.

With only slight, and from our point of view unimportant variations, the same administrative pattern holds for both Sweden and Denmark. One interesting feature in Denmark, however, is that if the parents so desire they may establish a parent's council which shall have the power of school inspection and which may assist the Board of Education in the selection of teachers—this for primary schools only, appointment of staff and general supervision of the secondary schools being the direct concern of the Ministry.

One interesting feature which all these countries so far under discussion share in common is that—no matter whether the administration of education be centralized of decentralized—they have as their aim the formation of an intellectual elite, and they believe strongly in the advantages that can be gained from a strictly academic type of secondary education. As a result, education at the secondary level is generally considered far too important a concern to be left too much in the hands of the local authorities, and the State has increasingly made this type of education its special concern. The contrary can be said to hold in both England and the United States. On the other hand, the chief difficulty in both England and the United States, because of the persistence of their own peculiar traditions of local control of education, is that of implementing the ideal of equality of educational opportunity. All the other countries, centralized or decentralized as their administration may be, are meeting with relatively greater success. It would seem that the most likely explanation for this is that education in these other countries has always been held to be an important instrument in securing the people's allegiance to a particular form of government and to a particular way of life that on its own showing made the people in turn happy, prosperous (to varying extents), and therefore contented. Thus in Scandinavia the decentralized system was imposed on the people by a Lutheran Church which seriously held that Christian salvation came through enlightenment of the people and that the only way to work at the people's level was through the smaller parish community. In France a highly centralized system was imposed *admaiorem Francorum gloriam*, the hierarchical system of the Catholic Church, and in particular of the Jesuit Order, being the obvious model to follow—as indeed in all predominantly Catholic countries. Russia—the only country to adopt the American unitary system of education—makes it work much more effectively through a form of centralization and through gearing it to the Marxist ideal. Holland and Belgium are in the midway position between extremes of centralization and decentralization, with State control acting as a "harmonizing" influence, and the Germans are hoping to move increasingly towards this.

England and America, each in their own particular sphere, have manifested a widespread opposition to uniformity and educational prescriptions of any kind. In both countries there is strong filling against delegation the control of education to a central national authority, an equally strong belief in local control as a method of stimulating voluntary effort on the part of the community. None the less, both countries have had to realize that the extreme form of decentralization they have enjoyed has in the long run militated against securing equality of opportunity, and have had to make definite moves towards some further form of centralization to harmonize over-all endeavour. Little more than twenty years ago there existed in the United State about 1,27,000 separate local administrative bodies for education, with more member on the boards of education in some State than there were teachers, and ranging in size from localities with a single school to a system like that of New York City with about 36,000 teachers. In England there were no fewer than 315 local education authorities, some very progressive, some extremely backward. England has now managed to reduce this number of local authorities to 146 and the number of local boards in the United State is being rapidly diminished. In England also, the Education Act of 1944, replacing the old Board of Education by a Ministry of Education, had given greater powers of determining policy to this Ministry which has in turn assumed a larger share in the financial support of education. Over the last thirty years or so moves have been constantly made to secure a greater participation by the Federal Government in the provision of funds for education, but—apart from funds for various special types of education, mainly vocational—any attempts through Federal aid to equalize educational opportunities or to establish reasonable standards throughout the whole country have been resisted through fear of Federal control. The fundamental problems for both England and the United States are thus those of how to increase funds for education from the national purse without interfering with the rights of local authorities to adapt education to local or regional needs, and how also to maintain satisfactory standards of education uniformly throughout the country.

If the American Federal Government has played virtually no part in education, neither can the State governments themselves be said to be in a position to excercise the same control within each state that is exercised by the *Land* within

Germany, for example. Within each state there is a Board of Education responsible to the legislative power for issuing general directives and programmes of education for the training of teachers, and for meeting roughly 30 percent of the total cost of education. The rest of the money has to be found by the separate L.E.A's which vary greatly in size, population, wealth and efficiency. It is, therefore, the L.E.A. that determines more particularly the actual programme of studies and decides what salaries are to be paid, the local costs for education (about 70 percent) being met out of the local rates and taxes on a special budget. This is the direct result of the Jefferson championing of democracy which, it will be remembered, argued that education was a function of government—of local self-government. In a word, the Jeffersonian approach means that the history of education in the United States is the history of the education of the public itself, and that progress must, depend on the ability of the general public to realize education's value and significance. Hence the emphasis, in all local communities, on education weeks, press publicity school demonstrations, public education meetings, school exhibitions, parent-teacher associations. Education must be kept constantly in the public eye. The taxpayer must know that he is getting value for his money, and a healthy rivalry must be fostered between neighbouring communities both to stir the sluggish and to lead to further experimentation. More redently, as, the disadvantages under which the smaller and poorer communities have to work have been more acutely realized, these have been encouraged (wherever practicable) to pool their resources and build a common school to which children may travel from the more distant parts by bus. Where there is no adequate high school accommodation, arrangements are being increasingly made with the nearest authority, capable and willing to absorb an extra population, to take the high school children of the "foreign" L.E.A. on a *per capita* basis of payment. Over the whole of this the Federal Office of Education in Washington keeps an approving eye and confines itself in the main to carrying on the job it was assigned when first created in 1867: that of collecting and diffusing such statistics and facts as are calculating generally to promote the cause of education throughout the U.S.A.

The central authority over education in England and Wales is the Ministry of Education, with a politically chosen Minister who has a seat in the Cabinet, and a staff of permanent civil servants divided into two groups": those who serve at the administrative central headquarter, and those who act as be kept constantly in the public eye. The taxpayer must inspectors and who are assigned to areas administered by local authorities. The Ministry does not maintain, provide, or directly control any kind of educational institution, but through its inspectorate it none the less exercises considerable influence. The work of the inspectors—who are servants of the Crown and not of the Minister—falls into three clearly defined areas: that of inspecting schools, consulting with local authorities and teachers and going advice where necessary; that of representing the Minister in their local areas on administrative matters; and that of advising the Minister in matters of educational theory and practice and of being responsible for the Ministry's publications. Prior to the passing of the Education Act of 1944 only state-aided schools were subject to inspection; under the terms of the Act *all* school without exception must be open to inspection and must conform to minimum requirements as laid down by the Ministry. The function of the L.E.A.'s is to provide a full range of educational opportunity at the primary, secondary, technical and further education levels, and they are responsible to the Ministry for the proper conduct of the schools they establish. Just as each L.E.A. in the United States has its superintendent of school, so in England there is the chief education officer. The important difference between the United States and England, however, is over the matter of finance: fully two-thirds of the total expenditure on education in each L.E.A. in England comes from national funds; in the United States the Federal Office of Education contributes almost nil, the local state boards only 30 percent, the L.E.A. round about 70 percent.

It is in many ways an interesting object lesson for the Americans to note that, despite the large sums devoted to education from the State funds in England, to L.E.A. still retains considerable independence of action. On the other hand, the Education Act of 1944 brought England much closer to European practice by replacing the former President of the Board of Education by a Minister and Ministry of Education, and by giving the Minister much more positive functions. In addition to inspecting and allocating grants (as formerly) the Minister is further enjoyed to "promote the education of the people of England and Wales." He can compel the L.E.A.'s when necessary and advisable to adopt a definite line of policy. And the Act itself, in order to iron out glaring inconsistencies, actually commanded local authorities to provide facilities—such as nursery school accommodation and schools for handicapped children—that had not formerly been readily available. It is unlikely, however, that there will be any significant further move towards more complete centralization. The peculiar English traditions of local government and of voluntary service at that level are too firmly entrenched.

Appendix - I

Tenth Five Year Plan (2002-2007)

Education

Our performance in the field of education is one of the most disappointing aspects of our developmental strategy. Our of approximately 200 million children in the age group 6-14 years, only 120 million are in schools and net attendance in the primary level is only 66% of enrolment. This is completely unacceptablee and the Tenth Plan should aim at a radical transformation in this situation. Education for all must be one of the primary objectives of the Tenth Plan. The Sarva Shiksha Abhiyan, which has been launched to achieve this objective, indicates a strong reiteration of the country's resolve to give the highest priority to achieve this goal during the plan period. It should also be our resolve that the process of integrating our educational system with the economic needs of the people and of the nation must begin at the primary school stage itself. The objective of education is the total development of a child's personality, in which character building and physical education, including sports, are crucial ingredients. Assertion of the dignity of labour and vocationalisation of curriculam are essential to ensure that a disjunction does not take place between the educational system and the work place.

Universalizing access to primary education and improvement of basic school infrastructure must be a core objective of the Tenth Plan. This would mean targeting the provision of one teacher for every group of 40 children for primary and upper primary schools, opening of a primary alternate schooling facility with in 1 km of every habitation, provision of free textbooks to all SCs/STs children and girls at the primary and upper primary school, management and repair of school buildings through school management committees, provision of opportunities for Non-Formal and Alternative Education for out of school children in the most backward areas and for unreached segments of the population in respons to local needs and demands articulated at the grassroot level.

Mere establishment of schools and hiring of teachers will not lead to an improvement in education if teachers remain absent as happens in many parts of the country, especially in rural areas. It is therefore essential that control over schools and teachers should be transferred to local bodies which have a direct interest in teacher performance. States should be encouraged to implement the 73rd and 74th Amendments of the Constitution, which facilitate the transfer of management of primary and upper primary schools to panchayats/local bodies. Planning, supervision and management of education would have to be through local bodies at district block and village levels. Efforts should also be made for social mobilization of local communities for adult literacy compaigns and for promotion of primary for adult literacy campaigns and for promotion of education.

Concerned users of public services have a self-interest in monitoring and improving public services. Where panchayats and other local bodies are not effective, it may prove more productive to set up parents group with representatives of the local bodies and teachers to monitor the delivery of basic education to the rural areas. These parent-teacher groups must be empowered to do this monitoring and unforcing accountability on absentee teachers and disappearing school supplies.

Steps would have to be intiated to fill up all the existing vacancies of the teachers through in a time bound manner, with defined responsibility to local bodies and communities, and to remove legal impendiments in the requirements of para-teachers. For quality education, provision of adequate academic support/training to all the teachers will be necessary. In this connection, the use of IT needs to be explored in terms of teachers' capacity building, as also for spread of literacy through TV, media.

The Mid-Day Meal Programme has made a difference in attendance and retention wherever a proper cooked meal is served. The practice of only providing grains followed by some State Governments, and that also not according to the prescribed norms in all cases, is vitiating the very purpose of the scheme. The State Governments must make efforts to provide hot cooked meals. If it is not possible to cover all the primary schools, efforts must be made to cover all schools in the backward and tribal areas, so that at least the children who badly need this extra nutrition are covered.

The University and Higher Education Sector also needs attention. Although the number of universities has expanded, and many of the universities continue to maintain high standards of education, it is matter of serious concern that the expansion in quantity has been accompanied by a fall in quality. Modernization of syllabi, examination reforms and greater attention to issues of governance of universities and colleges, all require urgent attention. Part of the problem facing universities is the inadequate provision of budgetary resources from the government. Since budget resources are limited, and such resources as are available, need to be allocated to expanding primary education, it is important to recognize that the universities must make greater efforts to supplement resources from the government. University fees are unrealistically low and in many universities have not been raised in decades. This policy is only starving the universities of the minimum resources needed to ensure quality education and is not in the interest of the students. A substantial hike in university fees is essential. Resources raised through adjustment of fees can be supplemented by contributions from industry, constituting funds/trusts like the Bharat Shiksha Kosh, etc. It is also necessary to encourage the establishment of private universities.

Laws, rules and procedures for private, cooperative and NPO supply of education must be modernised and simplified so that honest and sincere individuals and organisations can set up universities, colleges and schools, Oppressive controls on fees, teacher salaries, infrastructure and staff strength must be eliminated. The regulatory system must be modernised based on the economics of information and global best practices. Given the weak criminal justice system in our country, the regulatory system must also put the greatest emphasis on fraud detection and punishment while letting normal individuals to function more freely.

These considerations apply with even greater force to the technical educational system. Both technical and management education need to be managed strategically in order to provide broadbased, multi-disciplinary education incorporating composite skills and knowledge to meet the challenges posed by globalisation.

Appendix - II

Primary Education

Primary education is the education a child receives in its formative years, when it is 5-9 years old and classes I to V. The map, based on the 1981 Census data, projects information about this age group. However, the age group of children in the primary classes generally tends to be 5-11 years, and all data that accompanies the map is based on this wider classification.

In the last 35 years, the number of primary schools in the country has more than doubled, from 209,671 in 1950-51 to 509,143 in 1983-84 and it is still increasing. The annual rate of increase between 1950 and 1984 has been 2.7 percent. But the number of children is also increasing!

Almost every village in the country now has a primary school, and some have more than one, with towns and cities having several. The number of pupils in classes I–V has increased greatly over the years, from 19.2 million in 1950-51 to 35 million in 1960-61 and 81.1 million in 1983-84. By 1989-90, this school-going strength is likely to reach about 96 million. With the increase in enrolment, the school-going percentage to total population in age group 6-11 has also been going up, from 42.6 in 1950-51 to 83.1 in 1980-81 and 91.8 in 1983-84. The annual rate of increase between 1950 and 1984 has been 4.5 per cent.

India's performance in primary education is catching up fast with world norms. In 1982, India's primary school enrolment was 87 per cent as against a world average of 95 per cent. This increased to 92 per cent within the next two years. Barring the high-income oil-exporting countries which have a primary school level of enrolment of 76 per cent and low income countries where enrolment is 85 per cent, all other countries now have universal primary education, with the gross enrolment in some groups of countries exceeding 100 per cent as some pupils enrolled are below or above the countries standard primary school age. East European countries' have a gross enrolment of 104 per cent!

Census (1981) statistics based on a 5 per cent population sample, however, do not reflect this rosy picture. They indicated that only about 33 per cent of India rural children and nearly 60 per cent of urban children were attending primary schools. Kerala in both cases registered the largest percentages: 74.3 per cent from rural and about 79.1 per cent from urban areas. In all other major states, the children attending primary schools in rural areas were less than half the total number of rural children (Tamilnadu being the only other exception, with 54.2 percent). The enrolment in urban primary schools in six states was below the national average of about 60 per cent (Bihar, 51.2 per cent; Gujarat, 57.8 per cent; Madhya Pradesh, 55.3 per cent; Orissa, 56.9 per cent; Rajasthan, 49.1 per cent and West Bengal, 56.1 per cent) Kerala (79.1 per cent) and Tamil Nadu (70.1 per cent) had the highest percentage of children attending primary schools in urban areas.

Primary School Enrolment[1] : 1980-81

State	Male	Female
Andhra Pradesh	3,141,226	2,821,509
Assam	1,158,806	843,628
Bihar	4,661,879	1,886,668
Gujarat	2,619,470	1,785,218

Haryana	7,60,019	393,767
Himachal Pradesh	2,06,571	2,23,432
Jammu & Kashmir	350,682	196,888
Karnataka	2,462,459	1,879,092
Kerala	1,707,195	1,921,540
Madhya Pradesh	3,532,218	1,719,580
Maharashtra	4,770,331	3,623,128
Manipur	116,612	92,066
Meghalaya	1,04,732	9,5413
Nagaland	97,460	77,913
Orissa	1,632,604	1,112,104
Punjab	1,145,694	936,070
Rajasthan	2,132,994	6,72,309
Sikkim	24,715	17,071
Tamil Nadu	3,489,913	2,844,117
Tripura 168,866	123,608	
Uttar Pradesh	6,842,232	2,961,561
West Bengal	4,057,313	2,403,260
Union Territories		
Andaman & Nicobar	14,835	12,356
Arunachal Pradesh	39,340	18,921
Chandigarh	16,397	14,303
Dadra & Nagar Haveli	8,448	5,311
Delhi	353,151	354,648
Goa, Daman & Diu	82,475	71,638
Lakshadweep	4,009	3,442
Mizoram	31,949	29,627
Pondicherry	44,874	34,809
INDIA	**45,780,119**	**28,585,706**

Note: Estimated

Male pupils attending primary schools outnumber female pupils in all the states except Kerala, where male and female children attending classes I-V are each about 75 per cent of the child population. The next highest male and female enrolment is in Tamil Nadu, about 64 percent males and 55 per cent females. The lowest level of male enrolment in primary schools is in Uttar pradesh and Bihar. Madhya Pradesh, Rajasthan and West Bengal also have enrolments considerably lower than the national average of 44.3 per cent.

The national average of enrolment of females in primary schools is 32.2 per cent. Five major states of the Union have enrolments lower than the female national average: Bihar, Haryana, Madhya Pradesh, Rajasthan (the lowest in the country) and Uttar Pradesh.

The differences in primary school enrolments in rural and urban areas is also least in Kerala. This is mainly attributable to low drop-out rates. The next-best enrolment in both rural and urban areas in male as will as in female pupils is in Tamil Nadu (rural: male, 60 and female, 48. 1 per cent; urban: male, 72.1 and female, 68 per cent) This state is doing much better than these 1981 figures indicate, following the introduction of the Nutritious Meal scheme: the current policy of feeding daily 200,000 children between 2-9 years of age is believed to be responsible for the lowest drop-out rate on the country.

The expenditure in 1980-81 on primary education amounted to about Rs 15,283 million, 48.5 per cent of all expenditure on education (including Sports and Youth Welfare,) emphasizing the status now being accorded to primary education in the country. In several states, a substantial sum of money has been expended on primary education, notably Rs 1715 m or 49.4 per cent of state expenditure on education in Uttar Pradesh , Rs 1790 m or 46.4 per cent in Maharashtra, Rs 1174 m or 49.9 per cent in Tamil Nadu and Rs 1149.4 m or 54.5 per cent in Kerala; but it was Bihar that spent the highest amount (73.5 per cent of Rs 1509 m) of its outlay on education in the primary sector.

The number of teachers in primary schools in the

country has been on the increase, keeping pace with student enrolment and educational institutions. In 1950-51 the strength of teachers was 537, 918 which increased to 1.35 million in 1980-81 and 1.39 million in 1983-84, an annual increase of 2.9 per cent for the period 1950-84. But experience shows that while enrolment is still not 100 per cent as desired under the commitment to universal primary education, the number of teachers is inadequate, even for the present enrolment, although expenditure has been going up steadily.

To overcome the problem of low enrolments in primary schools, attention must be given to alleviating poverty and improving social and economic conditions before attempting to impose universal education. The New National Education Policy is expected to do better on this count.

Sources:

1. Basic statistics Relating to the Indian Economy, vol.1: all India, August 1986 and vol,2: states, September 1986, entre for Monitoring Indian Economy
2. Would Bank's Would Development Report 1986 Oxford University press
3. Seventh Five year Plan 1985-90 vol.II Planning Commission.
4. Key Population statistics Based on 5 per cent sample Data, paper 2 of 1982, Census of India, 1981.
5. Statistical Abstract India 1982 and 1984, Ministry of Planning. Quoting from Ministry of Education & Social Welfare.

Appendix - III

Secondary Education

In India, the educational drop-out rate is highest towards the end of the primary school years (age 5-9). Students continue to drop-out throughout the years of secondary education. Students receiving secondary education are in the age group 10-14 years. The data projected on the map is for this age group, according to the Census of India age group classifications. However, the age group of students in the secondary classes (including classes xi and xii) tends to be 11-17 years, and all data that accompanies the map is based on this wider classification.

The time series data for the number of schools and students in secondary education repeat the general pattern of change in primary education: there is an increase with the years, and with the increasing number of schools, in the number of pupils. But the similarity ends there, for secondary education has both smaller numbers and fewer schools. And the number of students that move into secondary education from primary education has always been much smaller than the number in the primary streams.

The number of secondary school students in 1950-51 was 4.3 million. This rose to 9.6 million in 1960-61, to 28.04 million in 1980-81 and to 40.3 million in 1983-84. The annual rate of increase in enrolment has been 7.3 per cent. The number of students in the secondary stream is expected to be around 42 million by 1989-90. Correspondingly, the number of secondary schools increased from 20,884 in 1950-51 to 66, 920 in 1960-61, 164,202 in 1980-81 and 181,580 in 1983-84. There were 212,000 teachers in the secondary stream in 1950-51 which swelled to about 1.9 million in 1983-84, with an annual rate of increase of about 7 per cent over these years. Throughout this period, students in the secondary stream were outnumbered by students in the primary stream. Not all students from the primary stream move into secondary education year after year; a sizeable number of the drop-outs are absorbed by the child labour pool in both rural and urban areas.

SECONDARY SCHOOL ENROLMENT – 1980-81

States	Male	Female
Andhra Pradesh	1,129,692	526,759
Assam	4,99,940	304,332
Bihar	1,475,584	347,299
Gujarat	998,749	579,681
Haryana	476,362	161,031
Himachal Pradesh	175,067	73,883
Jammu & Kashmir	162,044	74,544
Karnataka	930,237	523,209
Kerala	1,259,143	1,169,558
Madhya Pradesh	1,387,451	451,641
Maharashtra	2,052,416	1,108,873
Manipur	45,815	30,101
Meghalaya	38,012	31,584
Nagaland	34,385	24,814
Orissa	610,048	273,820
Punjab	630,609	388,213
Rajasthan	849,142	192,726
Sikkim	6,384	2,962
Tamil Nadu	1,483,604	879,315
Tripura	54,741	39,419
Uttar Pradesh	3,104,296	790,042
West Bengal	1,284,101	684,230

Union Territories		
Andaman & Nicobar	6,825	4,763
Arunachal Pradesh	9,076	3,186
Chandigarh	13,310	10,658
Dadra & Nagar Haveli	1,625	791
Delhi	284,265	204,741
Goa, Daman & Diu	49,491	36,625
Lakshadweep	2,263	1,248
Mizoram	20,901	17,813
Pondicherry	27,108	17,743
INDIA	**19,049,792**	**8,955,604**

Note: Estimated

The world average for secondary enrolment is 59 per cent (1983) whereas in India it is about 33 per cent. But even groups of countries which have registered universal education in the primary years, register lower enrolment ratios in the secondary years. East European countries have a high of 91 per cent and industrial countries follow closely with 85 per cent. In these cases, the ratios are attributable to students branching off into vocational streams rather than giving up education. On the other hand, all low income, middle income and oil-exporting countries are below the world average due to students dropping out from schools.

The national average for enrolment in secondary schools in 1981 was 50.5 per cent, with 44.3 per cent in rural areas and 71.6 per cent in urban areas. The regional pattern of total secondary school enrolment is similar to that of the primary school situation, with three states—Kerala (86 per cent), Maharashtra (62.6 per cent) and Punjab (62.9 per cent)–having the highest enrolments. Gujarat (60.6 per cent) and Tamil nadu (55.5 per cent) fare better than other states of the union. This performance is also reflected in the rural and urban shares of the states (Kerala: rural, 85.4 and urban, 88.7 per cent; Punjab: 58.7 and 75 per cent; Maharashtra: 54.2 and 80.3 per cent; Gujarat: 54.3 and 75.9 per cent; and Tamil Nadu: 47.5 and 71.6 per cent); and in male and female enrolment (Kerala: male, 87.9 and female, per cent; Maharashtra (73.1 and 51.2 per cent; Punjab: 69.2 and 55.6 per cent; Gujarat; 70.4 and 50 per cent; and Tamil Nadu 65.9 and 44.6 per cent).

The national average for secondary enrolment of males is 62.1 per cent and for females 37.5 per cent. The male attendance in rural areas is 57.8 per cent and in urban areas 77 per cent. The female attendance for rural areas is 29.2 per cent and for urban areas 65.6 per cent. The lowest male attendance among the major states is in Andhra Pradesh (51.6 per cent), and the lowest female attendance is in Rajasthan (18.7 per cent). The latter state also has the lowest secondary school attendance (40 per cent).

It appears from these facts that girls are at a disadvantage not only in primary education but also in secondary education. This inequality has persisted through the years and has never been really questioned. But 'gender justice' is now being more fully realized and is being translated in to a new educational policy.

The expenditure on secondary education, as an aggregate of state/territory expenses in 1980-81, was Rs 10,163 million and this was 32.3 per cent of the expenditure on all education (including Youth Welfare and Sports) in the country. The share of union territories was Rs 547 million (51 per cent of the total expenditure in the territories). Most states and territories have an expenditure on secondary education exceeding the national average in terms of percentage, the states with less than 30 per cent of their educational expenditure on secondary education are Andhra Pradesh (29.5 per cent), Bihar (16.8 per cent), Karnataka (21 per cent), Kerala (28.4 per cent) Tamil Nadu (26.1 per cent), Manipur (29 per cent) and Nagaland (20.9 per cent).

Sources: 1. Basic Statistics Relating to the Indian Economy, Vol. I: All August 1986 and Vol.2: States, September 1986, Centre for Monitoring Indian Economy.

2. Key Population Statistics Based on 5 per cent Sample Data, Paper 2 of 1983, Census of India 1981.

3. World Bank's World Development Report 1986, Oxford University Press.

4. Statistical Abstract India 1982, and 1984, Ministry of Planning, Quoting from Ministry of Education & Social Welfare.

Appendix - IV

Higher Education

Education is a concurrent subject in the Indian Constitution. The central and state governments have, over the years, invested ever increasing sums of money on it. A disproportionately large part of this expenditure is devoted to all types of higher education, the benefits of which accrue only to about 5 per cent of the Indian population.

Higher education is education provided by collegiate institutions, university and their equivalents which falls within the scope of the University Grants Commission (UGC). It therefore generally covers students in the 17 -plus age group in such institutions alone. Students in higher secondary schools and technical diploma– or certificate granting institutions (the 15-17 age group) are not covered. In this chapter, however, we have estimated data for the 15-24 age group as a whole, where applicable.

About 15 per cent of all students who complete secondary education go in for higher education. The expenditure on such education in 1980-81 was Rs 4722. 4 million, 15 per cent of the total educational expenditure in the country. The total expenditure on all education (including art and culture, scientific services and research) in 1970 -71 was Rs 7930 million and in 1980-81, Rs 31,480 million, a four-fold increase in 10 years, even after making adjustments for differing budget classifications. This has gone up to Rs 59,800 million in 1984-85, a 90 per cent increase in just four years. During this same period per capita expenditure has gone up from Rs 15 in 1970-71 to Rs 47 in 1980-81, and has shot up to Rs 80 in 1984-85.

There were 47 universities and institutions deemed to be universities in India in 1960. These had increased to 139 in 1983-84 and had 220,177 teachers working in 5246 colleges affiliated to them. Of these, about a fifth (48,694) are in the university departments/colleges. The average growth rate of enrolment during 1970-71 was 4 per cent per annum (the total enrolment in 1979-80 was 2.7 million), with differential growth rate for various faculties. Veterinary Science registered 7 per cent growth per year and Law 6.3 per cent. Commerce had the third highest growth rate, 4.6 per cent, while Medicine had the lowest, 0.5 per cent. The UGC has in its survey revealed that 1680 colleges in the country have less than 500 students each, and 520 colleges between 100 and 200.

HIGHER EDUCATION ENROLMENT—1980-81

States	Male	Female
Andhra Pradesh	390,650	136,744
Assam	123,382	39,516
Bihar	372,623	61,321
Gujarat	250,692	114,577
Haryana	71,765	29,920
Himachal Pradesh	15,828	5,296
Jammu & Kashmir	30,878	14,773
Karnataka	327,117	113,613
Kerala	147,533	122,293
Madhya Pradesh	179,592	57446
Maharashtra	558,808	236,812
Manipur	13,785	7,709
Meghalaya	8,296	5.540
Nagaland	2,921	1,067
Orissa	113,233	25,170
Punjab	92,147	52,905
Rajashtan	250,254	55,849

Sikkim	437	164
Tamil Nadu	350,804	178,856
Tripura	12,055	6,349
Uttar Pradesh	1,410,968	208,639
West Bengal	411,139	157,365
Union Territories		
Andaman & Nicobar	996	659
Arunachal Pradesh	875	155
Chandigarh	19,301	9,346
Dadar & Nagar Haveli	90	64
Delhi	107,063	71,068
Goa, Daman & Diu	11,073	6,126
Lakshadweep	209	97
Mizoram	3,073	2,107
Pondicherry	6255	3,000
INDIA	**4,901,322**	**1,722,393**

NOTE : Estimated

The inequality between sexes is again clearly discernible in collegiate education. However, this has shown gradual improvement over the years, from 14 women for every 100 men enrolled in 1950-51 to 23 in 1960-61 and 41 in 1982-83. In terms of faculties, the ratio is different. In Teacher Training, the majority are women. There are also substantial numbers of them taking Arts. In both Science and Medicine, about 28 per cent of the enrolment is female, but specialized faculties such as Engineering, Agriculture and Law have low enrolment of women. The overall enrolment of both men and women increased 10-fold, from 360,000 in 1950-51 to 3.55 million in 1983-84, an increase of 7.2 per cent per year.

Data in total enrolment in all types of higher education show an increase in enrolment from 425,000 in 1950-51 to 6.624 million in 1980-81, an almost sixteen-fold increase. The increase was continuous, being nearly three-fold over the decade 1950-61, a little over three fold over 1960-71, and nearly two-fold over 1970-81.

Enrolment in all higher education by individuals of the age group 15-24, accounted for various percentages in the major states in 1980-81: Uttar Pradesh and 8.8 per cent, Maharashtra 7 per cent, Karnataka 6.4 per cent, Andhra Pradesh and Tamil Nadu 5.7 per cent each, Gujarat 5.3 per cent, West Bengal 5.2 per cent Rajasthan 5 per cent and all others between 2.6 per cent (Madhya Pradesh) to 4.8 per cent (Kerala).

In all major states male enrolment is greater than female enrolment. It would seem that greater emphasis is being given to male education than to female education in these states. The greatest disparity (11.9 percentage points) is in Uttar Pradesh, which has 14.3 per cent male and 2.4 per cent female enrolment. The least disparity is in Punjab which has 2.9 per cent male and 1.8 per cent female enrolment. Kerala does almost was well, having 5.5 per cent male and 4.2 per cent female enrolment. Madhya Pradesh (3.8 per cent and 1.3 per cent) Haryana (5.1 per cent and 2.5 per cent) and Orissa (4.7 and 1.1) also show less disparities is on this count. In most states however, the disparity is about 4 to 7 percentage points: Andhra Pradesh 8.5 per cent male and 3 per cent female, Bihar 6.4 and 1.1, Gujarat 7 and 3.4, Karnataka 9.1, and 3.4, Maharashtra 9.3 and 4.4 Rajasthan 7.8 and 1.9, Tamil Nadu 7.7 and 3.9 and West Bengal 7.2 and 3.0.

If the student / teacher ratio is considered an indicator of educational welfare in higher education, then those states with fewer students per teacher may be said to enjoy greater welfare and vice versa. In this count, Sikkim (4 students per teacher), Nagaland (6), Andhra Pradesh and Manipur (7 each), Jammu & Kashmir, Kerala, Meghalaya and Tripura (9 each) all fare better than other states. Almost all the union territories, barring Chandigarh (14) enjoy such welfare and are well below the national average of 13 students per teacher. Much worse off than the national average are Rajasthan and Uttar Pradesh (27 students per teacher each), Karnataka (24), Madhya Pradesh (20) and Gujarat (19).

Sources. 1.Report & Tables Based on 5 per cent Sample Data, Part II Special, Census of India.

2.Statistical Abstract India 1984, Ministry of Planning .

3.Report for the year 1983-84, University Grants Commission.